■ A Summary Of This Book

"Do unto others as you would have them do unto you; it will return to you."
Confucianism, Hinduism, Sikhism, Judaism, Christianity, Buddhism, Islam

• • •

"There is *no neutral* ground in the universe: every square inch, every split second is claimed by God *and* counterclaimed by Satan."

C.S. Lewis, from *Christian Reflections*, 1967

• • •

"The line divid⋯ e heart of
every human be⋯ y a piece
of his own heart

A⋯ *Archipelago*

"There is no such ⋯⋯ as good versus evil; there is only the eternal struggle between those who *can* feel and those who *cannot* feel."

Alexander Tadich, *in conversation with his friend Jack*

• • •

"I'll always remember that there are Bulls as well as Bears; we know a lot about Bears."

Mikhail Gorbachev, last USSR president, NY Stock Exchange, May 1992

• • •

"Keep your bowler on your head and your eye on the diabolical criminal masterminds."

Emma Peel's last words to partner John Steed, TV show *The Avengers*

• • •

"Here's the deal! I want each of you to buy 5,000 shares between $6 and $7 per share. I'll give you each 1,000 shares free as a Frequent Buyer bonus. We'll all get rich!"

The Rampaging Bull said to Jack and me, Chapter 11, pg. 146

My Brokers Gossip

"I'll bet The Rampaging Bull enrolled you in his Frequent Buyer Plan to pay you off for encouraging your clients to buy his shares," my broker Milan slyly asked my other broker Bungee.

Chapter 11, page 153

■ Read This First

When I woke up on Oct. 20, 1987 I discovered that I had lost six figures in paper profits on my favourite penny stocks.

My stomach churned.

My head throbbed.

My gut twisted.

I wanted to punch someone.

I couldn't be consoled by the knowledge that almost everyone in the market had lost money. I didn't care about everyone else. I cared about me. I was depressed. I was angry. I was experiencing "Naive Beginner's Shock".

I eventually calmed down. I had learned an expensive lesson in the ways of the financial world while still a young man. I wanted to know what went wrong. I looked for books to help me make money or at least avoid another crash. I couldn't find the books I needed. I had a vision instead. That's when I assembled a team of experts with 200 years of experience to help me write this book— my blueprint for trading in penny stocks.

1. WE HAVE IT ALL!

RAMPAGING BULLS: *Outfox Promoters At Their Own Game On Any Penny Stock Market* is, to my knowledge, the only complete handbook ever written for the penny stock market.

■ You will learn the underlying dynamics that rule penny stock markets—or any markets for that matter.

■ You will discover the closely guarded secrets of speculators that you can use immediately—or tomorrow when the markets open.

■ You will discover that 90% of the *top* promoters and stock-brokers in penny stock markets exhibit similar characteristics that you can turn to your advantage.

■ We will show you how to evaluate a stock promotion and determine *when* to *buy*, *sell*, and *short* a stock!

■ You will discover the important personality characteristics needed to win as a stock investor.

■ We will improve your chances of making money on the stock market and entertain you at the same time.

■ We'll even send you a software package to make your evaluation of companies easier! Photocopy the two-part order form at the back of the book, fill it out, and mail it in.

2. FINAL PITCH

If I haven't convinced you to buy this book yet, I have one final pitch. Suppose I invite you to meet a dozen experts on the penny stock market who are willing to discuss what they know? Suppose I said you only have to buy a round of drinks. Would you jump at this chance to discover the secrets of making money? Sure you would!

Would you learn any secrets as your bar bill tops $100? No! Every expert, despite promises, will tell tall tales, laugh at other investors, and try to convince you to invest in his deal. The experts don't want to discuss their deepest secrets in public, with strangers, and/or with potential clients. They also don't want you to compete with them. It's an old story repeated every day.

I want to *save you the hundreds of dollars* you might spend entertaining a troop of experts or the *thousands of dollars* you might lose on their promotions before you learn the penny stock game.

My team and I offer you some amazing tips and theories to help you win on penny stock markets. We have illustrated our ideas through the fictional adventures of typical Naive Beginners (Jack, Vic, Dave, and me); The Rampaging Bull (Bob Holstein); hardworking but unconscious brokers (Bungee and Milan); a conscious but reclusive broker (Oswaldo); and the deal of a lifetime—B.H. Beane International. What are we going to charge you for these compelling truths? Less than the price of one fancy drink in an upscale downtown bar.

Is the penny stock game worth learning?

You bet! Remember: penny stocks are a better bet than government lotteries, casinos, animal racing, cockfights, or sports pools. You'll understand this as you read this book.

Every major company was once a private junior company or a publicly listed penny stock. No matter what circles you travel in, chances are that you'll be tempted more than once with a penny stock deal that holds the promise of instant riches.

When you finish reading this book you will understand, perhaps for the very first time, how the rich get rich; why the search for excellence is usually a promotional stunt; why many people are unethical; why many authority figures can be and are dangerous; how corruption spreads; why everything falls apart; how to know when someone is conning you; how to recognize a well structured deal; who to do business with; and how to ask the hard questions to get the information you need.

In short, we'll teach you how to beat The Rampaging Bulls at their own game.

We are on a quest. Join us. Keep reading as we unravel a mystery, discover the ways of The Master Trader on penny stock markets, and share a few laughs.

Alexander Tadich,
a windy sleepless night, 1 a.m., April 26, 1992

■ Read This Next

by Mark Wayne

If you read this book, one of two things will happen.

You will be equipped to take advantage of penny stock opportunities when they arise, as they always do, or you will decide never to invest in penny stocks.

Either way, you'll be better off than you were before.

That's why I heartily recommend **RAMPAGING BULLS:** *Outfox Promoters At Their Own Game On Any Penny Stock Market* to any reader who has ever invested or considered investing in penny stocks.

Alexander Tadich has written instructive and fiendishly funny fictional stories as part of a comprehensive and fast-paced review of the penny stock market's inner workings. You could invest in penny stocks until you qualify for an old age pension (or until you run out of money or margin) and never acquire the vital information and insight in this original book.

This book is an eye-opener, even for experienced stock players, because it covers *all* aspects of the penny markets—not just the limited area in which a particular player may have expertise.

As if this wasn't enough, this information is then synthesized in an easy to use series of questions and formulas which you can use to evaluate your own investment opportunities. By using these formulas, you will not only be able to separate the winners from the losers but you will also be able to determine when to buy and sell. It's incredible, but true.

I have been an avid investor since I was about 15 when I was taken under the wing of a very honest broker who introduced me to the principles of value investing which the legendary Benjamin Graham carefully outlined in his seminal works, *Security Analysis* and *The Intelligent Investor*, a half century ago.

These principles seemed sound to me then, as they do now, because they called for value, safety, and patience over the long run. The difficulty, as we all know, is that a long run investment in an undervalued company can be very boring for a young person with limited funds and lots of ambition. I soon turned my attention to penny stocks because I was haunted by Benjamin Graham's startling revelation that he had made more money on one speculative deal, at a certain point in his life, than he had made from all his conservative investments put together.

I researched hundreds of junior companies and read every piece of information I could find. To make a long story short, I didn't do very well. It wasn't because I wasn't smart or because I didn't try hard enough. The reason is beautifully summarized in Chapter 3 of this book *You Don't Know; You Don't Know!* I had no idea about the underlying dynamics that rule penny stock markets (and perhaps the major stock markets) and the pivotal role played by the infamous promoters represented in this book as the highly entertaining Bob Holstein—a.k.a. The Rampaging Bull. I wish I had this book when I was starting out.

Don't misunderstand me. I'm still very much a follower of the value investing techniques defined by Benjamin Graham. I have to be. As the founder of a $110 million mutual fund in Canada, I'm involved with a group of people who pay very careful attention to blue chips, value, and safety when they invest the hard earned money of other people.

But let's be honest. Many of us feel the need to risk our *own money* on penny stocks that will make us a "killing". This is the irresistible lure and danger of penny stocks throughout the world.

Fortunately, we now have **RAMPAGING BULLS:** *Outfox Promoters At Their Own Game On Any Penny Stock Market* as a pathbreaking guidebook to help us in our quest.

Mark Wayne is the founder of a $110 million mutual fund, a Chartered Financial Analyst, lawyer, and an avid penny stock dabbler.

"Most people don't understand how hard it is to get to the top . . . In fact, most people don't know what they don't know," The Rampaging Bull told us while smoking an after dinner cigar.

Chapter 11, page 145
Chapter 6, page 78

RAMPAGING BULLS™

BULLS™ Alexander Tadich

Outfox Promoters At Their Own Game In Any Penny Stock Market

Calgary   San Francisco   Houston   Barcelona   London

■ Catalogue.

Tadich, Alexander

RAMPAGING BULLS: *Outfox Promoters At Their Own Game On Any Penny Stock Market*

Includes Bibliographical References
ISBN 0-9694626-1-1

1. Penny Stocks 2.Speculation 3. Business/Finance I.Title

HG4551.T33 1992   332.63'228   C92—090071—2

Publishers Note
   This publication is a work of fiction. No characters in the book are in any way shape or form based on any specific company, person, or persons living or dead. Any similarity to any person is strictly accidental and/or coincidental and should be considered as such.

   This publication is designed to provide accurate and authoritative information with regard to the subject matter. It is sold with the strict understanding that the Publisher and Author are not engaged in rendering legal, accounting, financial or other professional advice. As such the Publisher and Author cannot be held responsible for any actions or initiatives taken by the reader as a result of having read this book. If any professional service is required, the advice of a professional should be sought and is recommended.

First Printing - July 1992, Printed in Dominion of Canada.

Rampaging Bulls, No Bull Guide are trademarks pending.

Elan Publishing Inc., Box 21009 Dominion Post S.W., Calgary, Alberta, Canada   T2P 4H5

In Memoriam - loving grandparents Luka and Maria, Radovan and Kata; uncles Milisav and Miljko; and loving uncle to Adam and Alexandra, Mark Hueniken

 **Dedication**

Michael

a loving and supportive father
who fought the great delusions of the 20th century
September 3, 1914 — April 26, 1990

■ Table of Contents

Naive Beginner Turns Promoter

"These guys are for real. The financiers are big money people from Florida, California, and New York. I think I'm going to buy more shares," Jack said while dreaming of great wealth.

Jack Meets the Rampaging Bull

1

. . . And Comes Back Excited

SUNDAY, MARCH 8—The Year Of The Rabbit

Jack met The Rampaging Bull by accident. Things always happen that way. There was something about The Rampaging Bull that warned him to watch out. Jack, of course, didn't watch out. That is why we have a story to tell. That is why we have a mystery to unravel.

I am not a hard-boiled private detective—yet. I'm Jack's friend. I know the whole story intimately because I got involved in this adventure with Jack. Vic, Dave, Bungee, Oswaldo, and Milan also got involved because of Jack. We couldn't help ourselves. We all recognized, very early, that this adventure was going to have a significant impact on our life. We did, however, survive, recoup some of our money, and continue to learn lessons every day. It hasn't been easy.

Jack and The Rampaging Bull were standing next to each other by the buffet table at a $100 per plate dinner sponsored by a local women's group, Victims Of Hatred And Sexual Harassment In The World. This organization, like so many that have sprung up in recent years, includes people from every ethnic background eager to make speeches about man's inhumanity to man—and women. This is noble, but not effective, since intolerance is a common genetic defect.

The Rampaging Bull turned with a full plate of pasta and bumped right into Jack. Jack spilled his drink on his trousers.

"Whoa! I'm sorry," said The Rampaging Bull.

"No problemo," said Jack. What else could he say to a man dressed in a Giorgio Armani suit, an Yves St. Laurent tie, a Polo shirt, a Gucci tie pin, a Rolex watch, and Rockport shoes? The Rampaging Bull thrilled Jack because he looked like a man who shops in expensive stores.

"I'll make it up to you. My name's Bob. Why don't you join my table over there?" said The Rampaging Bull with an intensity Jack believed was sincere. Then he left with his plate of pasta intact.

Jack returned to his table with a plate of cottage cheese, roast beef, and no drink. Vic and Dave were looking at him. They wanted to know why his trousers were wet. Vic and Dave are low key, honest, careful, and don't take many chances. They are family people. Between the two of them they have five kids, two wives, three dogs, two houses, large mortgage payments, and stable jobs. They aren't major players in our adventure, but they are important.

Jack noticed The Rampaging Bull at his table with seven other people—all distinguished looking. They were laughing and talking loudly as if they belonged there.

The co-chairpersons of the evening's gala, Professor John R. Van Guilder and Melanie Melonovsky, suddenly asked for the lights to be dimmed. They now had the attention of 300 people in the room. Van Guilder, an engineer and university professor, dressed in a style common to people who have large government salaries—tweed. I'm describing clothes because so many people consider clothes to be an important clue to status and ability. I think, as you might expect, that this is bogus.

Jack also noticed that Van Guilder looked stressed. This is important information for us later.

Van Guilder was talking about the 100 million people from several ethnic groups killed in a dozen genocides by maniacs during the 20th century. It was compelling stuff. Van Guilder was suddenly more interesting, to Jack at least, when he stopped in the middle of his presentation to point at someone. "Before I continue, I just want to thank Mr. Bob Holstein for his kind financial contributions that made this evening possible. Mr. Holstein, take a bow."

Jack's new "friend" Bob stood up and bowed. Bob looked at the crowd, smiled, and said: "Thank you Professor. I believe in this organization's work. Any movement or idea that encourages charity and kindness to others is good."

The audience cheered.

"Hey, that's not my idea. Jesus said that. That's the Dalai Lama's philosophy too. I'm with them," Bob laughed humbly as he waved at everybody with the same intensity as he had used to apologize to Jack moments earlier. Bob even seemed to wave at Jack as if they were old friends from highschool. Jack waved back. Bob sat down. Everybody clapped. Jack was impressed.

The evening had more of the same. There was much talk about being more caring and sensitive to the poor and the hungry throughout the world. When the party broke up, Vic and Dave had to go home—they had families to worry about.

Jack stayed behind. He was curious about this man Bob who could entertain seven people as well as another half dozen people who were pulling their chairs to his table. Jack went over too. That was his first mistake.

The Rampaging Bull, while smoking his after dinner "George Burns" cigar, was telling his friends around the table about his project to help farmers and ranchers in North America become energy self sufficient. Many people looked impressed. Jack vaguely recognized a few people in the group as prominent people in the community.

"Think of it . . ." Bob was saying as Jack sat. ". . . what is the biggest problem farmers and ranchers have? The cost of energy! Imagine if farmers could produce all the energy they needed without public utilities? Wouldn't this revolutionize farming? Wouldn't this reduce subsidies? Wouldn't this put more money in the farmer's or rancher's back pocket? You bet it would!" Bob said with conviction.

"We have developed a highly sophisticated . . ." Bob paused and laughed. ". . . and patented product, I might add, to make this scenario a reality. We want farmers to join our renewable energy bandwagon," Holstein said with an earnest face. "We propose to help farmers and ranchers turn cow dung into methane gas like they are doing in India and China."

Everybody laughed. Jack laughed. Bob smiled.

"I know it sounds wild. But we are in difficult times. Farmers need all the help they can get," said Bob, a budding "Man Of the People".

Bob leaned over to whisper his next few sentences. Everybody at the table leaned closer to Bob.

"I shouldn't tell you this. We will invite 500 farmers to get into our program during the coming year at no cost." There were "oohs" and "aahs" from the assembled group.

"There is more. We are also arranging financing to recruit 5,000 farmers for our program within the next 12 months—at a reduced rate. I can't tell you the financing details. Some things have to be secret," Bob laughed.

The audience laughed. Jack laughed. This was getting interesting. Then Bob lowered his voice even more. A few people moved closer to hear every word. His cellular phone rang, but he ignored it. He waited for the ringing to stop out of respect for his listeners.

"Methane gas is the wave of the future. You can get it from wood, dung, coal, natural gas, and canning plants. Did you know 100 million people in India and China are already doing this? We are going to add the managers of the two largest farms in the world to our board. These farms get all their energy, which is methane gas, from fermented dung produced by their pigs and cattle. Methane gas from organic waste already represents three percent of total world energy use. This is equivalent to several hundred million metric tons of coal!" There were more "oohs" and "aahs".

"This technology hasn't taken off in North America, up to now, because our energy costs have been low, farm income was steady, and things looked good. Farm income is now dropping rapidly and any savings farmer/ranchers can make might keep everybody in business longer. Things are changing," Bob said.

Bob looked at everybody in the room carefully. Most of the people were quiet, as if they were about to write cheques. A woman at the table was holding her breath while a piece of chocolate cake dangled from her fork. Bob wanted, Jack thought, everyone to feel the significance of this moment deeply because he had deemed them worthy of receiving this vital news.

"We have the backing of several major agricultural organizations. There is an automobile company, whose name I am not at liberty to divulge, which is reviewing our project," Bob paused.

"This unnamed automobile company has been developing a methane gas engine for years. You can't use methane gas in ordinary internal combustion engines. Methane gas corrodes everything. The company hasn't been aggressive about developing the methane engine because it might cost consumers a bit more initially and petroleum gas has been cheaper. But we have arranged meetings with this automobile company to discuss a joint venture agreement. Our company's success does not depend on the development of this methane gas engine—but it shows we have hit a nerve." Then Bob paused, like a great comedian just before he delivers a punch line.

"There is enough cowshit in North America, according to the experts, to heat one million rural homes. Who knows how many homes we could heat if we added all the pigshit, dogshit, horsehit, and catshit to our equations?" said Bob. Everybody broke out in laughter, including Bob. Jack couldn't stop laughing until he told me the story the next day.

"This is big. I need you all to keep this confidential," Bob said as if everybody at his table had received top priority clearance from the C.I.A.

"The stock of our company, B.H. Beane International, is 25 cents. It's going to be 35 cents Wednesday. Next Friday it's going to be 50 cents. A week Monday it's going to be 75 cents. In three weeks it's going to be $2. The price will top $5 in two months. Then the price of the stock is in God's hands. You didn't hear this from me. Somebody, nudge, nudge, could consider my talking to you about this before the public finds out as illegal," Bob laughed.

Nobody laughed this time. Jack thought everyone was trying to figure out how much money they could spare to buy B.H. Beane International shares.

Jack said he started daydreaming about 100,000 Beane stocks at 25 cents increasing in value to $2 per share. Although Bob was still talking at this point, Jack couldn't concentrate on the rest of Bob's presentation. His mind was electrified by thoughts of expensive cars and dining with beautiful women in his own restaurant. When Jack regained his composure, he managed to hear Bob's last sentence.

"We will be making a series of announcements that will thrill the world. I can't tell you everything," Bob finished. Everybody was silent. They didn't know what to say. An elderly man topped up Bob's wine glass. The silence was awkward. Everybody then started talking about something else just to break the silence. Nobody brought up Bob's story again. Jack thought everyone considered it bad manners to ask questions after Bob had offered the hottest stock tip in years. Bob pulled out his solid gold-looking business card holder and offered Jack his business card.

"Thanks for sticking around. If your pants are ruined I'll be happy to pay for the dry cleaning. If necessary, I'll get my tailor Gino to make you a new pair of pants. If you ever need anything, just drop by the office," Bob said. Jack looked at the card. It read: "Bob Holstein, president, B.H. Beane International." Jack also noticed that Bob was constantly fidgeting with his Rolex watch.

"It just goes to show," Jack said later, "that interesting things can happen when a man in a fancy suit makes you spill your drink." Now that I think about it, Jack was right.

MONDAY, MARCH 9—the next day

When Jack finally phoned me the next morning you can imagine what he said. I couldn't get a word in. Jack was almost delirious from all the excitement. Jack told me he had also phoned Vic, Dave, and another half dozen friends about B.H. Beane International.

"Jack, there are a million scams in the universe," I heard myself saying as if I had intimate connections with all the scams in the universe. "This is probably just another bogus deal. It's almost spring—stock promotions always start in the spring, last all summer, and end during the late fall. The promoter then takes a winter holiday," I said, amazed that I knew so much about promotions.

Jack said that he had just got off the phone with Bob Holstein. "He personally told me this stock is going to the moon," said Jack who was suddenly an expert on biogas conversion technology.

"Just watch what happens. Good grief! Holstein even told us what is going to happen. The stock is moving to 35 cents by Wednesday. Friday it's moving to 50 cents. Next Monday it's moving to 75 cents. In three weeks it's moving to $2. The stock will top $5 in two to three months. Then the price of the stock is in God's hands. You didn't hear this from me," Jack told me as if he was "The Man" behind the deal.

I have always liked Jack. What's not to like? He is enthusiastic; energetic; committed to helping others; does not smoke; drinks Friday nights with friends after work; loves his parents; is courageous about helping the weak; is so sincere that he confuses people; and once he makes his mind up about something he can become single-minded. In short, Jack is my friend. That is why I make allowances for many of his ideas and usually get sucked in as well.

The Rampaging Bull Hooks Jack

"Jack! Jack! The share price is going to the moon!" The Rampaging Bull said to the Naïve Beginner.

RAMPAGING BULLS: Outfox Promoters At Their Game On Any Penny Stock Market

WEDNESDAY, MARCH 11—two days later

I didn't buy any stock. I checked the trading in B.H. Beane International. Sure enough, the price of B.H. Beane International had increased to 35 cents per share. I had barely put the newspaper down to get a coffee when the phone rang.

"See," said Jack. "You could have made some serious money. I bought 30,000 shares at an average price of 29 cents. Not bad eh?" I was in shock. Jack had invested about $9,000 plus commissions because of a man who had made him spill a drink on his trousers. Vic phoned me.

"What am I supposed to do with Jack and Dave. They are both frothing at the mouth in their excitement over B.H. Beane International stock. I'm not sure if I should phone a psychologist or invest," said Vic.

"My broker says there are 100,000 shares bid at 35 cents while there are only 20,000 shares offered at 40 cents. This thing looks like it may go up substantially," said Vic.

"Are you going to buy stock?" he asked. I said no. He said he was thinking about it. That scared me. Vic, who never took a chance on anything, was now thinking about investing in a company that was proposing to turn dung into methane gas. Then Vic told me that he had mentioned this deal to a few of *his* friends. I couldn't imagine how many people from that ill-fated dinner had repeated the story. A dozen people can easily talk to a 100 people who can talk to another 1,000 people about buying B.H. Beane International stock. I was silent on the phone. Vic was silent on the phone.

"Why don't we just watch what happens. What's the rush?" I said. Vic mumbled something and hung up.

FRIDAY, MARCH 13—the time bomb goes off

Vic was still mumbling Friday at 8:30 a.m. when he phoned.

"I presume you have read the newspaper and the stock pages," Vic said. I picked up my copy of the local newspaper sitting on my desk. I knew I was in for a treat. Vic's broker had told him more than 100,000 shares of B.H. Beane International stock were bid at 48 cents and about 50,000 shares were being offered at 55 cents. The local newspaper had published a story with a photo of Bob Holstein and the manager of the local farm co-operative.

The headline proclaimed: "Philanthropist Wants To Help Farmers Become Self-Sufficient."

Holstein was starting to look like a populist who knew how to get people activated. I didn't know what to do.

"What the hell!" said Vic. "Dave bought 50,000 shares at 42 cents," he said. I coughed. Then Vic told me that he had bought 20,000 shares at 47 cents. I coughed again.

Jack phoned. He was shrieking in my ear.

"I have just doubled my money. Buy some. I don't want you irritated at me later. This stock can go the moon. You just don't understand this deal. These guys are for real. They are discussing the development of a methane engine for tractors and combines; they want to give 5,000 farmers the special biogas digester free as part of a major test; they have financing in place; the financiers are big money people from New York, Florida, and California; and there is talk about listing the stock on a major stock exchange," Jack said in one breath.

"And—I think I can arrange for you to meet Mr. Holstein. He said it was O.K. with him," Jack told me.

I still didn't buy any stock though the temptation was enormous. This promotion was getting out of hand. I phoned my broker, Bungee, who groaned when I asked him about B.H. Beane International. I had three brokers at the time mainly to help me shop for bonds, mutual funds, and the odd Blue Chip.

"You too?" he asked. Bungee told me that every broker in his firm was getting calls from clients wanting to get a small piece of this Beane stock.

"I think the stock might top $2 in three weeks," I told him. I didn't add that Bob Holstein had mentioned this to Jack. Bungee laughed at me. Bungee is moderately street smart himself. He isn't a genius, but he is reasonable, courageous, and rarely susceptible to major mood swings.

"The stock might go to 50 cents or $10 for all anybody knows," Bungee corrected me. "I don't think you should buy much of the stock because it is volatile," he said. I then told Bungee that Bob Holstein had predicted a $2 Beane stock at the black tie dinner just a few days earlier and that it was obvious Holstein was showing some promotional skill.

"I think he is going to fulfill his promises, at least in the short term. He wants to seduce the big money people," I said as if I knew. Bungee agreed as if he knew. We both sat quietly on the phone wondering what to do next. One thing was for sure. Absolutely everybody on this stock exchange had heard about the fateful night when Bob Holstein had whispered a few tips to his friends. I wondered if everybody had heard about Jack spilling his drink on his trousers. I decided not to ask.

Then Bungee said: "I heard from Holstein's broker that Jack spilled a drink on his trousers." That's when I decided to buy some Beane International shares. If something as meaningless as this was getting around, I decided that the share price might go over $2.

"Get me the best price you can Monday morning," I told Bungee before I hung up. Then Jack phoned. "I think we've found a pot of gold," Jack said. I got nervous because Jack was already showing his greedy fangs unlike me, the great altruist. I was about to make a large investment in a company developing new ways to handle cowshit and there I was accusing Jack of greed.

MONDAY, MARCH 16 — I get involved

Bungee phoned to tell me that he had bought 5,000 shares of the stock at 65 cents for my account just before it topped off at 76 cents — one cent higher than Bob Holstein had predicted.

"You couldn't buy more shares?" I asked.

"That is enough for God's sake," he said while I started thinking about 100,000 shares at 65 cents going up in value to $5. I asked Bungee if he knew anything about Holstein. I was hoping he would confirm my good judgement.

"I think he's a nobody," Bungee finished.

I phoned Milan, my second broker. Milan knew something about Holstein. Milan explained that he had met Holstein at a reception. Apparently Holstein had spilled some roast beef and gravy on Milan and the two of them had used that small but deeply significant moment to become phone friends.

"I can't tell you much about Holstein," said Milan.

"Do you think the stock is going to $5," I asked. Milan laughed just like Bungee. Milan is a good man who doesn't have the killer instinct that other brokers seem to have. But Milan is a fast learner. In fact, everybody I know says Milan is the smartest man they have ever met. I know what you are thinking. Why would a smart man become a stockbroker?

"You have your heart set on this stock don't you? I'll buy you 5,000 shares for fun. That way you can't blame me too much when the stock drops," he said. I told him to buy 10,000 shares between 80 cents and 90 cents. Milan didn't say anything because he was surprised that I would buy a penny stock.

I then phoned Oswaldo, my third broker, for more information on Holstein. Oswaldo, much more street smart than Milan or Bungee, said that he knew a lot about Holstein. I asked if he could tell me over the phone or would he prefer to tell me over a coffee somewhere. He said I could buy him lunch. He also told me it was obvious that I, like everybody in his office, was excited about the Beane stock.

"You want me to buy you 5,000 shares so you can feel good about being part of the madness. The stock is trading at $1.25 you know," he said with his voice lowered as if I should know better. I told him to buy me 10,000 shares. He laughed.

"You have it bad. Have you ever heard of the children's fairy tale, *Jack and the Beanstalk*?" Oswaldo asked.

"Sure, who hasn't. Are you telling me that Jack and I are a couple of twits?" I asked while looking at my phone receiver as if I had misunderstood Oswaldo.

"Whoa! Relax. Don't be so defensive," Oswaldo said.

"Jack and his widowed mother, who lived in a poor tumbledown cottage, had to sell their cow to get through a long hard recession. Jack, on his way to market and unprepared in the ways of the world, met a little broker by the side of the road. The little broker offered to take his cow in exchange for some magical beans that would lead him to a pot of gold. Jack, like the country bumpkin that he was, made the trade, took the beans home, and got a tongue lashing from his mother for being so foolish. The beans, as you know, did grow into a tall beanstalk that Jack climbed to the Giant's house where Jack did scoop gold coins," said Oswaldo.

I got irritated at Oswaldo. He noticed my irritation.

"I'm supposed to give advice. It's my job," said Oswaldo as he continued telling me the story.

"Jack, displaying greed, went back two more times. He took gold coins, the hen that laid the golden eggs, and the golden self-playing harp. This wasn't easy for Jack, the speculator-in-training. The Giant was no fool, could smell blood, and liked to eat children for dinner. Jack hid in the copper cauldron on his third visit—until the Giant fell asleep. Jack then finally stole the golden harp.

"The harp, as harps tend to do, woke the Giant up. The righteously irritated Giant chased Jack down the beanstalk. But Jack chopped down the beanstalk, much like short sellers chop down promoters, before the Giant got to the bottom. The Giant, according to legend, fell into a financial hole so deep that he never got out," Oswaldo said as he cleared his throat.

"This fairy tale has dubious lessons for children because Jack was a greedy little S.O.B. who would have gone to jail in real life. *Jack and the Beanstalk,* however, is an excellent adult fairy tale for investors who want to learn about the stock market.

"I hope you can see the similarities between Fairy Tale Jack and you. You and your buddy Jack, for instance, are as enthusiastic and committed to B.H. Beane International as Fairy-Tale Jack was to climbing the beanstalk. The two of you, *like* Fairy-Tale

Jack, haven't even thought about losing money, starving to death, or being eaten by the Giant. The two of you are not, *unlike* Fairy-Tale Jack, going to tell your mothers or wives about your involvement with Bob Holstein and B.H. Beane International. Your mothers or wives would bring you back to reality with a severe tongue lashing much like Fairy-Tale Jack's mom did for him," said Oswaldo.

"So where does that leave us?"

"In deep dung," Oswaldo said.

Oswaldo had hit the nail on the head. Jack and I were about to learn some hard practical lessons in the stock market. We were Naive Beginners who didn't have the benefit of a good tongue lashing. That is why I have prepared the equivalent of a series of mother-like tongue lashings in Chapters Three through Nine.

I have realistic expectations. Fairy Tale Jack didn't listen to his mom, I didn't listen to Oswaldo, and you probably won't listen to me. You don't even know me. You might be more inclined to listen to me after you read Chapter Two which explains why I wrote this book.

If you'd like to delay reading the mother-like tongue lashings until after you finish our compelling story, skip Chapters Three to Nine. Continue reading our adventure with Jack and The Rampaging Bull uninterrupted from Chapter Ten. We don't mind as long as you read Chapters Three through Nine eventually. They are a key part of your training.

Let's have some fun. You might even learn something.

Beginner's Shock

2

. . . And Why You Should Read This Book

Oswaldo's warning, when he told me the Old English fairy tale *Jack and The Beanstalk,* haunted me on Tuesday morning October 20, 1987 when I read the stock pages. All my penny stocks had declined in value dramatically on Black Monday. I felt like Jack did when he brought home magical beans instead of cold hard cash—inept and disillusioned.

Jack and I had believed the strangers who had promised us magical wealth for our hard earned assets. The stock market crash brought me back to reality much like Fairy Tale Jack's mom brought him back to reality with a severe tongue lashing for being so naive.

Instead of selling my shares when they increased in value, I had repeatedly gone back to buy more. That is what happens to Naive Beginners who get lucky. They invest more. They don't realize how lucky they were. Eventually they lose money and pay for the Giant's dinner. They find out the hard way that there are not enough magical beans to go around.

I believed then, as I believe now, that you and I can improve our chances of winning if we understand the dynamics of the stock market.

■ A. FIGHTING BACK

That is when I decided to fight back. I asked many investors if they had some survival tips about the penny stock market. I discovered that few people know much about the penny stock market mainly because they have never taken the time to evaluate themselves or the market.

I searched for the definitive text on speculating in penny stocks. I couldn't find anything that fully explained what I needed to know. There are, of course, many books about stocks, finance, and what to do with your money. It's almost a growth industry of its own. These books, however, are all about investing in senior companies. They are written, for the most part, by criminals seeking redemption, financial consultants looking for clients, or major communication companies cashing in on their prestige. I was disappointed.

I did, however, find a handful of authentic thinkers who I interviewed and a few authentic books which I mention later for further reference. I started making notes and thinking hard about my own experiences. The result is this book **RAMPAGING BULLS:** *Outfox Promoters At Their Own Game On Any Penny Stock Market* — the only book of its kind.

The investment strategies required for senior companies are often different from those required for penny stock companies which are the majority of listings on most stock exchanges. The companies listed on senior stock exchanges usually have real assets, revenues, employees, "bread and butter" type products, a track record, pay dividends, and spend enormous amounts on management salaries in good times or bad.

Junior companies listed on penny stock markets are just starting out; have a revolutionary and usually untested product; have volatile price swings; offer excellent opportunities for fast capital gains or losses; pay no dividends; pay promoters to "hype" stock; sometimes have revenues; and usually trade at low prices.

I wanted to learn how to trade penny stocks because I know that every senior company was once a penny company which made a fortune for somebody! This book is my blueprint for making money on penny stocks.

■ B. BACKGROUND TEAM

My background team includes several people whose combined experience in penny stocks exceeds 200 years. My team includes stockbrokers, financiers, floor traders, entrepreneurs, lawyers, and managers. I spent hundreds of hours collecting background information from these warriors who are trying to succeed in a difficult environment. They didn't offer their time freely. I had to give some of them a piece of the action. I thank a few of them at the back of the book; most have asked to remain anonymous because they like it that way.

At first they laughed at me.

■ "The penny market is too elusive to understand. Nobody has ever written a great book on the penny stock market," they said.

■ "Investors aren't smart enough to understand a book on penny stock markets," they said.

■ "Even if they read the book, investors are too lazy and greedy to remember the tips," they said.

■ "Too many investors believe everything they hear," they said.

I didn't disagree with any of these ideas. I did, finally, convince my background team that there are enough people out there who are genuinely interested in penny stocks. I shared some of my ideas with them. They got excited. I got them talking. My thesis is authentic, original, and even a bit shocking.

I wish I could say that I became a wizard, that I went on to make millions, and that I am now relaxing on a beach somewhere.

I haven't, I hope, and I might. The adventure continues.

■ C. OUR READERS

We prepared this book for the 55 million investors in North America and millions more in 60 other countries who buy stocks. Some people buy directly through stockbrokers. Others buy indirectly through mutual fund managers.

The typical stock investor in North America is 45 years old, earns $38,000, has 15.5 years of education, is either a man or a woman, and has a stock portfolio of about $7,000. The typical stock investor is a very ordinary person — like me and you.

This also means that the typical investor is similar to Fairy-Tale Jack — totally unprepared to cope with larcenous promoters who operate on every stock exchange. Isn't the growth of mutual and pension funds proof that many people feel inept to trade stocks by themselves and prefer to let *experts* do it for them? Commentators tell us large institutions, such as mutual funds, have increased their share of trading on stock markets from 16% in 1965 to well over 50% in 1992. This growth in *expert* trading will continue into the 21st Century. Doesn't this mean that typical investors are increasingly unsure, less self-reliant, and more dependent on the abilities of mutual and pension fund managers? Doesn't this mean that the fine art of speculating is being abandoned by large numbers of investors?

We want to reverse this trend just a bit. We want you to make a small speculative effort by yourself in growth and penny stocks with a broker you trust. We believe that everyone wants and maybe even needs at least one good speculation now and then to give them zest, excitement, and a chance to be part of the action. This also will make you a more worldly individual who understands the wily scams of promoters in almost every sector of our society. It's important if we expect to maintain a healthy market economy with lots of buyers and sellers. Yet we want you to keep in close touch with your mutual fund managers and your brokers who specialize in "safe" senior stocks.

◼ D. OUR INSPIRATION

Who are these wily penny stock promoters? Their backgrounds vary—some are greater and some are lesser. The most compelling we dub, The Rampaging Bull!

The Rampaging Bulls, with well defined personality traits, are always excited and upbeat about their favourite stock. They don't believe in bear markets, recessions, depressions, layoffs, or cutbacks. These people believe that any stock they get involved with is a great opportunity and that there is an *investor* born every minute. Few people can resist The Rampaging Bulls. They have power. They have charisma. They can sell anything, including magical beans to trusting investors. They are, after all, promising to make you as rich as they are or as rich as *you think* they are. This book will help you beat this easy to recognize, but hard to understand, promoter and the other types of promoters we identify.

The characters in this book are purely fictional. They represent a composite sketch of people operating everywhere today who, while intriguing, display predictable behaviour. Discovering these patterns has been our biggest joy. We approach our subject with wonder, not malice, and a desire to level the playing field.

In short, we consider this to be an upbeat book.

■ E. SPECULATION IS INCREASING!

The promoters are doing a good job. Even while increasing numbers of investors are placing themselves under the protection of professional fund managers, the remaining investors are becoming even more speculative.

This seems like a contradiction. It isn't. Increasing numbers of investors are afraid of being speculative on their own, but they don't hesitate to urge their money managers to take chances "as long as they get results". Many professional mutual fund managers, faced with a demanding and greedy investment public, are becoming more speculative and at times take major risks. It's amazing. Consider the following:

■ Many senior stock exchanges have loosened their regulations to list penny or speculative stocks and develop more business. You will find many penny stocks trading on senior stock exchanges.

■ Could properly priced shares suffer a $500 billion or 22.6% one-day decline in value on the New York Stock Exchange during Black Monday October 19, 1987? Weren't the shares overpriced by speculators?

■ Could properly priced shares suffer a $14 billion (in 1929 dollars) or 12.8% one-day decline in value on the New York Stock Exchange October 29, 1929? Weren't the shares overpriced by speculators?

■ Banks in the market economies lent enormous sums of money to speculators who wanted to buy and flip companies and real estate during the past 20 years. We discuss this later in detail.

■ The typical daily volume on the New York Stock Exchange in the 1960s was 6 to 7 million shares per day; in the 1970s was 40 to 60 million shares per day; in the 1980s was 100 to 120 million shares per day; and in the early 1990s is 150 to 200 million shares per day. Isn't this speculative frenzy even if you allow for inflation in your calculations?

■ In the 1960s 12% of shares on the New York Stock Exchange changed ownership at least once each year? Today, 80% to 90% of shares change ownership at least once each year. Isn't this speculative frenzy?

■ There's even an investment theory which says activity on senior stock exchanges can be predicted by activity on junior stock exchanges. The theory states that if the number of annual Initial Public Offerings or Blind Pools on penny stock markets reaches historical highs then a bull market on senior stock exchanges will collapse. Doesn't this imply that speculative frenzy on senior stock markets spawns speculative frenzy on junior markets?

■ The Toronto *Globe and Mail* reports that Canadians spend 30 times more on legal gambling than on going to the movies. In fact, the newspaper says legal gambling on lotteries, bingo, horse racing, charitable casinos, raffles, and other games topped $10 billion in 1991 and will continue to grow. This makes Canadians among the most compulsive gamblers with per capita spending of about $400 on games of "no" chance. This doesn't include illegal gambling. Yet just 30 years ago, the only gambling was on horses!

Speculation is part of our life. There is no doubt about that.

■ F. CRIME ON INCREASE

Increasing white collar crime is partially caused by speculative frenzy throughout society. This seems to be a genetic law. Consider what commentators have discovered:

■ Credit card fraud is increasing at 20% to 40% per year according to credit card companies. Criminals are *manufacturing* fake cards; stealing cards from the mail; and soliciting by phone to get credit card numbers.

■ No wonder banks, according to various reports, are more afraid of fraud, which includes bad cheques, than robberies.

■ Regulators tell us that tens of thousands of people lose hundreds of millions of dollars in phony gold mines each year. Authorities believe North American investors lost $250 million in 1988.

■ *The Washington Post* and *Newsweek* claim the U.S. Congress and Senate add billions of dollars each year to the federal budget for payoffs, perks, rewards, and bribes to their hometown friends and associates. The situation is so bad that several senators declined to stand for election in 1992 because they think government graft and corruption is incurable!

■ One of the largest brokerage firms on Wall Street says it employs four people under the names Scoop, Hook, Ferret, and Cy Spy to make sure everyone behaves ethically.

■ We were shocked to discover 500 or more North American companies spent more than $1 billion to bribe foreign officials according to the TV show *Wall Street Week* with Louis Rukeyser.

■ We couldn't believe that managers of 115 companies, among the 500 largest in North America, were convicted of at least one major crime or paid civil penalties for serious misbehaviour during the 1970s according to *U.S. News & World Report*.

■ The R.C.M.P. in early 1992 said, on the Canadian television show *Marketplace*, that home repair swindlers scoop more than $350 million a year from lonely southwestern Ontario seniors every year. This means that home repair swindles may top $9 billion in North America each year!

■ Do North American entrepreneurs launder $5 billion to $15 billion each year through the North American and international financial system as estimated by the U.S. Justice Department?

■ The U.S. President's Commission on Organized Crime claimed that the "Mob" siphons $50 billion U.S.

■ Estimates exist that white collar crime costs $40 billion to $100 billion each year.

■ The U.S. taxation authorities believe $9 billion in taxes is lost each year through insider trading, embezzlement, and fake bonds.

◙ Shrinkage, better known as shoplifting and employee theft, costs over $8 billion every year according to the U.S. Commerce Department. Each shoplifter, by the way, steals about 49 times during his or her career before he or she is caught.

◙ A 1988 survey by the American Council on Higher Education of 290,000 first year students in more than 500 colleges found the top goal of 75.6% of students was "to be well off financially". What will happen to the ethics of these students under the pressure of extreme competition when they discover that there aren't enough magical beans to go around? Their chances of maintaining their integrity will be about the same as that of a camel going through the eye of a needle.

◙ Only 39.4% of these same 1988 students surveyed said that "developing a meaningful philosophy of life" was most important to them. This was down from the 82.9% who believed this in 1968.

Indeed, you as the buyer must be aware. White collar crime and speculative activity engineered by promoters will continue to be a way of life on the planet through the next century. This is our dark and brooding vision of a future that promises even more pain, and lost investments, for ordinary people. Laws will not and cannot change this because the managers of the justice system don't have the staff and, sometimes, the will to bring everyone to justice. The very people running the financial and judicial system are often unethical! We can improve things only if we get a grip on ourselves by becoming informed and self-reliant.

RAMPAGING BULLS: *Outfox Promoters At Their Own Game On Any Penny Stock Market* will be relevant as long as there are stock markets and larcenous promoters to seduce Naive Beginners.

You Don't Know; You Don't Know!

3

. . . First Tongue Lashing and Great Insult

You have to know what you *don't* know when you play the stock market. Jack and I, for instance, had no idea what we were doing. That Jack could be so easily impressed with Bob Holstein's fancy suit said a lot about Jack's lack of judgement and the failure of the educational system.

We didn't even know what questions to ask. No one had ever explained that the underlying force behind all stock markets is the *degree of promotional activity* going on at any given time.

The greatest insult you'll ever receive from a professional stock trader goes something like this: "You don't know what you are doing. In fact, *you don't even know what you don't know.*"

If you hear this phrase directed at you, get out of the room immediately. Go hide. You have been offered *The Great Insult*. This insult, in short, places you in the same company as all the other Naive Beginners held in contempt by the stock market pros.

The stock market pros, when they direct the Great Insult at you, rarely complete the thought. If you ask them what you don't know, they will laugh.

". . . I need a lifetime to explain," the professionals might say.

The stock market pros know penny stock market activity is a product of what major and often twisted promoters and managers are doing. Economic conditions, income statements, and balance sheets are secondary. Stock market pros buy and sell based on their assessment of the promoters involved. The background information complements or detracts from the promoters strengths.

This fundamental rule of the penny stock market applies to the senior stock exchanges as well as the penny stock exchanges, we think, though this opinion is not universally held.

If a stock market pro, on the other hand, insults you as a "slimeball", "a sleazeball", "a crook", a "highway robber", "an asshole", or a "jerk" consider yourself complimented. This may mean that these people respect and fear you as a person of great illumination who understands the workings of the market.

▧ TWO-MINUTE DIGRESSION

The Great Insult has wider implications in all areas of our life. If you aren't interested in this digression, then skip to the next chapter.

The ultimate vanity is to think that you know enough to succeed. Almost all of us, at least initially, fall into the trap of thinking we know enough to survive in the markets or, for that matter, in any field of activity.

Most of us recognize, eventually, that this just isn't true.

The educational systems of the world, to their shame, have never managed to develop guidebooks or courses that encourage students to recognize that the things they don't understand can ruin them. Most of us now recognize that educators teach students to believe the fictions and delusions of their time rather than to be self-reliant and independent thinkers.

Imagine if we all had one special class to discover the right *questions*, but not the answers, about government, thought, organizations small and large, medicine, economics, ethics, ambition, arrogance, religion, hygiene, chess, baseball, diet, auto mechanics, and so on. Suppose the teacher urged us to make these *questions* part of our quest. You already know what would have happened. You and I would have discovered answers much faster with less pain.

No wonder there are so many lost souls who don't know what they don't know. Very few knowing people in authority want to share the important *questions* because the questions usually lead directly back to them and their behaviour. Think about it. Every person, religion, ethnic group, profession, organization, media organization, or government tries to manage questions to obscure reality and history. This giant worldwide effort to limit questioning, and therefore critical thinking, has put at least seven professions or industries into constant turmoil: journalism, public relations, advertising, entertainment, education, religion, and the technology of communication.

Confucius once said that most people don't understand anything until their mid-30s or early 40s. Some, unfortunately, don't understand anything until the day they die. Think of the parents who have struggled to make their children understand the things they have experienced. Think of the children who suddenly wake up in their 50s full of regret and remorse for not listening to their parents who tried to share their experiences with them.

You can't skip over this requirement. This is part of your training. A great athlete, a great writer, a great thinker, a great warrior, and a great stock market investor always knows his limitations and works to overcome them.

You have heard of the titles "apprentice", "journeymen", and "master". This is an old idea that needs to be reinstated in all fields of activity—especially the stock market. I can't imagine an "apprentice" investor getting the best of a "master" promoter unless he is lucky.

There is nothing more tragic than when an "apprentice" stockbroker passes himself off as a "master" stockbroker just because he has a license. What a comedy! Since many stockbrokers don't last longer than five years in the brokerage business, you can rest assured that many brokers are apprenticing at your expense.

The questions we pose in this book summarize what a stock market investor needs to know as a superior speculator.

4 | Discounters and Promoters Rule

. . . Second Tongue Lashing

Discounters and promoters rule the stock market.

There is no penny stock market without them. They provide the energy that allows real value and ideas to be discovered and developed. The promoter *and* discounter represent opposing forces that create balance.

You as a stock trader must become a promoter or a discounter depending on the situation. You may on any given day be a promoter *and* a discounter.

The promoters and discounters, however, can make serious errors. When they make errors they lose, investors lose, companies lose, and society loses. Here's how.

■ A. THE PROMOTER

The promoter can be good and/or bad. Naive Beginners and many experts misunderstand this important distinction. You should never automatically react negatively to the word "promoter". A promoter is the type of person who generally looks at a glass of water as half-filled.

1. The Good Promoter

This is the kind of person who has a sharp eye for value, for what people need, and for what people want. This promoter explains to others the merits of a product, a cause, a political party, a religion, or a company. There is no doubt in our mind that this is an important public service. Far too many people just don't understand the value of the things around them, especially new things. This promoter *as a Bull* helps people understand the value of these things.

The little man on the side of the road who offered Jack the magical beans which grew into a beanstalk was essentially a "good" promoter. The little man knew Jack needed help to discover the value of beanstalks as a way to find gold and pay debts.

Consider a fictional mining company whose geologists have been working on a property for several months. The assays of core samples from the property are positive and the managers believe there is enough gold to develop a mine.

A promoter, in this instance, will do a substantial public service. He will tell investors this property can become an operating mine, provide employment, increase the local tax base, and make investors rich.

2. The Bad Promoter

Suppose the promoter goes too far. Suppose the promoter promises things that don't exist. Suppose a promoter says he saw geese which lay golden eggs and heard self-playing golden harps near the mine. This is bad.

This is essentially what the Criminal Incompetent and the Rampaging Bull do—over promote to steal your money. The Rampaging Bull over promotes his stock by overstating his case or, what's worse, lying. The investor eventually discovers, after he overpays the stock, that the promotion is false.

If you get too excited about this gold mine and bet the family farm or the farm's only cow, then you might suffer. That is why The Rampaging Bull, as the promoter gone bad, is a danger and menace to society.

■ B. THE DISCOUNTERS

Discounters also can be good or bad. They are the type of people who look at a glass of water as half-empty. Yet the good discounter, like the good promoter, is also looking for true values as a *bear*.

The bad discounter, like the bad promoter, also misstates the value of everything.

1. The Good Discounter

The discounter as a professional trader provides a public service when he recognizes the gold mine promoter for what he is—a Rampaging Bull. The discounter warns his friends, neighbours, and others about what The Rampaging Bull is doing. The discounter helps everyone in this type of situation especially investors who naively believe that the stock is worth a fortune. The discounter as a professional trader and public servant, which we want you to become, buys, sells, and shorts to force an inflated stock price to more realistic levels.

The discounter also provides liquidity in the stock market which allows you to sell a stock—even if it is at a lower price.

When the discounter helps the stock price drop to more believable levels he is helping the company, investors, the community, and himself find true value. The bad promoter will fight back for a short time to keep the share price inflated.

2. The Bad Discounter

The discounter can be a danger to society when he looks at everything as if it lacks value. The discounter gone bad is a cynic, a rebel without a cause. This is the person who believes that people have no redeeming virtues; that this company can never find a gold mine; that everyone is lying; that nothing can be improved; that the world is doomed.

The discounter gone bad would never have invested in Xerox because nobody could possibly develop a copying machine; in Eastman Kodak because nobody could develop a camera; or in Henry Ford because nobody could mass produce an automobile.

The discounter as a cynic is a danger to society, himself, and to anyone who believes him. He doesn't want us to dream and/or try to make dreams happen. The cynical discounter, disguised in many ways, is afraid of risk. He makes it difficult, and sometimes impossible, for any promoter or entrepreneur to produce or discover anything of value or beauty.

■ C. FINAL COMMENT: THE UGLY

We have discussed the good and the bad.

We owe it to you to discuss the ugly for a moment. The ugly usually happens when you, as a Naive Beginner, lose money with a promoter or discounter who is bad. This doesn't have to happen.

There is a constant struggle between these opposing forces: The discounter as public enemy; the discounter as public hero; the promoter as value enhancer and public hero; and the promoter as a Rampaging Bull and worldwide menace.

The essence of a stock market is to allow these four opposing forces to struggle against each other so that value can be created for society. It is almost impossible for a Rampaging Bull to have absolute power in a free market which allows discounters to sell and/or short The Rampaging Bull's stock.

In a highly controlled company, organization, social club, religious group, market, or society, however, The Rampaging Bull can limit the discounter's ability to sell and/or short his "position". This means that resources will be invested inefficiently to the detriment of everyone.

Your job as an investor is to decide who is playing what role during any and every promotion on junior or senior stock markets. Some people can play several roles at the same time. If you understand this, things won't turn ugly for you.

5 | The Big Picture

... Third Tongue Lashing

There are six major themes you need to understand before you can practice the fine art of speculating on penny stock markets.

We can teach you about three themes. We can help you understand the various tips and techniques, use and avoid leverage, and recognize The Rampaging Bull.

We cannot teach you about the other three themes because they all have to do with your personality. These three themes include courage, coping with your needs, and understanding what makes you blind. We never said learning the fine art of penny stock speculation would be easy!

■ A. THINGS WE CAN TEACH

1. Tips And Techniques

This entire book is about tips and techniques. The secrets we share with you might not work for you immediately because of your personality. Don't worry. You'll understand eventually if you keep your sense of humour.

2. How To Use Leverage

Using leverage should come under the heading of tips and techniques. We give leverage a separate heading because this idea plays such a central role in the stock market.

If you are not an expert trader then we have a very simple rule: don't use leverage. The reason is simple. Leverage allows you to lose more money than you have. If you follow this rule, you will cut your losses in half.

You are using leverage when you borrow money to earn money. You can do this in the stock market when you open a margin account with your broker. The broker agrees to lend you a specified percentage of your account's value—usually 50%. You don't have to sign a promissory note, visit a banker, go through a credit check, or any other troublesome action usually associated with borrowing money. All you have to do is think big, tick off a small box on your application, and sign the margin agreement that you probably won't read because it is written in what seems like Old English.

You'll probably think that you will use this margin account wisely. You might use it wisely at first, but you will slip up. Trust me. You'll quickly join the wild and exciting world of panic selling as you discover that you have over-extended yourself.

Leverage isn't just dangerous for penny stock investors. The supposedly sophisticated big time investors have also been seduced and financially strangled by leverage gone wrong.

i. The First Nightmarish Example

The entire U.S. savings and loan, and much of the banking, industry made many bad loans during the 1980s in real estate and other deals. American citizens may have to pay $500 billion to cover these losses now slyly referred to as the "S & L Crisis". This is no crisis. The disaster has taken place. These losses, which may never be properly tallied, are larger than the *combined annual Gross Domestic Product* of over one-third of the U.N.'s member states or *60 times larger* than the *annual foreign aid* given by the United States.

Yet no political or business leaders are going to jail for this— except, of course, for a few of the most obvious criminals. How did this happen? Banks loaned enormous amounts of money to developers, among other wheelers and dealers, who lacked assets other than the buildings or land they were in the process of developing with borrowed money. Try to imagine the phone conversations.

Only the naive, the incompetent, or the greedy would have loaned money on these deals. Banker errors affect every person, directly or indirectly, who does business in or with America.

ii. The Second Nightmarish Example

Many companies were taken over and wrecked by merger and acquisition artists who borrowed and raised money to take over companies they didn't have the slightest ability to operate. This is "The Leveraged Buyout" or "LBO".

A Leveraged Buyout occurs when a bigshot promoter, usually with a track record but inadequate amounts of money, borrows money to buy a company whose assets act as collateral for the loan and payoffs to bankers, government officials, and other intermediaries.

Does this sound crazy? It is crazy. The original shareholders got a short term profit. Virtually all of the other people who jumped on the bandwagon as bondholders or equity investors lost money. Yet all the LBO experts are always trumpeting how they enhanced share values! All of this corruption and larceny was made possible by the use of leverage!

Cash rich people will have countless opportunities to scoop up quality assets and companies at bargain basement prices through the 1990s because their previous owners went bankrupt as "Leveraged Buyout Specialists". Almost every major financial magazine is *now discussing* "restructuring", "debt reduction", "deleveraging", and "the advantages of equity issues over bond issues." There is justice in the marketplace.

3. Recognizing The Rampaging Bull

i. The Definition

The Rampaging Bull is the most exciting promoter on the stock market—or anywhere for that matter. That's why we single him out for a deeper analysis.

Most people don't understand him.

He thinks he's perfect and a misunderstood man of destiny—and behaves as if he is.

Psychiatrists think he needs counselling though there may be no cure for his condition—most commonly a malignant narcissistic personality disorder. Consider some of the symptoms commonly associated with this person:

■ an extremely powerful will;
■ intelligence and/or cunning;
■ a deep need to feel and be perfect;
■ lack of tolerance for other people's imperfections;
■ a willingness to take shortcuts and cheat;
■ an inability to respect anyone;
■ a willingness to blame and judge others when things go wrong;
■ a need for status (takes credit for everything);
■ a willingness to manipulate and break every rule to achieve power and dominance;
■ an obsession with unimportant details;
■ an easily aroused rage;
■ a tendency to swear (some more than others);
■ a conviction that he or she deserves all the money;
■ an inability to relax with friends;
■ an inclination to sulk when he does not get what he wants;
■ a willingness to pay lip service to propriety or correct behaviour, especially in dress, because it helps to get things done;
■ an inability to understand ethical principles that require each individual to behave responsibly toward others and oneself.

This is a terrifying list of characteristics.

The Fairy-Tale Giant, challenged by Fairy-Tale Jack, was probably a malignant narcissistic. The Giant was brutish, pushed his wife around, hoarded money, liked to grind bones, didn't respect others, made his own rules, was willful and greedy, could smell blood, and was totally self-indulgent. Yet he was smart enough to develop a self-playing golden harp and a hen which could lay golden eggs.

The personality of the Fairy-Tale Giant might not match exactly that of the malignant narcissistic, but it is close. The Giant was, obviously, a formidable enemy and one very troubled "dude".

How the narcissistic personality disordered can avoid facing their imperfections while aggressively reminding everyone else about their imperfections is a complete mystery to us! Despite their deep-rooted problems, these people never willingly go to psychiatrists or psychologists because they believe they are "perfect". Instead, they make life miserable for others who seek psychiatric or psychological help because of them. This is the great untold, and unrecognized, tragedy of life.

These people make the search for excellence in most organizations impossible and hopeless. The malignant narcissistic cannot tolerate excellence in others because it competes with the malignant narcissistic's own view of himself or herself. The malignant narcissistic will hire consultants, with appropriate hoopla, to go through the motions of creating an "excellent" organization as long as he or she can maintain complete authority. Excellence to the malignant narcissistic means everyone listens to him or her!

Rampaging Bulls are not, however, lazy or stupid. They often exert themselves and sometimes go through tremendous hardship to gain status or respectability. These people are so completely dedicated to themselves and their personal gain that others exist only as an audience or as someone to be used and abused along the way.

Rampaging Bulls like each other's company. When they meet, they instantly recognize each other. They will work together to steal from *you* though they don't trust each other.

Don't ever think you can be this person's friend or that he or she will ever respect you. If The Rampaging Bulls respected anybody, including you and their parents, goodwill could break out overnight. Wars, ethnic violence, religious fanaticism, and mean spirited laws would all be banished from the planet.

As stockbrokers and promoters, The Rampaging Bulls believe their clients are weak, fearful and, in turn, greedy. This thrills them because they believe they can make money from their clients' weakness forever. These Master Promoters believe their clients will always come back for more abuse.

These people are supremely confident even when they don't know what they are talking about. This tricks most of us into thinking they actually know something. If you can recognize these people for what they are, you can turn it to your advantage.

ii. The Reason

How do The Rampaging Bulls have this incredible horse sense? There is some debate among psychiatrists as to whether these people are born or developed. Some psychiatrists believe these people, as the personality disordered, have been unloved or abused as children. Their hostile mean-spirited behaviour, psychiatrists tell us, might be a defence against a world which gives them little or no love. These people develop an overblown view of themselves as a defence against self-loathing. Once these people become adults, they have no way of changing without dedicated and trained help.

Other psychiatrists believe this lack of feeling may be genetic which implies there is no cure. Who knows? Who cares?

Psychiatrists have classified as many as 11 personality disorders under various headings such as narcissistic, histrionic, antisocial, paranoid, dependent, borderline, and compulsive. Psychiatrists say that more personality disordered classifications are yet to be discovered.

Some personality disordered people have coping problems, are stupid, are brutish, and so on. But all personality disordered people, however, have a problem with "feeling". If we use a scale that defines a person's ability to feel we can understand the personality disordered better. We rank the altruists, who have the greatest ability to feel, at the higher end and the psychopaths, who have no ability to feel or understand morality, at the lower end.

The personality disordered, which include the malignant narcissistics, fit somewhere between these two extremes of being able to feel—usually at the lower end. The personality disordered are, to be blunt, almost all "bad" and in a few cases extremely "evil". We define evil, by the way, as behavior which limits other people's liveliness, free expression, joy, and freedom of movement.

Your job is to survive intact. These people make a mockery of the words humane, free will, ethics, and conscience. The literature is extensive. You don't need to get caught in this person's soap opera, designed to prove how wonderful they are, while they stomp all over you. Unfortunately many people find Rampaging Bulls interesting to watch. Who isn't fascinated by a cobra, a tiger, a scorpion, a panther, or a tarantula?

You should only be interested in beating these "evil people" at their own game. It's more fun that way and *you won't need a psychiatrist* (or if you do, you'll be able to afford one).

iii. Prevalence

Malignant narcissistics are, for the most part, already in control. They are the ones causing war, revolutions, pain, and sadness.

The cult classic movie, *The Invasion Of The Body Snatchers*, summarizes our attitude, although not the reality, about what is happening and will continue to happen through the 21st Century. The 1956 original and 1978 remake, based on the novel by Jack Finney, are science fiction paranoia at its best. Pods from outer space infiltrate a small California town to replicate and replace humans with their unfeeling lifeform. This is an overstatement to be sure.

But The Rampaging Bulls, in their quest for status, money, and power, can and often do become powerful. They are involved in many professions. They can be, and have been, prison wardens, priests, bishops, popes, gangsters, political party bosses, patriarchs, monks, mayors, rabbis, ayatollahs, gurus, doctors, dentists, teachers, senators, psychiatrists, educators, television evangelists, publishers, fund raisers, editors, journalists, politicians, police officers, soldiers, generals, dictators, civil servants, lawyers, accountants, managers, presidents, and some authors.

Wherever there is power, they stand in line. They always advocate how something or somebody is superior to something or somebody else. They want you to buy into their promotion, denigrate and abuse others, and make them rich.

Most of the people involved in the "S & L Crisis" and the "LBO" binge were either psychopaths, malignant narcissistics, or criminal incompetents feeding on the insecurities and stupidities of the naive and weak. Just scan the apologetic books these people have written as proof of how troubled and mentally ill they really are and were.

It's hard to estimate how many personality disordered people there are. They rarely ask for help. Yet the National Institute of Mental Health in the United States thinks at least one percent, and maybe more, of the population is personality disordered thanks to an exhaustive 1984 study of 10,000 people.

We tend to think the number of personality disordered people is much higher—anywhere from one to five percent and perhaps substantially higher. Review the characteristics we outlined earlier. How many people do you know with these characteristics? Chances are you know several. Frightening isn't it?

iv. Why Don't You Know About This?

Most of us don't understand how prevalent these people are because the news media and educational systems have lost the will to shine a bright light on their activities.

A growing number of media companies is already owned and managed by Rampaging Bulls themselves.

Many journalists, tragically, do recognize that they can't write freely because of stringent libel laws or cranky but powerful lobby groups. Small wonder that news organizations offer "boring, pandering, and filler" stories on sports, entertainment, lifestyles, accidents, and local heroes. In fact, this type of reporting has been dubbed "McNews" and is well on its way to become the dominant type of journalism in the 21st century.

No wonder newspaper readership is down; magazines are fighting to stay alive; and TV is losing viewers! The age of the crusading journalist who leaps tall buildings at a single bound and runs faster than a speeding locomotive as he or she unveils *true* corruption has been over for some time. Everybody knows it. A *handful* of journalists is trying to keep the flame of truth alive and save the journalism profession from disgrace.

Some media, of course, take more gambles than others. Unfortunately, many so-called "hard" TV news shows usually discuss safe topics which trick people into believing great injustice is being revealed. Hah! No media will tackle bigtime Rampaging Bulls who have strong community support unless the evidence is extremely heinous. The Rampaging Bull's libel lawyers are eager to threaten everyone in sight. Should anyone be surprised that many good journalists often drink too much as people burdened by the injustice of it all? In fact, the American Institute of Stress, according to the *Los Angeles Daily News* and *In Health* magazine, tell us that journalists and stockbrokers are in the top 10 most stressful jobs.

v. Other Psychological Classifications

Since we are on the topic of psychological classifications, we might as well mention other mental disorders that have an impact on the stock market.

Addiction, stress, neurosis, hysteria, depression, anxiety, phobia, obsession, and psychosis that includes manic-depressives and schizophrenics are the mainstream of psychiatry and psychology. People suffering from these disorders are generally "sad" and/or "crazy". They do get help often—unlike the personality disordered who, as "bad" people, rarely get or ask for help.

Many master speculators and investors have commented that the stock market is manic and/or depressive—"bullish" and/or "bearish". This can only happen, as far as we know, if unstable people are encouraged to invest by Rampaging Bulls. Is this true? The National Institute For Mental Health in the U.S. reported in 1984 that 20% to 25% of the population has a mental disorder.

Who are we to argue? It all makes sense to us. Some of these people must be stock market investors. People suffering from the better understood and curable mental disorders are often the targets of The Rampaging Bull's seductions.

If we add all the Naive Beginners and just plain stupid people, whose numbers elude us but may be outrageously high, then you can understand why the stock market is so volatile.

vi. Cures

There is no proven cure for psychopathic behaviour, malignant narcissism, and/or any of the related personality disorders. Nor are we looking for a cure. These people may reform, however, after a major life trauma. But don't bet on it.

We want to help you beat these people at their own game if and when you get involved in the penny stock market. But there is good news. The stock market allows you to beat them. We believe a free market and an open society, with less severe libel and slander laws, are the only ways to lasso Rampaging Bulls managing political, religious, social, and corporate organizations.

Nobody can overvalue their services, their company, or themselves for very long in a free market where discounters force prices to more realistic levels. That's why Rampaging Bulls and their followers are always trying to control, convert, and subvert the market and the people in it.

vii. Lesser Bulls

Many promoters do not qualify as Rampaging Bulls. These weaker promoters are generally less willful and ambitious.

Some are Criminal Incompetents because they are inept at doing anything complicated. They are willing to do almost anything to promote their deals as if everything is perfect.

These lesser bulls are less powerful than The Rampaging Bull although they are equally irritating, can cost you much money, and often talk and act like a Rampaging Bull.

viii. Greater Bulls

There are promoters who are superior to The Rampaging Bull. We discuss them later and dub them Successful Entrepreneurs and Warriorpreneurs.

ix. Conclusion

We recognize that you might get offended by what we have written because you may be a romantic who thinks the best of people. We respect that. Be patient with us. Consider our proposition as it applies to the stock market. Test it. Our goal is to make money as speculators, not change the world. The world is too big for you and 'me to save or change.

Remember, the true Rampaging Bull has supreme confidence in himself or herself and doesn't care about what we have to say about him or her. The Rampaging Bull is convinced that our advice will fall on deaf ears. He or she may be right because almost everybody in their arrogance has ignored the warnings of the great sages since the beginning of time. There is, however, hope for you because you are reading this.

■ B. THINGS WE CAN'T TEACH

We include the next three themes, not to teach you, but to remind you how your personality might affect your ability to succeed in the penny stock market.

1. Courage

Courage is a necessary, but not a sufficient, characteristic for winning on the stock market. So how do you get courage?

The Cowardly Lion in the classic story of *The Wizard of Oz* didn't *get* courage when he received a medal from the Wizard. The Cowardly Lion had, unknowingly, already displayed tremendous courage when he led his team into the malignant narcissistic Witch's castle to save Dorothy. The Cowardly Lion's genuine affection for Dorothy awakened his courage.

Jack discovered he had courage when he went into the Giant's house three times because he wanted to save his mom.

You will find the courage you need to win in the stock market once you are on the right track. This will only happen with homework, experience, and wisdom.

2. The Great Needs

We can't teach you to manage the four most common needs: security (not wealth), sex, love, and fun. Too much is bad; not enough is bad; just the right mixture is good.

Your goal in the stock market is to add to your security, not to create it or lose it. You cannot expect to make or save yourself financially on one great stock market gamble. Fairy-Tale Jack was fighting for his security—the most basic of needs—and to regain his mom's respect and love. Don't count on becoming as lucky as Fairy-Tale Jack.

3. The Great Blindness

We also can't teach you how to overcome The Great Blindness. You won't win big on stock markets unless you become more aware. Consider this ancient Chinese axiom which essentially tells you to get tuned in as soon as possible:

■ A warrior who doesn't know himself or his enemy must lose.
■ A warrior who knows himself but who doesn't know his enemy has a 50% chance of winning.
■ A warrior who knows his enemy and himself will win most of the time.

There are five emotions which keep you blind. Consider them carefully:

■ vanity (or narcissism),
■ anger,
■ fear,
■ sympathy,
■ and laziness.

These characteristics are very similar to the *Seven Deadly Sins*. They were first developed almost two thousand years ago by Christian monks in the Egyptian deserts who neatly summarized their ideas in the *Philokalia*, a highly entertaining collection of books. The sins, or transgressions against God, included:

■ pride (or vanity or narcissism),
■ jealousy,
■ anger,
■ laziness,
■ inordinate desire for "stuff" (covetousness),
■ inordinate desire for food (gluttony),
■ and inordinate desire for sex (lust).

Jealousy, inordinate desire for food, and inordinate desire for "stuff" are all byproducts of fear. The degree of fear you have about life will determine your level of greed. Greed, as you know, is the grease that makes the stock market a very efficient and high powered machine which can run anything over.

To be sympathetic is good. However, if you consistently forgive everyone who wrongs you, and you keep doing business with them, you will eventually go bankrupt on your way to heaven.

You might win for a short time even if you are vain, angry, or lazy. You might even get rich with these traits. You will, however, eventually lose everything unless you develop self awareness. A vain, angry, or lazy investor is essentially blind.

These ideas are taught by every world religion. In fact, the world's religions have identical teachings, we think, on the topic of awareness or illumination. It is a tragedy that most religious leaders don't discuss these similarities. They focus instead on differences to increase their market share and gross revenues. You can make a fortune on the stock market if you understand and follow the *teachings*, instead of the many *narcissistic administrators*, of the world's religions.

Fairy-Tale Jack, for instance, was lucky his greed didn't trip him up in the Giant's house. Jack's greed, covetousness, and recklessness could have led him to his doom. He could have easily ended as the Giant's dinner. Remember, this was just a fairy tale. Any investor going back to a stock promotion to squeeze out more gold for a second or third time will likely lose everything.

■ C. CONCLUSION

We want to teach you at least two things in this book:

■ How to recognize The Rampaging Bulls and the other promoters for what they are.

■ How to defeat The Rampaging Bulls and other promoters at their own game.

If you recognize that you are weak and that promoters are using this against you, then you can make money.

If you don't or can't recognize your shortcomings, reading this book won't do you much good. You can memorize every theory in this book; then you'll get a phone call from a promoter telling you about the last of the great deals. You'll invest. You think you won't, but you will.

Suppose the product is revolutionary?

Suppose four major firms want to test the product?

Suppose two of the biggest promoters are getting on board?

Suppose the product can be sold all over the world?

Suppose the stock is "cheap"?

Suppose the investors are rich Taiwanese, Arabs, or newly emerging Europeans?

Suppose the stock is going to double in two weeks?

Suppose . . . Suppose . . .

You are already excited. I probably can sell you this stock in less than an hour. Suppose the share price becomes a little more expensive? You still might buy this stock because the share price increase has validated the promoter's story even if you didn't originally believe anything you heard!

You may be afraid that you will never get another chance for an investment like this. You want a piece of the action. You want the promoter to think you are smart. You are at this point a Naive Beginner like Fairy-Tale Jack who traded his last remaining asset for magical beans. Fairy Tale Jack, to his credit, adapted very quickly to the reality of doing business with the Giant.

We want you to become a courageous trader and speculator who is willing to learn about himself, the penny stock market, and The Rampaging Bull.

6 | A Penny's Many Faces

. . . Fourth Tongue Lashing

From a distance all penny stocks look the same.

Up close, penny stocks vary as dramatically as senior stocks. We identify seven categories of penny stock companies in this chapter. Once you figure out a company's category, your chances of being a successful speculator improve dramatically.

Remember: sympathy, laziness, vanity, anger, and fear always rear their ugly heads to throw you off course.

■ A. THE CENTRAL THEME

The central theory for all penny stock companies can be summarized as follows: *Entrepreneurs list a company on a stock exchange to finance a new venture they believe will succeed. Management promotes the share price to attract investors and keep as much control of the company as possible. Management, paid in "inexpensive" share options, uses the capital to develop a profitable company whose share prices will eventually be worth the promoted share price.*

The reality is something else again.

■ B. BASIC CHARACTERISTICS

Actively traded companies listed on penny stock markets, for the most part, have the following characteristics:

■ marginal or no sales;

■ some money in the treasury recently raised from speculators willing to take a risk;

■ debt which will be paid when the company "takes off";

■ no dividend record;

■ little or no hard book value;

■ some "goodwill" or other intangible assets;
■ little, if any, inventory;
■ few or no full time employees;
■ "a terrific story with superior potential" to change the world;
■ expectation of near term profits "once the New York mail order company puts the product in its catalogue" or when "a major ore company" builds a mill on the property;
■ a talented marketing and management team that includes "a former Blue-Chip executive".

Most of these points overlook whether the company's management is competent, honest, and willing to follow through on promises. Yet these issues should be a major concern to investors because incompetence can lead to desperation and, in turn, criminal behaviour.

You may find it impossible to believe that penny companies can be classified. Trust us, they can. Don't Eskimos have more than two dozen ways to refer to snow? A company with these characteristics will never be evaluated, however, by any major analyst. Analysts only want to know about companies that have cash flow, profits, and existing products.

■ C. COLLECTING INFORMATION

To classify penny stock companies, you have to collect information. We are not asking you to become a private investigator although this is a good idea. Meet as many people involved with penny stocks as possible to help you on your quest.

·You can collect your information ten ways described below. We summarize the questions you need to ask in Chapter 19, *In Search Of Warriorpreneurs*. The Warriorpreneurs, who we discuss in detail, are rare and the most evolved business people.

■ **Option 1 — Visit your broker. Discount what you hear**.

Always ask your broker to research a key piece of information on a company especially if the broker has been promoting the stock. This will force the broker to think about what he says.

■ **Option 2 — Visit the company. Discount what you hear.**

A visit will eliminate the "telephone aura" that a sharp manager or promoter can build for his company. Sharp promoters can even buy a tape recording of a hectic office background! Presidents of companies listed on penny stock markets are much more inclined to speak to investors than the presidents of companies listed on senior stock exchanges. They need your money.

■ **Option 3 — Listen to what other financial people say about the company. Discount what you hear.**

■ **Option 4 — Develop a file on each promoter's activities in the market to help you judge what he might do in the future.**

Keep track of the highs, lows, and length of each promotion.

■ **Option 5 — Visit the stock exchange to review and/or copy all the public filings. Interpret what you read carefully.**

Look at the quarterly and annual reports; 10-K and 8-K forms required by The U.S. Securities and Exchange commission; technical reports; and the prospectus. Read the section called "Risk Factors" at least twice. Chances are that one or more of these risks will sink the company.

■ **Option 6 — Write letters to the securities commission or the stock exchange to ask about any penalties levied on corporate managers, promoters, brokers, or anyone else involved with securities.**

Keep in mind that the stock exchange will never comment on anything potentially damaging to a company or person unless the stock exchange or securities commission has held formal hearings and penalized the troublemaker. You won't know if the regulatory authorities are investigating someone.

Brokerage firms, which own most stock exchanges, want promoters, entrepreneurs, and Rampaging Bulls to succeed. Success means profit. Profit means jobs. Some brokerage firms are more honest than others. Some are managed by psychopaths or Rampaging Bulls who will do anything immoral but nothing illegal. Don't expect the stock exchange to get your money back if something goes wrong.

Do recognize, however, that most stock exchange staff want to help you even if there are limits to what they can do. The stock exchange managers also like to keep the securities commission happy. The securities commission, usually made up of lawyers and former police officers, is a government body that doesn't care about profits and pays attention to serious problems.

■ **Option 7 — Visit the manufacturing plant, gold mine, or oil well if you are thinking of investing substantial sums.**

If the property is 600 miles from the nearest road or if the plant isn't operating because the "bearings haven't arrived from Japan" don't worry. You haven't missed "the deal of a lifetime".

■ **Option 8 — Phone the local, regional, or federal police.**

This isn't something that's easy to do. We all avoid talking to the police. But the police are your friends unless the officer is himself a malignant narcissistic. Police will talk off the record sometimes to people they trust or to people in responsible positions. The police are real people who fight a losing battle against malignant narcissistics and criminals. If they believe you can help them in the war, they will help you as far as the law allows. If, however, you look and act like a whiner nobody will speak to you.

■ **Option 9 — Go to lunch with corporate managers and review the information you have collected about them.**

This is an excellent way to get new information. Most penny stock company managers need to talk. The managers feel a deep need to justify themselves. They need help. If they offer you a position on the board of directors during your first meeting, don't invest unless you are very rich.

If the company managers argue; ask you to pay for lunch; or order expensive meals you should reconsider your investment. Memorize the questions in Chapter 19, *In Search of Warriorpreneurs*. That's what you want to know.

■ **Option 10 — Contact the Credit Bureau and the Better Business Bureau.**

Discount what you hear because useless, petty, and incorrect information is in these files sometimes.

D. CLASSIFICATIONS

Let's be frank. Chances are that you won't do anything to get background information. You might convince yourself that you do not have enough time. Just keep this in mind: proper due diligence will help you decide what trading technique to use, how much risk to take, and whether to buy or short sell. This makes all the difference between losing or making money.

If you can identify the type of company you are dealing with, you will be able to predict whether managers and/or promoters can raise money; can promote share prices; will use money appropriately; and will succeed in developing a successful company.

1. Category One — Waiting For Godot

This category resembles the famous play by Nobel Prize winning writer Samuel Beckett, *Waiting For Godot*. This is a "theatre of the absurd" play about people waiting for something to happen, which of course doesn't happen. This type of company is to be pitied rather than invested in. There is no promoter; there is no believable chance for investors to get excited; and the highly stressed managers may be working elsewhere full time.

The trading charts for this type of company are flat much like the heart monitor reading for a dead person. In short, these companies also can be described as "Flatliners".

The managers spend their time with lawyers and accountants who produce paperwork for the stock exchange and the securities commission to maintain the company's listing.

The managers also spend much of their time negotiating unsuccessfully with brokers, government, and private investors to get financing. The managers hang out at inexpensive bars, drink large pitchers of beer, and look depressed. The company does help its lawyers, accountants, and the regulatory agencies live well. But that's about it.

This stock trades in pennies per share on the rare occasion when it does trade. You should not buy this stock unless you want to finance, manage, and build this venture yourself. You will then

The Stylized Trading Charts

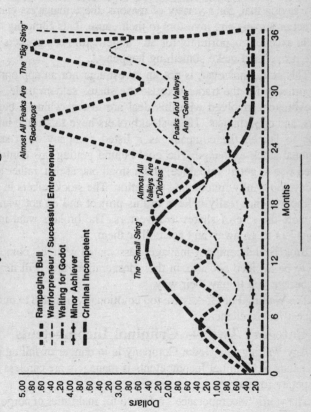

Dollars

Legend:
- Rampaging Bull
- Warlorpreneur / Successful Entrepreneur
- Waiting for Godot
- Minor Achiever
- Criminal Incompetent

Almost All Peaks Are "Backstops"

The "Big Sting"

The "Small Sting"

Almost All Valleys Are "Ditches"

Peaks And Valleys Are "Gentler"

Months

RAMPAGING BULLS: *Outfox Promoters At Their Game On Any Penny Stock Market* negotiate with managers to receive warrants, options, and other incentives to complement the shares you buy.

The managers of these companies could spend their time better by working for someone else instead of waiting for a miracle. Waiting For Godot managers may be worthy and able. We are only saying that, for a variety of reasons, these managers cannot attract promoters and investors to their cause. This company may be an excellent opportunity for an "angel with deep pockets" to take it over and make something happen.

This stock, however, is not an investment nor an appropriate opportunity for the trader because the shares seldom trade. The stockbrokers involved with this deal are losers, whiners, beginners, and opportunists. These stockbrokers have raised the initial cash to launch the company as a listed company on a small regional stock exchange. The goal behind getting this company listed was to get an initial fee, and a small one at that, rather than to develop a fully functioning operation. The stockbrokers in this example do not really believe in this project and do not want to promote the sale of shares to investors. The brokers want these managers to go away and not bother them.

Brokers and company managers associated with this company are to be avoided because, in their desperation, they will lie and encourage you to pay their way.

The Waiting For Godots are too emotionally troubled to pursue a quest for excellence.

2. Category Two — Criminal Incompetents

Any Waiting For Godot Company is in danger of falling into the hands of Criminal Incompetents if managers are careless and desperate for money.

The word "incompetence" refers to the inabilities of corporate managers and promoters to develop a company successfully. The word "criminal" refers to the willingness of the promoter and/or managers to act unethically.

The Criminal Incompetent Company's trading charts usually look like a "giant bubble". Initial share prices are low, increase during the promotion, and then rapidly decline as everyone recognizes this company won't succeed. This company also can be termed a "Bubble Company" and the people who invest can be termed "Bubbleheads". If the promotion is exceptionally short, the trading chart looks more like a "Spike".

The Criminal Incompetent promoter, because of his vanity and aggressive tendencies, often subordinates the operations of this type of company to meet his needs. The desperate and generally honest but naive corporate managers, meanwhile, are busy trying to develop the product.

There may or may not be a product. If the product is still conceptual, the Criminal Incompetent promoter can weave any story. If the product is functional and a prototype is available, The Criminal Incompetent promoter will describe the product as a miracle. We define the word "functional" as referring to something which is yet to be sold commercially.

The Criminal Incompetent promoter knows very little about, and has under budgeted for, sales, marketing, production, and distribution. Getting the product distributed is typically more expensive than the cost of start up, design, prototype development, and testing. The amount of money needed usually is beyond the ability of brokers and promoters to raise. You should always evaluate the extent of the real costs for development.

The Criminal Incompetent Company has a promoter who in public, at least, is working hard to raise money, get the company functioning, and keep everybody excited. The Criminal Incompetent talks big.

"Hey! I know some well-connected California distributors. Don't worry. They'll help us. They'll love our product. It's a cinch. I'll fly down and arrange the deal."

The minute you hear the word "California" from a promoter who lives in Idaho, British Columbia, or Wisconsin look out. This man is making a pitch; he is not being candid. He may have met the California distributor. Making a deal to distribute your product, however, is a much more arduous task than making a few phone calls. The California distributor is probably another Criminal Incompetent who shares a Beverly Hills office with other crooks who need an upscale address.

"You wouldn't believe what the Spiegel (or Eaton's, American Express, L.L. Bean, Sear's, Montgomery Ward, or several hundred other mail order) people said. We are in their next catalogue. This means we'll get $2 million in sales," might be another typical statement by the Criminal Incompetent.

The typical promoter believes most people are too lazy to confirm claims. He may provide you with telephone numbers and contact people at the mail order company. If this happens to you, don't assume anything. Phone the contact person at the mail order firm. You will often get a completely different story. This shouldn't surprise you. This is par for the course.

This promoter's relationship with brokers, who are supposed to praise this stock to clients, is uneasy. Many lower level brokers, who need business and are in debt for any number of reasons, will help sell this stock in exchange for shares. The brokers, usually, dislike the risks in this deal. The brokers want to make a quick buck and get out of this promotion while still keeping their clients.

The Criminal Incompetent promoter's goal is to pump the share price above the market average. He wants to unload his stock and his options, raise money through a share offering, and do it all again. He wants to look good while doing it so he can get a larger company to hire him next time.

The stated business reason for puffing up the share price is to help the company raise money through a share offering without giving away company shares at low prices.

Every company wants to raise $200,000 at a share price of $1 instead of 25 cents. Unfortunately, the cost of promoting the shares to $1 may use up much of the money raised in the public offering.

The offering takes place at the same time as the promotion. Since the managers and promoters are incompetent, the share price usually drops, slowly or quickly, after the money is raised and the options are sold.

Naive Beginners will be stuck with overvalued stocks. The company will have some money but not enough to get the job done. Everyone will be hoping for something to happen to give their shares value. The company may bump and grind its way to obscurity over the next few years.

The company will, unless the managers get extremely lucky and start selling their products commercially, revert to being a Waiting For Godot Company whose shares never trade.

If the financing is complete and the share price, for some reason unknown to you, keeps increasing in value, then you may have lucked into a good promotion. This promotion may be a Rampaging Bull's Company or The Good Try Company marked by a higher degree of commitment to a stock promotion. You can consider further involvement in a stock promotion if the share price remains firm after a public or private placement. The managers and promoters might work hard during the next one to three years. This assumption should be reviewed often.

The Criminal Incompetence Company offers a good opportunity to make money. The share price may reach as high as $1 to $3 before dropping back to 20 cents. A well trained speculator will buy, sell, and perhaps short shares to make a profit. The trader recognizes that the Criminal Incompetent is on a roll and worth following for a brief ride.

A company in this category cannot be expected to offer responsible communications to investors. Communications will be, for the most part, lies. Releases will have phrases such as, "fully expect", "early indications are", "gold is visible", and "management is optimistic". In short, these people are too stupid, greedy, and twisted to understand the quest for excellence as worthwhile.

3. Category Three — Minor Achievement

This type of company is managed by the naive, moderately competent, and somewhat honest. There is generally no promoter on the team because the managers probably don't believe in "promoters". These managers, unfortunately, don't understand that "company fundamentals" by themselves might not excite anybody to buy.

This company may have progressed from the conceptual stage to the test marketing of a prototype or design and construction of a pre-production model. The product might be in local stores. The local newspaper may have written a story on the product as an excellent example of local entrepreneurs diversifying the economy. A few people may have purchased this product which is usually not an important utility but some fad product or service. The managers, often honest people, have somehow managed to raise enough money to develop a product that is "functional".

A resource company in this category may have found oil, gold, zinc, or whatever. The resources, however, just happen to be 600 miles from the nearest road. The managers might be negotiating with the "Japanese" or some "major resource" companies to develop the mine or wells.

The corporate offices may be more attractive than the Waiting For Godot Company. A secretary may be on duty. The company may still have some money left from a secondary financing or a government grant. A local broker, acting as a mini-promoter, might have moved the stock from two cents to 60 cents because the company has a "real" product.

The company may report some revenue; is upbeat about future revenues; and may have a small profit or loss for the year. The stock is probably trading below the high of 60 or 70 cents when a small public offering was completed. The company seems like a classic penny stock with some potential.

This level of development generally exceeds that of the Criminal Incompetence company which usually has yet to decide if the product is functional, never mind commercial. Unfortunately this company must be classed as a "Minor Achievement" company and approached with great care if you are a trader. Here's why.

Despite its revenues and small profits, this company is in trouble. The costs of getting the product to a *national* market successfully far exceed the costs of start up, paperwork, manufacturing, creative design, product testing, and local distribution.

The Minor Achievement Company has gone through the motions of distributing its product locally but cannot expand its distribution without a very substantial infusion of capital. Yet the Minor Achievement Company is unable to attract major investors with its less than committed broker acting as promoter. The more honest management team is also resisting the Criminal Incompetents who want to subvert the company for their own profit. This is a good move for the long term. Unfortunately, there is nobody on the team able to move the stock higher for a financing.

For the company to be a success it has to attract substantial investment to develop the mine, drill the well, or get the product to market. Marketing and advertising a gadget to people who are overwhelmed with major advertising by large companies is not easy. The Minor Achievers, although they are selling locally, have to attract the support of major distribution organizations which are picky about new products. They need a champion who can promote the product and the stock successfully. This is how they fail.

This company offers a few more money making opportunities than the Waiting For Godot Company. The local broker acting as a mini-promoter cannot take the share price higher than the market average. As the shares approach the average price of shares on the stock exchange you should be preparing to sell. The broker/ promoter associated with this company is a risk avoider. The broker, concerned with his career as a securities dealer, does not have the inclination or the time required to help this company succeed. The broker as sponsor is willing, however, to raise moderate amounts of money and undertake a moderate stock promotion to kick start the company to a higher category.

The lower level broker sponsoring the Minor Achievement Company may have a few hundred clients who he "places" in this stock. His clients must buy and sell according to the broker's dictates. If the clients don't listen, they lose money.

The broker acting as a promoter invites, for instance, 75 clients to buy 10,000 shares each at 25 cents; 75 clients to buy 10,000 shares each at 40 cents; and 75 clients to buy 10,000 shares at 55 cents each. You should notice that 2,250,000 shares have been sold for about $800,000. Some of this money goes to the broker and his firm as commission; some to the company treasury; and some to clients as capital gains.

You'll notice, if you play with the mathematics, that the broker/ promoter's clients cannot make money unless other people buy the higher priced shares.

The money raised is typically not nearly enough to get the job done. The managers, usually, don't realize that they may be in trouble from the beginning. The managers assume that they will attract financial support at later stages of development because they have support initially. This assumption is foolish.

The trading charts for this type of company show a "Ripple" instead of a "Bubble" like the Criminal Incompetent Company or a "Flatline" like the Waiting For Godot Company. The "Ripple" suggests that share prices went up moderately for a short time before they settled slowly to a lower price. In short, everyone is waiting for a "Ripple" in the trading charts as the share price settles to the share price before the promotion—about 15 cents to 40 cents. Sophisticated traders will not get heavily involved.

The Minor Achievement promotion can last longer, however, than the promotion by the Criminal Incompetence Company. The Minor Achievers may develop a promotion that lasts six months to a year or longer. They don't have as much pressure to keep the share price at outrageously high prices.

The Minor Achievement Company is willing to share information with investors because the company has a story. The communications, however, may be too conservative. Managers don't want to be seen as promoters. Traders or investors have to read between the lines to get excited. The managers don't realize what it takes to get investors excited about the company's possibilities.

Special Example Minor Achievement

The small resource company, as a Minor Achiever, might have cash flow big enough to provide a salary and cover expenses for managers. These managers recognize that their company will never grow into a major operation. They just don't have enough financing or opportunities to drill big wells. That's why these managers usually don't want to promote the share price.

You should not invest in a public company whose revenues are steady, small, and only cover salaries for top managers. The share price will not increase soon. This company exists for the sole purpose of providing an easy living for its managers. If you look closely, you'll be amazed how common these companies are.

4. Category Four — The Good Try

The category four company is a unique phenomenon because it makes a good effort to succeed.

Category Four is a major advance from the Minor Achievement Company. The company is also a step below the Successful Entrepreneur's Company, described later, which actually has profits, a price/earnings ratio, and a chance for continued growth.

The Good Try has a more competent management team usually educated, well trained, intelligent, and able to promote. The idea of "goodwill" as an asset may be relevant for this type of company. The people in this company generally do not share any similarities to the Fairy-Tale Jack's Giant with his narcissistic personality disorder.

The company has a realistic chance to succeed with a strong team of brokers to finance the company and keep the share price stable. A promoter might be on the team to complement the managers and brokers. The company may have raised between $200,000 and $1,000,000 to promote, market, advertise, and overcome market resistance facing its new product.

The brokers on the company's team may be successful corporate builders who specialize in helping companies get a start— and have done it. These people recognize that it takes years for a company to get results through careful and dedicated work.

The company may have also successfully test marketed the product locally or regionally and found strong market support. The managers might have solved production or sales problems.

The stock promotion with a Good Try company may last one to three years allowing everyone time to buy, sell, short, and hedge the stock successfully. The share price might climb from 15 to 60 cent levels, associated with a Minor Achievement Company, to well over $2 and perhaps even over $5. Sometimes a Good Try Company may have a stock trading at over $5 for as long as three years. This, of course, confuses everyone including professional traders into thinking that this may be a successful company.

The trading charts for the Good Try often feature "Several Bubbles" with share prices increasing and declining several times like the Successful Entrepreneur's Company which we discuss soon. This shows that the promotion team wants to develop the share price as a way to raise more money. These people are not short sighted con-men.

Experienced short sellers may lose money if they launch an attack on the share price prematurely. Short sellers will undertake extended investigations into this company to answer the questions in Chapter 19, *In Search Of The Warriorpreneurs,* before launching an assault on the share price. If the company managers maintain corporate secrecy while pretending to commune with investors then the Good Try has a chance to keep its share price high over an extended period.

The Good Try Company will eventually collapse because the market does not accept the product; the company does not adapt the product to changing conditions; or the company competes with a giant corporation which has decided that this new product is a threat to its products.

The Good Try has barely entered the game and is already being threatened with bankruptcy because a giant conglomerate decides to create and *market* a similar product. When a billion dollar conglomerate decides to market a competing product this triggers an avalanche of fear among Good Try managers. The conglomerate's product will appear on store shelves in the Gobi Desert while the Good Try Company is still trying to get in local stores.

If the Good Try is a resource company the situation is similar. There may be sufficient gold reserves in the ground but the "recovery factor" was too low; the development expenses were too high; or the grade of ore declined rapidly after a short period of production. These problems can only be discovered after the company gives it a "good try".

The Good Try is a company on the verge of success but fails to succeed because of what, in short, makes capitalism what it is—a hard to predict adventure. Don't misunderstand us. We are not suggesting that managers in this sort of company are saints—far from it. In comparison to the Criminal Incompetents and Rampaging Bulls, these are hard working people with a product that might succeed on the open market.

For any broker or promoter to develop a Good Try is a major success in the securities industry. The Good Try managers inspire respect from competing brokers and envy from Minor Achievement, Waiting For Godot, and Criminal Incompetence managers.

The brokers and promoters involved with a Good Try are welcomed in any bar frequented by financial people. They are stars because they have helped every professional stock trader make money during the promotion.

These people may succeed in the future because they may understand that the quest for excellence includes failure as part of the learning process.

5. Category Five — Rampaging Bull's Company

The Rampaging Bull's Company is a major advance from the Criminal Incompetence category but is not as socially redeeming as the Good Try and the Successful Entrepreneur's Company.

The managers and brokers of The Rampaging Bull's Company are more corrupt and larcenous than those associated with a Minor

Achievement, a Good Try, or a Successful Entrepreneur's Company. They are essentially a much more polished and skilled version of the Criminal Incompetents.

The promoter, "The Rampaging Bull", sits on his throne in all his glory. An entire state or region or nation is enthralled with this company. This is the Giant who claims he has invented a self-playing harp and/or developed a goose that lays golden eggs.

The Rampaging Bull's Company raised several hundred thousand and perhaps several million dollars to finance everyone's salaries, bonuses, offices, and some product development or exploration. The company's offices are plush; everybody is calm; and the secretaries are attractive and efficient. This always convinces everyone that the company must be real. And why not? There is lots of money in the bank from Naive Beginners. There is, however, no revenue from sales. This company has so much smoke and so many mirrors that nobody knows what's going on.

The smoke can include letters of support, money in the bank, a charismatic leader, and many naive followers. The mirrors can include a technology that seems to work or reserves of immense mineral wealth which have yet to be revealed as being uneconomical.

The managers, for the most part, are competent although not inspired and have usually never been a success with real companies. The inspired person in this group is The Rampaging Bull. He carefully handpicks his associates for their ability to obey, follow orders, never say too much, and lie at appropriate times. The payoff is a handsome living—even if there is no commercial product.

The brokers involved in this type of company are thankful. The brokers can now dump all the Waiting For Godot, Minor Achievement, and Criminal Incompetence companies and move on to bigger deals.

"If you are going to be a crook, you might as well do it with the best," these brokers tell themselves. The brokers on the Rampaging Bull's team are not independent thinkers although they think they are; are not strong although they think they are; and are not smart although they think they are. You should not be doing serious business with these brokers because they only have one priority—getting you to buy and hold this stock.

The promoter, "The Rampaging Bull", has a lot of power. The promoter can attract hundreds of people, at the whisper of his name, to buy shares at $2 or more even if they are worthless. These people believe in the power of this Rampaging Bull to get people excited. They know he is a Master Promoter who can manipulate the price of the stock with great ability; hold a price he chooses against powerful short sellers in the opening stages of a promotion; and beat the most experienced traders. He can only be tripped up by an organized conspiracy of Master Traders or the passage of time if he doesn't develop a Successful Company.

Before we get carried away about The Rampaging Bull's abilities, we must emphasize that he needs a very exciting product idea which will "change the face of western civilization". This is a *vital* factor for success.

Some investors or traders in this company, however, don't even care if there is a product in the beginning stages of this promotion. The investors know the promotion can last three to four years with share prices fluctuating from $1 to $10 or more. The trading chart for The Rampaging Bull's Company will feature several bubbles with steep share price declines and inclines. This is bewildering to most investors. This will totally terrify the professional short sellers during the first couple years. They will wait on the sidelines before they eventually force the stock to a realistic price. The Rampaging Bull can write cheques for several hundred thousand dollars to prop up the stock. This scares his enemies and thrills his friends.

As far as the public is concerned there is a new product on the leading edge of its industry. This essentially means that revenues could become very large overnight. The Rampaging Bull's Company is always negotiating a deal with some conglomerate. You might hear the words "Japanese", "California", and "New York" in every other sentence.

The product can "be some kind of black box" in which certain magical things happen to produce something—anything. This "black box" is "patented", a deep secret, never explained, and if possible never shown to anybody.

We always hear that the development team, hidden away in their lab and rarely allowed to speak, is just about ready to make a breakthrough. Phrases such as "just another week"; "you should have seen the tests"; "Hitachi is sending spies to town, tell me if you see strangers in the area"; and "this is going to be the biggest thing in electronics, medicine, sports, or manufacturing during the last 100 years" are common.

When the developers come out of hiding they speak to financiers in the most convoluted way to terrify and confuse them. There may be a prototype they can show investors. The effect, product, or methodology is never completely demonstrated. The product "is top secret you know".

If the product is a resource, instead of high technology, then The Rampaging Bull's pitch might include the following lines:

■ "There is so much gold we've put security guards around the property;"

■ "You can see the gold from the plane for God's sake;"

■ "several major resource companies want to develop the property right away;"

■ "I can't let you buy more than 10,000 shares at $5. I'm serious."

The Rampaging Bull has two to three years to milk his audience before the stock price starts to decline. There is always a sense of mystery to confuse investors, traders, the industry, friends, relatives, the mining community, and managers. The only person who knows the whole story, and he is not telling, is the Rampaging Bull who is everyone's best friend. If clients don't invest, however, The Rampaging Bull can suddenly become everybody's rude and crude disciplinarian.

The traders do not dare short this stock in the beginning stages of the promotion because they have no idea how high the price will increase. Experienced traders will short this stock only after two to three years when The Rampaging Bull finally tires. Nobody can keep begging for $50,000 investments in a company which has, for some strange reason, not produced or mined a product.

When the experienced short sellers recognize that the Rampaging Bull is tiring they will come in for the kill and short the stock mercilessly. The traders believe there is no product and there may never be a product. Nobody, however, can ever figure out if there was, has been, or could have been a commercial product or proven resource.

If the company fails, The Rampaging Bull will whine in righteous indignation. It happens every time. The Rampaging Bull, incredibly, will whine to the media about scapegoats. The scapegoats include "eastern shorters", "western shorters", "cynics who don't know business", "wimps", "foreigners", and "saboteurs". This is a signal The Rampaging Bull is starting to stumble.

The Rampaging Bull, still a hero in certain segments of the financial community, can retire to his favourite bar and hold court about what went wrong. "Assholes tripped me up," the Rampaging Bull can say.

Everybody knows, however, that The Rampaging Bull has pocketed several million dollars in an offshore bank and is waiting to start his next big promotion. The Rampaging Bull smiles a lot in his new imported fancy-schmanzy four cylinder sports car when nobody is looking. He lives in a great home, tries to "help his friends" get their business started, and still eats in cafeterias when people are looking "because it is good to be real".

The Rampaging Bull is also making lists about which people to reward for their loyalty like a medieval despot handing out favours.

Everybody knows this and wants to be his friend. The Rampaging Bull, however, smiles at this fawning. He likes the leverage it gives him over people because for every dollar he hands out he will ask for $1.50 back. He'll laugh, be friendly, and ask personal questions while looking for weakness. It is a habit. He is building a dossier on how to use people. He is convinced he lacks real friends. He is right. He has lied and abused all his real friends on his way up. He must now buy everything. This makes him happy because he has no obligations. But he still needs to justify to his old friends that they should have stayed associated with him even if he abused them.

"It isn't easy getting to the top. People don't understand that," The Rampaging Bull might say.

The Rampaging Bull, at this stage, has now become a parody of the fictional heroes in the novels we suggest for further reading—in short, a true caricature. His enemies might joke about him as "Dracula", "Scrooge", "Stalin", "Citizen Kane", "A Little Hitler", or worse. It's amazing. It's pathetic.

A farsighted Rampaging Bull may recognize that his extreme vanity will create major problems. He may lose everything as his enemies conspire against him. He smiles at this thought. He is confident that this scenario is well into the future. He has bought half the city. Even if he loses everything, The Rampaging Bull believes he can win it all back. He will, however, begin to be much more security conscious—just in case.

That is why The Rampaging Bull avoids creating a paper trail or evidentiary trail for administrators of the justice system. The Rampaging Bull believes in the maxim: "no paper trail, no conviction."

Malignant narcissism can play strange tricks on an otherwise great mind. There is nothing you can do about this except maintain a sense of wonder and humour—if you haven't lost money. *Man does not always act rationally*, like economists insist. That is why things go wrong all the time.

The managers of this company, and especially The Rampaging Bull, have no idea what searching for excellence means. They only know this is a "cool" phrase to use in conversation with intellectuals whom they disrespect anyway. They will hire "excellence consultants" while laughing at them behind their back.

The only thing that can save The Rampaging Bull at this point is some traumatic event like a serious car crash, a disease, a death in the family, or "The Ghost Of Stock Promotions Past". These are among the very few things that might make a Rampaging Bull reform for a short period.

6. Category Six — Successful Entrepreneur

When a company finally gets real revenues and earnings which are expected to increase, it qualifies as a Successful Entrepreneur's Company.

The trading charts for a Successful Entrepreneur Company show share price increases which move steadily upwards with several twists and turns for profit takers. In the early stages of success this company has yet to "be discovered by major analysts" who, when they discover it, will promote the "hell" out of the company. This is the type of company that famous value investors like Peter Lynch, Benjamin Graham, Sir John Templeton, and Warren Buffett drool over. To find one of these companies at an early stage is to find a company whose stock can make you a multi-millionaire. If you buy this stock at $2 per share and every analyst in the world later thinks it is worth $40, you can think about retiring.

This company qualifies to be reviewed by major stock brokerage firms, pension funds, and everybody else as a "growth stock". The managers, however, should not be considered as "benevolent" people. More often than not, the managers of the Successful Entrepreneur's Company can be arrogant, selfish, and jerkish. These managers do, however, understand the idea of ethics or morality unlike The Rampaging Bulls and Criminal Incompetents. The managers of these companies, therefore, can behave ethically sometimes and especially when it suits their needs. The managers of these companies will do the right thing if they think their reputation as decent people will be undermined and if the cost of doing the right thing is low.

These people do understand excellence as a concept which can help them and their employees, even if they don't know how to achieve and maintain excellence.

7. Category Seven — The Warriorpreneur

We recognize there is an element of sensationalism to the way we classify this type of company. Humour us. During the initial stages a Warriorpreneur's Company is similar to the Successful Entrepreneur's Company.

The real difference between the two companies is how management approaches its employees, investors, suppliers, and associates. The Warriorpreneurs, almost ideal people and extremely rare, do the following:

■ reduce employee stress whenever possible;

■ isolate corporate bureaucracy from the company's champions who need elbow room;

■ plan details for achieving the strategic vision;

■ stick to the vision;

■ surround themselves with people of courage, ability, and benevolence;

■ listen to the visionaries;

■ listen to customers;

■ let people do their work on their own or as part of small teams;

■ encourage their troops;

■ reduce red tape;

■ have open communication at all levels of management;

■ are extremely fair but firm when necessary;

■ don't blame staff for everything that goes wrong;

■ consider work as play and almost a joy;

■ reduce management levels;

■ learn from experience.

The Warriorpreneur's style is analogous to how great fictional and real life heroes like Robin Hood, King Arthur, Davy Crockett, and Alexander The Great inspired their troops.

The Warriorpreneur, in short, is not jealous of his team and wants them to do as well if not better than he. The Warriorpreneur is well read and has achieved some wisdom.

The Warriorpreneur understands ethics as being a balance between courage, fairness, benevolence, prudence, and temperance. This means that he, as a humane and feeling person, commits himself or herself to being self-reliant and to fighting evil people. Evil people, to remind you, are unfeeling, narcissistic, ambitious, self indulgent, selfish, need to control or destroy others, limit liveliness, and create misguided movements.

In fact, the Warriorpreneur understands that the idea of being ethical means you must be a warrior. What else can you be? An ethical person must recognize the difference between good and evil, fight evil, and help the good even if he or she is the only person on the battlefield. He or she, as the warrior, does not believe the end justifies the means. The means and the end must complement each other and be moral.

This is romantic. This is breathtaking. Few people can do this. Ethics require too much energy and sacrifice from most people who are weak, ill, naive, narcissistic, or desperate.

James Bond, Robin Hood, Superman, Batman, Mike Hammer, Dirty Harry, Nero Wolfe, Sherlock Holmes, Perry Mason, Lovejoy, John Steed, Emma Peel, and other fictional heroes have shown that fighting evil is a lonely job. Most people prefer to watch heroes fight evil at the movies instead of doing it themselves day to day. The few ethical people left on the planet realize too many of their neighbours are easily seduced "Bubbleheads". *They don't know what they don't know.*

The Warriorpreneurs are the only leaders who can develop companies dedicated to *quality* and *excellence* as described by many thinkers including Edwards Deming, guru to the Japanese, and *In Search of Excellence* authors Tom Peters, Robert Waterman.

Unfortunately, there are very few, if any, major or large corporations in the Warriorpreneur category despite propaganda from the world's largest companies and their publicists. The Warriorpreneur Company, it seems, can only exist as a small tightly knit and cohesive team. Once a company achieves a certain critical mass the Rampaging Bulls, Criminal Incompetents, Waiting For Godots, and other leaches muscle their way in. The company then becomes yet another example of the modern corporate jungle. In fact, some think, as we do, that a team of 20 or fewer people is the ideal size to achieve excellence and keep a tight knit sense of family. There is debate on this issue.

Some large companies have tried valiantly to foster excellence by encouraging employees to think and act independently. This is, for the most part, a hopeless quest because big companies are crowded with Criminal Incompetents, Minor Achievers, Rampaging Bulls, and Naive Beginners all trying to crush the Warriorpreneurs and independent minded. The Warriorpreneurs almost always leave the "big" company to start "small" companies of like-minded associates which then grow. The cycle always continues. The larger the company, the more power, the less wisdom. Remember: Albert Einstein once said wisdom and power have rarely been combined and then only for a short time.

Larger Warriorpreneur companies can exist during the initial glory years. These years become the legend on which the company feeds forever. Future managers retell forever the exploits of the youthful warrior leader whose wisdom made things happen.

The Warriorpreneur's Company is, as you might guess, a true growth company with potential to make all investors rich. This is especially true during the early years. Everyone believes *excellence* is the essence of corporate culture. If you can find just one Warriorpreneur company, you will earn a fortune. When the Warriorpreneur finally sells the company hedge by selling shares, looking for another job, or looking for other suppliers.

7 | The Beast Never Goes Away

... *Fifth Tongue Lashing*

Keep one thing in mind: The Rampaging Bull never goes away—he's always lurking in the shadows to spread pain. There is no cure or vaccine against The Rampaging Bull. The only protection against The Rampaging Bull is to work with people who understand the nature and prevalence of this enemy and his lesser cousins, the Criminal Incompetents.

The Rampaging Bull's company, on the other hand, may have developed a functional product or resource, by accident or by skill. If this happens The Rampaging Bull moves his company to a senior stock exchange as a Growth Company. He searches for his people. They congregate. They work together. They can still promote, lie, and cheat. They can still develop "magical black boxes" which can change the world. They can still get people excited about investing and do everything they did on the penny stock market. It never ends.

It is just a bit harder to over promote a company that has revenues, a price earnings ratio, cash flow per share, book value, net worth, and a debt-equity ratio.

The Growth Company can be defined as a company with superior earnings which pays no dividend or a small dividend; which supposedly invests all extra cash into development; and is constantly being promoted for its potential.

Our goal, for now, is not to define the various subtleties of investing in Growth Stocks. This book can be helpful, however, when a Growth Company is being promoted. You can try every tactic discussed in this book. Managers are often available, as you might expect, to scoop your money. Growth Companies need promotion just like any penny stock to increase share prices and raise even more money for more growth.

If The Rampaging Bull takes over or develops a Growth Company you should not expect the company to succeed. The malignant narcissism of the top man subverts the efforts of the firm's champions. The Growth Company managed by a Rampaging Bull is usually a short to mid-term term phenomenon which offers excellent chances to earn capital gains on a quick sale. This company can only succeed in the long term through a stroke of good luck or if The Rampaging Bull hands management to more competent people.

The Growth Company managed by graduates from a Successful Entrepreneur or Good Try Company are the ones to watch. These former Good Try managers, now graduated to a Successful Entrepreneur Company, have the training, ability, talent, desire, and money to make a Growth Company succeed.

Mutual fund manager and author Peter Lynch says there are six classes of companies on the senior stock exchanges:

■ Blue Chip companies, which pay large dividends, are the elite of business; have large organizations; interest every business publication; and go out of business every generation.

■ Secondary Companies are solid well established companies with slightly less investor support than Blue Chip companies.

■ Asset Plays

■ Cyclicals

■ Turnarounds

■ Slow Growers

Slow Growers, analogous to Minor Achievers and Waiting For Godot companies on junior exchanges, are to be avoided. Asset Plays are companies with underused resources such as machinery, minerals, land, or people. Cyclicals, analogous to The Rampaging Bull's Company on penny stock markets, are usually manufacturing companies whose customers come in waves. Turnarounds, analogous to The Good Try on penny stock markets, are usually companies that might succeed. These companies need a promoter like The Rampaging Bull or the Warriorpreneur to give their stocks a jump start like any penny stock.

Blue Chip and Secondary Companies, on senior stock exchanges, do not offer as many opportunities for stock promotions. They grow slowly but pay dividends as part of their allure. These companies develop promotions and advertising to sell *product and their stocks*. These product promotions, many of which are crass and immoral, should be considered as important when shopping for Blue Chip or Secondary Company stock. A company with superior product promotion or advertising may be making money and may be a good speculation on the verge of greater growth. There are, apparently, 21,000 commercials produced for North American networks each year. The 100 largest companies sponsor three out of four of these commercials. This is power. This is the equivalent of a *cartel*. So pay attention to the TV commercials not as a consumer, but as an investor. The commercials can tip you off to very important trends which the huge corporations want to promote and develop. The smart investor should recognize this.

Should a Rampaging Bull, unfortunately, take over a Blue Chip or Secondary Company look for the following phenomena:

■ *outrageous salaries* for top executives 100 to 500 times larger than an ordinary employee;

■ deep *plush* carpets in executive offices;

■ *constant struggles* by lower echelon employees to get minimum salary increases;

■ cranky blue-collar workers who experience management *arrogance* every day and voice this *frustration* through strikes;

■ *abuse* of truly innovative people who often move on;

■ emphasis on *control* instead of *innovation;*

■ *stagnation* of product lines;

■ strange diversifications that contradict the company's philosophy;

■ a *climate of terror* rather than excitement;

▪ strict lines of communication from one management level to another which prevents *spontaneous communication* and praise for good employees;

▪ irrational decisions and *strange changes* in company direction;

▪ recruitment of overly ambitious and/or violent prone managers;

▪ constant efforts by managers to *ingratiate* themselves with outsiders as community boosters while they *rip out* the hearts of associates and employees;

▪ *systemic* lying to employees and the community;

▪ virulent *anti-union* attitudes;

▪ over emphasis on *secrecy* and *security*;

▪ *alienation* of staff from management.

When The Rampaging Bulls age their behaviour changes—but not by much. Here are some things an old Rampaging Bull does:

▪ delegates responsibility *without* authority;

▪ develops an even worse attitude of them versus us;

▪ complains that nobody can be trusted while he or she squeezes out high-level managers or employees he or she once needed;

▪ accepts even less advice than when he or she was young.

Does this sound like any political, criminal, or religious group you know about? Does thinking about this give you heartburn? The implications are scary for the future of the human race!

The United States Labour Department tells us that today's college graduates will change jobs 7.5 times—and that four of these job changes will be forced on the college graduates! Statistics Canada says these numbers are not available in Canada. Think hard. There are so many malignant narcissistics in charge of companies that the typical employee has to change jobs several times before he or she can find a happy niche!

Don't get confused here. Just because a corporate leader is celebrated, that doesn't make him or her a Rampaging Bull. The other factors we have listed must be present to varying degrees before you can conclude that the person in question is a Rampaging Bull. Do not expect any help from the media. They never, thanks to stringent libel and slander laws, describe a manager as a malignant narcissistic, a narcissistic personality disorder, or a "partial" psychopath—unless he or she is dead with no relatives.

The Rampaging Bull's sweet talking ways seduce the media. Journalists are gullible and like free food and drinks. Publishers need advertising dollars. Expect to see many glowing stories about The Rampaging Bull especially when he or she achieves critical financial mass and can afford to launch libel and slander actions against critics.

If a Rampaging Bull commits a crime or gets too pretentious, a frenzied and penitent media will rip every piece of meat from his or her bones like hungry piranhas. By then it's too late for traders and ordinary citizens to do much about foolish investments unless they can successfully short sell a stock.

Even many established brokerage houses, which pride themselves on correct behaviour, insist on sales quotas from their brokers. This means ethics have to be ignored in a competitive environment. The U.S. National Association of Securities Dealers reports a 35% increase in disciplinary actions against brokers and a 161% increase in arbitration cases between 1986 and 1992. Most of these problems are directly related to how young brokers are encouraged to act by their employers. The situation may get worse.

Don't expect help from anyone if you get tricked. Government and enforcement agencies have limited powers. You are on your own as a trader. *You* as a client must be able to *press* charges and *pay* legal fees. Don't ever forget those two words, *press* and *pay*. Every promoter believes you do not have the guts to do either when he or she takes your money. That's why you have to learn the fine art of memos, contracts, invoices, and paper trails.

Be cool. It's strange, not to mention scary, out there.

Caveat emptor.

8 | Coming Out Of The Chutes

. . . Sixth Tongue Lashing

The penny stock market investor must pass successfully through seven stages of development before he or she can claim to have graduated.

To experience these stages is like coming out of the chutes when the gate swings open. Every bullrider understands this special moment. The bullrider is sweating. The bull is sweating. Both animal and man are afraid, but excited. The adrenalin rush makes their heads spin. Neither of them knows what will happen, but both of them know that something horrible could happen.

You cannot advance from stage to stage unless you are ready or you will be trampled by The Rampaging Bull. The first four stages, which we review in this chapter, can be mastered by any beginner in a couple of years. You will know when you are ready to advance from one stage to another.

■ A. STAGE ONE — THE NAIVE BEGINNER

We have already described the Naive Beginner.

He has that reckless and unaware state of mind that I, the fairy-tale Jack, and my friend Jack had in the chapters titled *Beginner's Shock* and *Jack Meets The Rampaging Bull*.

Although the Naive Beginner is not prepared to invest, he will do it anyway. The Naive Beginner *does not know what he does not know*. Almost every stock market professional has a Naive Beginner investor story, about himself or someone else, to entertain dinner guests. This isn't funny, of course—nudge, nudge, say no more.

If you learn the fine art of speculating, all the other Naive Beginners can eventually make you rich. There is an endless supply of Naive Beginners. In fact, studies by a famous circus promoter have shown that one is born every minute. They are prepared to invest in or believe almost any fairy tale.

Many investors, unfortunately, never get beyond being Naive Beginners. We discussed some of the reasons in the chapters titled *You Don't Know; You Don't Know!*, *The Big Picture*, and *Discounters and Promoters Rule*. There is just one good thing about being a Naive Beginner—you can get lucky. Every once in awhile the Naive Beginner will meet a broker who will convince him to buy shares like the little man who convinced Fairy-Tale Jack to buy magical beans. These low-priced shares magically become high-priced shares and make the Naive Beginner rich for a little while. But, Beginner's Luck often turns into Beginner's Shock. We want you to avoid this by becoming a Careful Trader.

■ B. STAGE TWO—THE CAREFUL TRADER

Stage Two is exciting if done properly. Your goal in Stage Two as The Careful Trader is to increase your savings and earn more money than the bank offers you in interest. You will also learn to leave profit on the table for the other guy. This is crucial to your long term success.

Remember The Careful Trader's most important lesson: **a bear makes money, a bull makes money, and a pig gets slaughtered.**

Fairy-Tale Jack was a quick learner. Jack never scooped more gold from the Giant's stash than he could carry down the beanstalk. In short, Fairy-Tale Jack was not a pig.

The fundamental rules for becoming The Careful Trader are listed below. Chances are that you may think you are much more advanced as a speculator than these rules allow. Chances are, of course, that you are wrong. Re-read these rules as often as possible. Memorize them.

Rule 1 — You will never use the word "investor" again to describe yourself as a buyer and seller of penny stocks. You

are now a "trader". This very simple idea will liberate you. More than 80% of penny stock companies fail and their shares become worthless within three to five years. This means that you cannot expect to make money by buying and holding a penny stock. You must be active.

Rule 2 — Time is your enemy. This may be the biggest difference between buying senior stocks and junior stocks. Studies show that even if you buy senior stocks at the top of a market cycle you will often recoup your losses and go on to make money in the long run. Time can be your ally with senior stocks which can bounce back. Unfortunately, most penny stocks have a limited shelf life. You don't know the expiry date, but each passing day brings you closer to it. You must, therefore, never fall in love with a penny stock. You must be willing to take a profit or take a loss. Once a penny stock declines, it might never recover. If you learn nothing else in this book, remember this rule.

Rule 3 — Never buy more than 10,000 shares of a penny stock regardless how exciting the company may be. This allows you to move out of the market in one or two days of trading if things go wrong. This is a very difficult idea to master because you will always be tempted to buy more shares if you think the price will increase.

Rule 4 — If you don't know much about a stock never pay more than the market average. This gives you a fighting chance to make money if a promoter is serious about his stock. The average price of a share on a penny stock market usually varies from 40 cents to $1. Determine the average price of a stock on your stock exchange. If the stock you are interested in is selling well above the average price on the market, don't buy. Wait for another promotion to come along.

Rule 5 — Since you will likely ignore Rule 4, we will rephrase it. Buy most of your shares between 10 cents and 90 cents. This is about the average price of a stock on most penny stock markets.

Rule 6 — Only buy penny stocks that have an active and able promoter as part of the team. You must recognize that you can buy a penny stock whenever you want, but you will often find this stock hard to sell. A promoter will, you hope, create a market for your stocks when you want to sell them.

This rule must never be broken even if friends, relatives, acquaintances, and enemies beg you to buy their stocks. If you must be a "friend", which is an irrelevant idea in the stock game, then you must not pay more than five cents for a stock without a promoter. Nineteenth century San Francisco writer Ambrose Bierce, author of *The Devil's Dictionary* first published in 1906, defined a beggar as a rich man who got there because of his friends.

There are thousands of penny stocks that have no promoters and, as a result, have a small or non-existent market for their stocks. There are thousands of penny stocks that trade in North America on junior stock exchanges and on over the counter markets. There are not enough good promoters for every company.

Rule 7 — Never buy more than one stock at a time. You need to focus all your attention on the managers and promoters associated with any stock you buy. You can't afford to spread yourself thin.

Rule 8 — Learn how to leave something on the table for others, reduce your risk, and take a profit. A Careful Trader never tries to make a million dollars on any speculation even though he or she will hear stories about people who did. Always think of your profit as a percentage of your original investment. If you buy B.H. Beane International at 30 cents, sell it at a price which gives you a return two or three times higher than a bank. Don't wait for $20. Chances are better that you will see the stock at 20 cents.

In countries that don't have hyper-inflation, you might sell your 30 cent stock at a 30% profit after commissions. In our example, this means you will sell the stock at 40 to 50 cents. This is a difficult thing to do when the price of a stock goes up. You will be tempted to let the price of the stock go to the moon.

Rule 9 — If the 30 cent penny stock you bought drops in value, do not start whining. Sell when a stock loses 50% of its initial market value unless you have compelling evidence that the promoter is doing this as a ploy. The promoter might want to depress the share price before he moves the price back up. We will discuss this later at length. Compelling evidence of this tactic, however, does not include your unsupported hopes that the price of the stock price will increase.

The earlier that a significant share price drop occurs during a promotion, the less you have to worry that the share price has hit rock bottom.

A stock that has dropped by 50% of its value from 30 cents is probably being promoted by a weak promoter anyway. Sell. Take your loss like a warrior. Walk away. That is why you didn't buy hundreds of thousands of shares. You can sell out in one or two days of trading once you see that things are not turning out as expected.

Rule 10 — Never buy stock from a promoter on whose promotions you have lost money. You have learned a lesson. The promoter was weak. He couldn't get above the average price of a stock on the market you are playing. You will now search for a stronger promoter.

Rule 11 — You will probably ignore Rule 10 and revert to being a Naive Beginner. We all do it sometimes. Let's rephrase Rule 10. Never buy a stock from a promoter on whose deals you have lost money unless you can buy stock 30% lower than the highest share price of his worst promotion.

Rule 12 — Never buy shares from a promoter directly; always buy through a registered brokerage firm that must follow the rules and regulations of the local securities commission. The brokerage firm will deliver the shares you buy, a promoter might not.

Rule 13 — Buy shares recommended by a promoter only if he or she has connections with your country, province, state, or city. Avoid buying penny stocks listed on foreign exchanges from promoters you don't know—domestic or foreign. Deal only with brokers and promoters who live in your country, who nurture their public profile, who have a family, and who list telephones.

Rule 14 — Never guess what a promoter should be thinking. A Careful Trader will never buy or hold a penny stock because a promoter "would be crazy" to let the price drop below a certain price.

Rule 15 — If nobody takes responsibility for whispers and rumours by putting them in writing, then you should discount this information as much as possible. Every penny stock, during a promotion, trades because of "supposed insider information" which comes "from the horse's mouth". Yet few people have ever met the horse. You'll discover that nobody takes responsibility for this whispered information about a company's prospects, earnings, or current situation. The whispered, secret, and incredible "facts" are the promoter's major tool and should make you suspicious, not enthusiastic.

Rule 16 — If you have money don't get restless. Wait for the right promotion, the right promoter, and the right price. You will be vulnerable right after you make money on the stock market. You will be eager. You are on a roll. You will convince yourself that you can afford the risk because you are playing with "free" money. Don't be so eager to give back your winnings.

Rule 17 — Never let anyone talk you out of selling a stock once it reaches price levels you have set for yourself as an acceptable profit. Holding on too long is worse than selling too soon. Yet many investors would rather risk it all instead of collecting an "early" profit. Nobody has ever gone broke by taking small or premature profits. Yet this remains one of the hardest things to learn.

Rule 18 — Sell your shares if you buy because of a promised event which, for any reason, doesn't happen. The loss you suffer now will be much less than the loss you suffer later.

Rule 19 — Review a stock carefully if a promoter or manager fails to reach business targets and offers excuses on a regular

basis. **You may be getting a signal to sell.** The excuses might include:

- "The whole market is weak. It's just a correction;"
- "We have to go back to Taiwan for more meetings;"
- "We have a few details to work out in our negotiations;"
- "The pension funds are always slow to move;"
- "Investors are far too demanding. We need to keep control of the company. We need to find the right kind of investor."

Rule 20 — Buy at month end or on a Monday. Sell on a Friday and at the beginning of the month. There are many reasons for this phenomena. Promoters like to close the week with as high a share price as possible. The stock will look good in the weekend newspaper listings, generate trader excitement, and set the stage for heavy buying Monday. This of course does not always happen. Many speculators or insiders will try to unload their shares on Monday which can cause a price drop.

Once a share price reaches a certain level some brokerage firms will allow margin trading. The firm will advance you credit to buy a stock considered to be adequate collateral. This is exactly what the smart promoter wants you to do. The smart promoter will keep increasing the bids on the stock until about a week before the end of the month. Most brokerage firms review their client's margin position at month end. This is when bids for penny stocks decline rapidly. The promoters want to *force margin buyers to sell their shares at a lower price than they paid. This allows the promoter a chance to buy back cheaper shares.*

Rule 21 — Never buy escrowed or other restricted shares as a trader. Some shares are restricted from trading for a specified period. Restricted shares are for investors, not traders. A trader can't be handcuffed.

Final Comment On Careful Trading

The Careful Trader will win on most stock promotions launched by weaker promoters or Criminal Incompetents because he will sell before the promotion collapses. The Careful Trader, however, will miss the huge profits on stock promotions which do take the price to the moon. The Careful Trader, of course, doesn't care about what he missed. He knows there is always a new deal.

■ C. STAGE THREE—THE PROFESSIONAL

A Professional Trader is willing to assume a bit more risk because he has learned something as a Careful Trader.

He has learned something about promoters, managers, market players, and companies—but still doesn't want to get too deeply involved because he doesn't trust the typical promoter.

Rule 1 — Follow all the Stage Two rules with a few exceptions listed below.

Rule 2 — You can buy and sell more than one stock if prices are well below the average price on the stock market. A Professional Trader knows the principles in this book and can handle more than one stock at a time.

Rule 3 — Once the share price increases, sell some stock gradually. The Careful Trader sells all of his stock once the share price reaches a predetermined level. The Professional Trader wants to recoup his initial investment and take advantage of a good promotion. The Professional Trader tries to wring a little extra profit from a promotion.

Rule 4 — Once you recoup your initial investment, allow your remaining shares to ride the promotional wave as long as it seems appropriate. Don't buy more shares. A rising share price creates excitement that can build to a fever pitch. All trading discipline is usually ignored. Greed takes over. The Naive Beginner will often buy more shares at this point because the rising share price magically transforms his initial doubts into misplaced faith about the future of the company. If this happens to you, review Rule Two in Stage Two which states that you should never fall in love with a stock.

Rule 5— Sell when the price of your remaining shares reaches a level near the average of the market. Let's assume that the average share price on this stock market is about $1. When B.H. Beane International reaches 90 cents per share The

Professional Trader will consider selling off his remaining position. The ideal Stage Three Professional Trader is disciplined, not greedy, and controls himself. The Professional Trader can allow his remaining shares to drop as low as five cents in value before running the risk of losing money because he has already recouped his initial investment. By following Rule 5 The Professional Trader guarantees himself a healthy profit.

The key behind the success of this formula is simple. The Professional Trader never has too many shares. His position can always be sold in one or two days of trading. He has protected his investment as the price of the stock increases by collecting some profits. He has been easy on the promoter and sold his shares gradually.

Rule 6 — If you notice the stock is undergoing heavy trading volumes while the share price remains steady or drops, sell your entire position immediately. The stock promotion is usually finished when the trading volume increases dramatically, without a corresponding increase in the share price. The insiders are probably unloading their shares on "investors".

Rule 7 — Do a daily review of your stock positions because junior companies are unstable.

Final Comment On Professional Trading

The Stage Three Professional Trader will win on promotions conducted by weaker promoters because he believes the share price will not go very high. Since most promotions are weak or of moderate strength, The Professional Trader should do well.

The Professional Trader will usually sell prematurely shares being promoted by an unknown Rampaging Bull. The Professional Trader is trained to take his profits early.

If a Professional Trader follows these rules carefully then he or she can trade on penny markets with other people's money, take more profit than a Careful Trader, and still leave profit on the table for others. The Professional Trader might diversify some of his winnings into safe investments such as guaranteed income certificates, Treasury Bills, "deleveraged" real estate, or a sun holiday.

■ D. STAGE FOUR—THE DILIGENT

The Diligent Trader devotes more time to investigation than The Professional or Careful Trader and thus takes more risk.

When we use the word "diligent", we mean just that. One phone call to your broker does not qualify as a diligent investigation. We've discussed the things you can do to get information in Chapter Six, *A Penny's Many Faces*, and we will discuss the questions to ask in Chapter 19, *In Search of the Warriorpreneur*. But first ask yourself if you would keep buying this stock if its share price declined 10% to 30% quickly. If you hesitate to say yes, you haven't done enough diligent investigation. A true Diligent Trader knows that this stock is a winner regardless of price fluctuations. In fact, a price decline encourages The Diligent Trader to buy more shares. This takes commitment and courage.

Fairy-Tale Jack, as a Diligent Trader, might have looked into the background of the little man by the side of the road who offered to sell him magical beans. Jack would never have made the deal if he had found something bad about the little man. But suppose Jack's investigation showed the little man to be a philanthropist with occult powers? Would Jack have then done the right thing by trading his cow for the magical beans?

The Diligent Trader can do the following:

■ He can buy more than 10,000 shares.

■ He can pay more than the market average.

■ He can let the stock ride the promotion longer before selling.

The Diligent Trader can do all this because he or she has thoroughly investigated the product, the company, the market, the economy, and the managers. The Diligent Trader believes this stock has big potential.

The Diligent Trader can make or lose more money than The Professional or Careful Trader because he is taking a bigger risk. The Diligent Trader can get stuck with a lot of overpriced shares if things don't work out. What would have happened had trading in B.H. Beane International been halted for illegal activity; had promoters ran away with the money; or had short sellers won the battle against The Rampaging Bull? This happens all the time. The Diligent Trader could have lost his entire and substantial investment because of the extra risk he took while trying to make a killing.

■ FINAL COMMENT

The Naive Beginner is a capital loss waiting to happen. The Careful Trader settles for a predetermined percentage gain as he learns the ropes. The Professional Trader wants a bigger profit as he unloads his shares in stages. The Diligent Trader is looking for an even bigger win based on his diligent investigations into the background of the company and its team.

No matter how good you think you are, you should start as a Careful Trader. The rules have been carefully designed to protect you against your own greed. Don't be in a hurry to advance to the next stage. A Careful Trader can "live long and prosper".

The next chapter covers some intriguing moves for more advanced players. If you have a conservative nature you might skip to Chapter Ten where our story with Jack, Bob Holstein, and B.H. Beane International continues.

You don't need to know what advanced traders can do.

Seriously!

9 | The Expert Bull Riders

. . . Seventh Tongue Lashing

The experienced speculator can try some amazing moves.

But you should have a good reason for trying these more sophisticated techniques. Frankly, we can't think of many. You should not try any of the manoeuvres in this chapter with "rent" money! This is vital. If more people followed this rule the world would be in better shape.

■ A. STAGE FIVE — LEVERAGE TRADER

The Stage Five Leveraged Trader is willing to take an enormous risk by borrowing money to trade because he is supremely confident (and greedy) about penny stocks, the promoters, and his abilities. The Leveraged Trader pays attention to all the rules in Stages Two, Three, and Four while adapting them to his needs.

We do not recommend this type of trading unless you are a very experienced trader who enjoys high risk.

Suppose Fairy-Tale Jack's diligent investigation into the background of the little man on the side of the road revealed he really was a philanthropist who helps poor families? But suppose Jack and his mom didn't own the cow to trade? Suppose Jack and his Mom had mortgaged the farm to buy a milk producing cow? Would Jack have done the right thing by trading the cow for the magical beans? Maybe, maybe not! Suppose Jack's information about the little man as a philanthropist was wrong? Suppose the little man was really a con artist? Why not, it happens every day! This clearly proves the danger behind using leverage recklessly. You can become bankrupt if you leverage yourself against your assets in a risky venture, especially if you still owe money.

1. Strategy One

Most brokerage firms will not allow you to borrow money by using stocks in your portfolio as collateral unless the share price reaches $2 to $5. Every firm has different rules.

Let's assume that your fully paid 1,000 shares of Beane International trade at $5; that the brokerage allows you to borrow on stocks valued at $2.50 per share or higher; that the margin rate is 50%; and that you feel like buying another 500 shares on credit. Here's how the brokerage firm views your account:

■ The current market value of your 1,000 shares at $5 per share is $5,000.

■ Your debt to the brokerage firm for buying another 500 shares at $5 is $2,500.

■ Your total equity is now $7,500 (1,500 shares at $5 per share).

■ The brokerage firm will allow you to borrow 50% of $7,500 or $3,750.

■ You've already borrowed $2,500; you can still borrow $1,250.

We want to address two dangers inherent in this strategy. Since this is a penny stock, the share price might easily decline from $5 to $3. The stock will still be marginable but the brokerage will now only allow you to borrow $2,250 (50% of your 1,500 shares now worth $4,500 at $3 per share). You would then have to write a cheque for $500 to increase the value of your account to $5,000 to maintain your $2,500 margin loan.

But what if the share price declines below $2.50? The stock will no longer qualify for margin. You must pay your entire $2,500 debt to the brokerage firm immediately (or by month end). You will then probably be forced to sell your share position in a panic to raise money. You might even lose more money than you started with. This is the horror when a leveraged deal doesn't work. See how dangerous this can be?

2. Strategy Two

The *smart* Leveraged Trader learns how to leverage *and* hedge. Let's assume you, as a budding Leveraged Trader, buy a secure $3,000 short term government bond such as a Treasury Bill from your profits on Beane International. You deposit the Treasury Bill, whose value will not vary, with your brokerage firm.

The $3,000 Treasury Bill sits in your account at the brokerage firm earning interest. This makes the brokerage firm feel secure. The brokerage firm allows you to buy penny stocks on credit in a margin account backed by this $3,000 Treasury Bill as collateral.

Let's assume that you buy 10,000 shares of another penny stock, let's call it Black Box Enterprises, at 25 cents per share on credit by using the $3,000 Treasury Bill as collateral.

You now have a $3,000 Treasury Bill earning interest and 10,000 shares of Black Box Enterprises bought on credit for $2,500 at 25 cents per share plus current interest charges.

This might be excellent use of leverage if Black Box Enterprises increases in value. If the share price increases, the interest charges on the borrowed money are more than covered by the capital gain from Black Box Enterprises.

If the Black Box Enterprises stock declines from 25 cents to 15 cents, for instance, the Stage Five Trader doesn't have to sell the stock he has bought on credit. In fact, the Stage Five Trader can hold the stock as long as he wants, if he pays the interest charges on his margin debt. The brokerage firm knows The Leveraged Trader can always pay for his Black Box Enterprises stock with his $3,000 Treasury Bill. This is why the asset used for collateral must be secure and independent of the stock market.

You should be aware that the interest charges on your margin loan will usually be greater than the interest accruing on your Treasury Bill. The spread will not be large, but there is a spread.

Black Box Enterprises, of course, might not rebound and you, as The Leveraged Trader, may decide to sell the Black Box Enterprises stock at the lower price for a loss. You will cash your Treasury Bill, pay the $1,000 loss if you sold at 15 cents per share plus commissions and interest charges. Pocket the balance from the sale of the Treasury Bill.

You, as The Leveraged Trader have lost—but not significantly. You survived this loss because you didn't buy too many

Black Box Enterprises shares. You *hedged* your bet by leveraging against a very secure asset that is immune to stock market swings. You didn't have to sell. You could never lose more money than you had available for investment.

3. Final Comment On Leverage Trading

The Leveraged Trader, because he is risking more, tries to get involved only with stronger promoters such as The Rampaging Bull. There is no point leveraging anything against weak promoters. That is why The Leveraged Trader must learn as many investigative tricks as possible to uncover the top promoters.

■ B. STAGE SIX — THE HEDGED TRADER

If Fairy-Tale Jack had understood the idea of hedging he would have done one of two things:

■ offered to hand over the cow to the little man on the side of the road only after the magical beans sprouted;

■ arranged to share whatever he found in the Giant's house without trading the cow. This would have been an excellent hedged deal if the little man had accepted the terms.

The Hedged Trader, who can also be referred to as the first stage shorter, operates between The Leveraged Trader and The Master Trader whom we discuss next.

The Hedged Trader, a.k.a. the First Stage Shorter, wants to profit as the share price *increases* and as the share prices *declines*. The Hedged Trader, generally, believes that the stock price will eventually decline at some point, but isn't sure when. Since eight out of ten penny stock companies fail and their shares become worthless, The Hedged Trader is on fairly safe ground.

The Hedged Trader is similar to The Careful Trader and The Professional Trader when he takes profits on the way up instead of waiting for the stock to hit $20. The Hedged Trader is a more advanced trader because he *positions* himself to profit from, what he believes, the *eventual* share price collapse. He does this by short selling some shares as the price increases. He establishes his short position on the way up because most stock exchanges will not let you short a stock in a declining market.

The Hedged Trader, however, should never short sell more shares than he owns. To short more shares than you own moves you into the high risk world of the Stage Seven Master Trader.

Let's assume The Hedged Trader buys 10,000 shares of B.H. Beane at 30 cents the same starting point we used for The Careful Trader and The Professional Trader. Let's assume The Hedged Trader believes the stock will not go over 75 cents and will decline. Let's also assume the stock increases to 60 cents.

The Hedged Trader sells 5,000 shares at 60 cents and pockets $3,000. He lets the rest of his 5,000 shares ride the promotion. The stock goes to 68 cents.

The Stage Six Hedged Trader isn't sure what is going to happen next like everybody else. He believes, however, that the share price will decline. Here is what he does.

1. Open Short Account "B"

The Hedged Trader opens a second account, a "Short" Account B. He instructs his broker to sell 2,500 shares of B.H. Beane, which he doesn't own, at 68 cents for a cash balance of $1,700. He thinks the price of the stock will eventually drop and that he can buy it back to cover his short position for less than he sold.

The Stage Six Trader also has a "Long" Account A. He still owns 5,000 shares of B.H. Beane International in this account originally bought for 30 cents per share. Two things can happen now. The B.H. Beane International share price can increase or decrease.

2. The Share Price Decreases

Let's assume that The Hedged Trader, after much soul searching, finally sells his 5,000 shares of B.H. Beane in his Long Account at 55 cents instead of 68 cents, the most recent high. The Hedged Trader pockets $2,750.

The share price looks like it will continue to decline. What does he do with his Short Account B? He lets it ride since he is making money as the stock price declines. He lets his Short Account ride for as long as possible. Suppose the stock drops to

20 cents. The Hedged Trader, recognizing his Prophet-like qualities, may decide to settle his Short Account B. The Hedged Trader buys 2,500 shares to return to the brokerage firm at 20 cents per share. You'll remember The Hedged Trader borrowed these shares to sell at 68 cents in his Short Account B. The Hedged Trader's profit is 48 cents per share or $1,200.

The Hedged Trader's total return for this entire scenario is $3,950 rather than $2,750 which he would have earned without shorting the stock.

3. The Share Price Increases

Suppose the price of B.H. Beane International stock increases from 68 cents to $1.20. The Hedged Trader recognizes that this promoter has strength. He was wrong to short when he did.

The Stage Six Hedger has four options he can choose. The right choice requires experience and intuition.

Option 1 — The Hedged Trader does nothing. He will make money as the share price increases because he owns more shares than he has shorted.

Option 2 — Let's assume he sells 2,500 shares at $1.20 to pocket $3,000. He also keeps 2,500 shares in his Long Account A to cover his Short Account B which is short 2,500 shares. He can hold this position for long as he wants. When the price bubble bursts, The Hedged Trader will sell his long position in Account A as fast as possible. The Hedged Trader can now profit from any further price declines because he has an outstanding short position.

Option 3 — He can sell all 5,000 shares in his Long Account A at $1.20 to pocket $6,000 as a financial cushion. He also has $1,700 in his Short Account B from the sale, at 68 cents per share, of 2,500 shares which he borrowed and must return. His total financial cushion is $7,700.

The Hedged Trader will do this only if he is sure the promoter has run out of bullpower. He has made enough money to cover his short position if the share price keeps increasing—for awhile. He is confident the share price will drop. This is a risky initiative and not recommended for a Budding Hedger. The share price could increase to $3 at which point The Hedger will start losing money. The Hedged Trader might then buy 2,500 shares at $3 for a heartbreaking $7,500 plus commissions. He settles his Short Account B by returning the 2,500 shares to the brokerage firm. The Hedged Trader will then consider himself lucky to have come out even. He has discovered that the promoter has staying power.

Option 4 — Suppose The Hedged Trader follows Option 3 but the share price increases beyond $3 while The Hedged Trader is still short 2,500 shares at 68 cents in Short Account B?

The Hedged Trader is now losing money because his financial cushion was only $7,700. The share price may continue increasing to $30 or more because the promoter may be a Rampaging Bull, a Successful Entrepreneur, or a Warriorpreneur.

The Stage Six Hedger can then become a Bullish Hedged Trader by buying twice as many shares for his Long Account A than he is short in Account B. Let's suppose the Bullish Hedged Trader buys 5,000 B.H. Beane International at $3.50. He now has a position similar to where he started in the first place with twice as many long shares as he has short shares. The Bullish Hedged Trader makes rather than loses money if the share price keeps increasing.

Suppose the share price declines from $3.50 after he bullishly buys 5,000 shares. The Hedged Trader has now been "whip-sawed" and will probably never short a stock again.

4. Final Comment On Hedged Trading

The Hedged Trader does better with promoters who are weaker. This trading style can be useful when share prices decline after a moderate increase. The Hedged Trader does worse when the stock is promoted by a more sophisticated promoter who can take the stock on an extended run.

If you plan on short selling penny stocks, Hedging is a worthwhile strategy to learn because it reduces the pain of making the wrong choices. The Hedged Trader makes smaller but less risky profits and is generally happy since eight out of 10 junior companies do fail.

■ C. STAGE SEVEN — THE MASTER

The *true* Master Trader knows all and sees all. The Master Trader makes his move on the merits, not arrogance, anger, resentment, or vengeance. The Master Trader is a careful evaluator because he risks substantial amounts of capital to take on The Rampaging Bulls at their game.

The Master Trader is, therefore, a realist—not a disillusioned cynic. A cynic rarely reaches this stage of trading. The disillusioned cynic believes that 10 out of 10 penny stock companies will quickly fail and their stocks will decline in value. The cynic can lose a fortune as a short seller. The Master Trader knows that many, *but not all*, penny stocks will fail sooner or later—only the timing is in doubt. He has taken it upon himself, as a local hero, to predict when things will go wrong.

How does he do it? The Master Trader has experience and superior information. He will even pay private investigators for information to complement his intuitive skills. The Master Traders lurk in shadows, caves, and fancy restaurants just like Fairy-Tale Jack hid in the copper cauldron to wait for the right moment to pounce and scoop the gold. The Master Trader's superior information allows him to buy or short sell with equal confidence. When The Master Trader chooses to short sell, he transforms himself into The Big Bear.

Every promoter recognizes the danger of the reclusive Big Bear with his or her claws, huge paws, and awesome power. The promoters don't want The Big Bear to notice them. That is why promoters and managers hide as much sensitive information as they can about their company during a promotion. Promoters don't want The Master Trader to awaken and transform himself or herself into The Big Bear who can short a promotion to pieces.

The Big Bears win consistently because they pick the right moment to short a stock. If The Big Bear picks the wrong time to short a penny stock, he can easily lose a fortune.

That is why our corporate stages of development are so important. The Rampaging Bull's Company or The Good Try should not be shorted for *two to three years*. The Rampaging Bull or the Good Try team will be busy raising money, promoting the stock, recruiting new investors, pleading for government grants, and holding regular press conferences. An over confident and cynical short seller might short a stock at $6 only to watch it go to $30. He discovers too late that promoters have power. This is not good— nudge, nudge; say no more.

The well trained and disciplined Big Bear shorts The Rampaging Bull's Company or The Good Try only after these companies have tackled the market and failed. The Big Bear gives these companies enough time to wear themselves out.

Most managers and promoters won't admit they have failed to develop their companies. The burden of bringing reality to the share price rests with The Master Trader and his well thought out analysis. He becomes very wealthy when the share price tumbles from $30 to $5 or lower.

You do realize, of course, that many Master Traders are not ethical people—surprise, surprise. Some Big Bears don't even bother to borrow shares from a brokerage firm to sell on the open market or declare their sales as short sales. This is usually illegal.

The Big Bear can tackle lesser corporate promotions, including those classified as Minor Achievers and Criminal Incompetents, by short selling their stock as early as possible. The Big Bear knows he can crush a weak promoter. The Master Traders, however, rarely waste their time with minor promotions because they have their eye on the activities of The Rampaging Bulls. Keeping track of The Rampaging Bulls is almost a full time job.

Here is what The Big Bear might have done in the examples we shared with you earlier. We use the prices we used previously to keep things simple. Keep in mind that The Big Bear will probably be doing these manoeuvres after a long period of time and at much higher prices.

Let's assume that The Master Trader bought 10,000 shares of B.H. Beane International at 30 cents for $3,000; sold 5,000 Beane shares at 60 cents to pocket $3,000; and sold 5,000 shares of B.H. Beane International at $1.20 to pocket another $6,000. As The Master Trader watched this stock increase in price he started growling. His investigations, for instance, might have convinced him that this stock was not worth the share price and had become a short selling candidate.

Let's assume The Master Trader unleashes his claws to become The Big Bear. The Big Bear sells 2,500 shares, which he doesn't own, for his Short Account B at $1.50 for a $3,750 balance.

This can be an excellent initiative since most penny stock markets have very few shares trading higher than 90 cents. The Big Bear must be *completely* convinced that the promoter can't promote the price any higher. This is an extremely dangerous initiative which can backfire because the Big Bear has a totally unprotected short position. The Big Bear must know the promoter, the company, and the players.

Suppose, however, the stock increases to $2.

The Big Bear has nothing to worry about if the price of the stock doesn't go much higher, too quickly. The Big Bear has a financial cushion from earlier profits on this deal which helps absorb a sharp share price increase—for awhile.

He has, however, a lot to worry about if the promoter suddenly shows terrific staying power and moves the stock higher. The Big Bear, in this example, might settle his Short Account B and lose some of his previous profits.

Let's assume, however, that The Big Bear has superior information because of his connections and investigations. The Big Bear also has a degree of courage the average trader does not have. The share price goes to $2. The Big Bear sells another 2,500 shares for his Short Account B at $2 for a cash balance of $5,000. He fully expects the price to decline soon.

Suppose the share price increases from $2 to $2.50. Big Bear sells another 2,500 shares for his Short Account B at $2.50 for a cash balance of $6,250. He has never been surer that the share price will decline. Let's assume The Big Bear repeats this process every time the share price increases.

You'll notice that Big Bear is relentless. He believes that The Rampaging Bull promoting B.H. Beane is a phony, that there is no pot of gold, and that the share price will decline.

You will notice also that The Rampaging Bull is relentless in his efforts to push the stock price higher. He wants to force Big Bear to buy at higher prices to cover his short positions.

The Big Bear must have substantial assets for this scenario to be allowed by any brokerage firm. The Big Bear has borrowed, more or less, 15,000 to 25,000 shares; sold the shares at prices ranging from $1.20 to $3; deposited about $25,000 to $40,000 in his short account; and expects to buy the shares back at a lower price for a big profit. This takes real courage and a big bank account as the share price increases to $3.50 or higher.

Let's suppose the price of the stock declines, as it usually does in real life. The Big Bear makes money at each drop in price.

Suppose, however, The Rampaging Bull turns out to be supremely gifted and convinces everyone to buy stock at prices over $3. If the Big Bear is strong enough he can keep shorting the stock all the way up. The Big Bear knows that his strategy will win eight out of 10 times and that he has large resources to survive.

A weaker Big Bear might lose courage, settle his account, and take a loss. When he buys shares at the higher prices to return to the brokerage firm, his loss might top $20,000 to $40,000. Keep this in mind.

A Big Bear usually has a *six figure trading account* which gives him clout. He can wait for the promoter to fumble his promotion which he often does.

The Big Bear will decide on the merits whether to continue the battle with the promoter over the share price. The Big Bear will take his loss if he decides that the company is worth over $3 or more per share—which is rare. The Big Bear evaluates the company's product, management, the promoter's courage and clout, and the mood of the market. He employs the tools and tricks common to industrial espionage which includes hiring private investigators.

If Big Bear discovers The Rampaging Bull's company is overvalued at $3 per share he will do something more horrifying to the promoter. The Big Bear will call on other Big Bears, who know and respect each other, to come out of their caves to fight The Rampaging Bull. The promoter can only win this titanic struggle if he is rich and his stock is widely held as part of a sophisticated promotion. The Big Bears will usually deliver a knock out punch. Here's the truth:

■ The promoters, strong or weak, will eventually lose every time against The Big Bears if the stock is overvalued.

■ The Big Bears are experienced bull tamers. They will corral Rampaging Bulls sooner or later. Later can come quickly if there are enough Big Bears lined up to do battle with The Rampaging Bull. If The Rampaging Bull tires and the share price declines from $30 to 75 cents, the Big Bears can earn a fortune as short sellers.

■ A bored Big Bear looking for action might short a minor promoter's stock. This means the weaker promotion for a Minor Achievement or Criminal Incompetence company will be finished sooner than expected. If you, as a Diligent Trader, discover the Big Bears are moving in on a stock you are playing, go with the flow. Sell your position. Try a short sale if you feel bold.

■ D. PERKS FOR PROFESSIONALS

Even the most experienced traders can become "Flyers" when they buy shares in a company before a broker and or promoter comes on board. We encourage you not to do this. The Flyer, like The Master Trader, has a superior network of associates who keep track of what promoters are doing, discussing, and even thinking. If The Flyer and his team discover that a promoter might promote a penny stock, they scoop a few shares on the open market.

The Flyers are not pigs. They hedge their bet by not buying many shares like Professional and Careful Traders. The typical Flyer might buy up to 5,000 shares of a stock before a promoter comes on board. The price of a stock must be very inexpensive because a penny stock without a promoter or revenues is essentially worthless.

The Flyer is risking no more than $500 to $1,000 on this venture. This is a lot of money for working people. For someone like a Careful, Professional, Diligent, or Master Trader this is a calculated risk. The Flyer must be prepared to write off this purchase in case the promoter decides against doing business with this company.

The Flyer has gone to the effort of getting superior intelligence on a company and on a promoter. The Flyer may, however, lose more than he wins.

Imagine the thrill of buying 5,000 shares for five cents per share and selling them for $2 per share. This stock will provide The Flyer enough of a financial cushion to try other gambles. This type of trading must only be made when the information falls into your lap, and is to be avoided under most circumstances.

▓ E. MOVING UP

Most of us want to get involved in the world's senior stock exchanges that feature blue chip, secondary, growth, cyclical, turnaround, and asset play companies. The share prices, unfortunately, are beyond the reach of most people.

The rules for trading in stocks of more established companies are generally different. However, traders and investors can apply many lessons in this book on senior stock exchanges.

The game still involves speculation; brokers try to manipulate the senior markets the way they try to manipulate penny markets; and the personalities are similar.

Recent and continuing securities scandals in Japan, the United States, and elsewhere have proved that Rampaging Bulls and Criminal Incompetents can emerge in any market wearing many disguises. We believe the degree of arrogance, vanity, and larceny among managers of companies listed on senior exchanges is comparable to the managers of penny stocks. There may be more Rampaging Bulls per capita as managers and promoters of companies listed on senior stock exchanges than there are on junior stock exchanges. Nobody has made a reliable estimate.

The typical company listed on senior stock markets is promoted six ways compared to only three ways for a penny stock.

1. Penny Stock

The typical penny stock has a much weaker promotion:

■ Brokers promote the stock;

■ Hired promoters hype the stock;

■ "Investors" gossip about the stock.

The company is too poor to hire advertising agencies. The press and analysts consider the company with contempt. This is an important distinction between senior and junior stocks.

2. Senior Stock

■ The typical senior company advertises products directly *and the company's stock indirectly;*

■ Stockbrokers promote the stock;

■ "Investors" gossip about the stock;

■ Analysts recommend the stock;

■ Business journalists review the stock;

■ Hired promoters hype stock.

Analysts or "analists", depending on whether you have a sense of humour, tend to search out managers and promoters who have done well in the past as people who should be watched in the future. This, if you think about it, is blatant promotion because it encourages brokers to sell their clients on what are "perceived" as hot stocks at inflated prices. This is precisely how The Rampaging Bull promotes his latest penny stock.

That's why we are in full agreement with the value investing rules of John Marks Templeton who chalked up tremendous results with his various Templeton mutual funds; Peter Lynch, the successful mutual fund manager and author of *One Up On Wall*

Street; Sydney Cottle, Peter Dodd, and Benjamin Graham as authors of *Security Analysis* and *The Intelligent Investor*.

These gentlemen believe, or believed, that the best thing you can do as an investor is to find public companies that offer superior value at low share prices before analysts do. This is analogous to buying a penny stock just as a promoter launches his campaign. The "investor" who finds a superior company on a senior stock exchange, trading at low share prices, can be certain this company will be discovered eventually by everyone.

University of Chicago Professor Eugene Fama suggested, in a 1964 thesis and in a famous 1970 *Journal Of Finance* article, that stock markets are too efficient for those looking for deals. Popular books and magazines such as *Worth, Forbes, Fortune, The Wall Street Journal, Barron's,* and Bruce Malkiel's *Random Walk Down Wall Street* have debated this theory. The market efficiency theory in short says: The price of a stock reflects, almost immediately and accurately, all available information. This means when you buy XYZ stock at $10 it's worth $10—no more and no less because all information has been accounted for.

We appreciate these ideas even though we don't think the market adjusts instantly to information or that all information is evaluated accurately. Nobody can accurately and quickly adjust to all information. There are more than 30,000 publicly traded companies in North America. There is too much information flowing at everyone. Everyone can't respond to everything instantly. The average broker is doing well if he can find time "once a month" to read, never mind consider, what his own firm's analysts are saying. There are thousands of deals out there.

We do agree, however, that the market responds to information. Everyone in the stock market will eventually discover a company that has a significant material change. The crowd will, sooner than later, discover these "value" companies, rename them "growth" companies, and bid the shares beyond their value.

The fathers of value investing believe material changes in a company will be reflected in the stock price when analysts, brokers, and press understand the deal and promote the "hell" out of it. They believe that a hard working investor can uncover some pretty hot deals well before the analysts and their promotion machines. Once everyone talks up a company, and in turn proves that the market is efficient, you will pay a higher price for the shares. Consider this:

■ The penny stock promoters are analogous to senior stock market analysts, business journalists, and advertising gurus who are all promoting a stock in one way or another.

■ Mutual fund, pension fund, and other institutional managers can manipulate prices of senior stocks among themselves much the way cash rich promoters manipulate penny stocks.

■ Mutual fund managers, pension fund managers, analysts, brokers, corporate executives, and the press can convince everybody a company is a "growth company" even when it is not. That is why these influence peddlers are regularly courted by company spokesmen as a vital component to becoming known as a "growth" company.

■ You can buy a senior stock before the promoters get on board while you must wait for the promoter to get on board a penny stock.

■ The "investor" in senior stocks can then follow all the rules of trading we have set out in this book for penny stocks and do extremely well.

In the end, we are all speculators. You can quote me.

■ F. FINAL COMMENT

If you are a beginner you may not have understood everything in this chapter. Don't worry, be happy.

We recommend that you graduate yourself to being a Hedged Trader and a Leveraged Trader only after a long and profitable apprenticeship as a Careful, Professional, and Diligent Trader. You will not deprive yourself if you never become a Hedged or Leveraged Trader.

You will need the rest of your life to become a Master Trader. You may, however, never qualify as a Master Trader because you can't overcome your greed or you don't have $100,000 to lose without sweating.

Learn what you can. Do your best. Use our Due Diligence Test in Chapter 19 as often as possible. Cultivate friendships with experts. Ask for help. Improve on what we offer. Remember that people have become more restless and speculative about everything.

Your government, for God's sake, encourages you to speculate and lose money every day. These speculations include lotteries, gaming casinos, bingo, horse or greyhound racing, pull-tickets, and future considerations for political donations during elections. Is this all *reckless* speculation? Certainly!

Expect to lose in penny stocks before you win. If you follow our guidelines your losses will be minimized and you will have a realistic chance of eventually becoming a winner.

More Beginner's Shock

10

... There Is No Other Way To Learn

I met Oswaldo at the 12 St. Bar and Grill for lunch. I wanted the gossip "on the street" about The Rampaging Bull. Oswaldo wanted me to buy him a pizza. We were both happy.

"Don't get too carried away with this Beane stock," said Oswaldo as the server delivered the gourmet pizza with anchovies, garlic, fresh tomato, and green peppers.

"I don't like penny stocks. I don't even like growth stocks— the ones with real earnings and a chance to go to the moon. They are always being promoted beyond what they are worth. I like high quality bonds, income stocks, and stocks that have yet to be discovered by analysts," he said.

I nodded my head. I couldn't disagree with his conservative approach to the stock market. I liked how Oswaldo was handling my account. I had, however, made up my mind to learn as much as I could about penny stocks.

"Isn't that what I am trying to do?" I asked. "I'm trying to get a piece of a company's future earnings at a price below what it might be worth in the future?" Oswaldo nodded his head unconvinced. I was buying lunch so he didn't want to fight.

"Sure. That's why I am saying don't get carried away. Holstein is a great promoter, not an administrator. There are no revenues. Don't get bogged down with too many shares. You are depending on too many factors to make money. You are relying on Holstein's talent to pick a company with a commercial product; ability to promote; ability to raise money; and ability to kick start the company to make everyone rich.

"If Holstein is committed to this deal you will have a chance to make money. If he's a flake, he'll pocket investor money, the stock price will drop quickly, and you'll lose money. This is a dangerous bet for any investor," said Oswaldo looking at me directly in the eye.

"I think you've just described the essence of the penny stock market," I said as Oswaldo took a bite of the pizza.

"I'm a genius. Pass the chili pepper," Oswaldo said.

Then Oswaldo laughed. He told me that the chances of making money at the prices I had paid for B.H. Beane International were good.

"Holstein is a good promoter. Holstein made his money with at least two boiler room operations. You know what they are—the outlaw brokerage firms that employ aggressive sales people to sell worthless stock while doing everything they can to stop clients from selling.

"Good grief! You should have seen him in the old days. He would phone clients with a garbage can over his head to simulate the sound of people talking in a mine. He'd tell his clients the gold mine looked like a jewellery store. If city crews were doing street repairs below his office windows he'd stick the phone out of the window and tell investors he was at the drillsite," said Oswaldo. I laughed.

"Holstein is flashy. He dresses well. People are so simple minded they think a man in an expensive suit is important. He also likes to get involved in groups that help the unfortunate or downtrodden. It makes him feel important. People down on their luck are also easier to manipulate. This biogas digester deal must have a couple of desperate inventors who will do anything to make a fortune," said Oswaldo.

"He comes off sweet and fun when he first meets you. But he has a hot temper if he doesn't get his way. He is smart. He likes to insult or make fun of people to their face because he thinks everybody is so insecure that they will come back for more. He *thinks* he is smarter than everybody. His ego is so big that he needs a van to move it from place to place," Oswaldo said.

I told him that's not the story I got from Jack who thinks Holstein is one of the coolest, nicest, and warmest people he has ever met. Oswaldo laughed. Then he ate some more pizza.

"Jack is smart, but naive. Jack is like 99% of the people. He doesn't know what he doesn't know," Oswaldo said. I got intimidated. I put on my knowing look because I wanted to be part of the magical One-Percent-Know-It-Alls Club.

"That's why the world is in a mess. Nobody understands people like Holstein. Every investor wants a promoter who will be kind to him or her but abuse everybody else. Researchers have done psychological tests on college students who were asked to subject other people, as test subjects, to pain. The college students didn't need much encouragement to hurt other people. This is extremely frightening. This is just another clue that people may be greedy and easily seduced "weasels" to quote a famous late night TV show host," said Oswaldo.

"Holstein is so cunning that he even spreads bad rumours about himself so he can deny them later. This always boggles my mind. He doesn't even tell his public relations consultants what he is doing because he thinks they are 'big dorks' who can't be trusted.

"Everybody thinks big-money foreigners will help his promotions. Brokers in my office say Holstein brokered a deal between the Mossad and the Arabs; that he is on a first name basis with the biggest U.S. mobster; and that he is part Chinese. This Chinese thing blows me away. His mother, according to this stupid rumour, is Chinese and her extended family is supposedly very *big* in Hong Kong," said an exasperated Oswaldo.

"Why would Holstein make these stories up?" I asked. Oswaldo looked at me. I was dangerously close to being demoted from the One-Percent-Know-It-Alls to the naive 99% group.

"Who do you think leaks all those embarrassing personal details about celebrities to tabloid magazines?" Oswaldo asked.

"The celebrities themselves??!!" I said incredulously.

"Celebrities recognize that positive stuff is boring. Celebrities try to get publicity by unveiling every stupid thing they can about themselves to get ink—through other people of course. As long as people talk about you, you are a commodity. Think about it. Who, but Holstein, would even think about spreading a rumour that he is Chinese? He doesn't even look Chinese for God's sake," said Oswaldo.

"I've tested people's gullibility. I actually told a few friends that I am a Chinese from Hong Kong. I wanted to test how gullible my friends are. They believed me," said an exasperated Oswaldo. This was intriguing stuff. When Oswaldo and I finished lunch, I phoned Jack to tell him I was ready to meet Holstein.

"By the way, if I told you I was related to the royal family of Burma, would you believe me?" I asked Jack. He wanted to know who Burma was.

FRIDAY, MARCH 20 — the press gets involved

Two days later the newspaper carried a story about B.H. Beane International Inc. with a photo of Holstein and the chairman of the food bank at a fund raising event. The news story explained that Holstein was negotiating with a major automobile company to develop methane combine and tractor engines; that the manager of the largest energy self-sufficient pig farm in the U.S. had joined the board; and that Holstein was planning to visit Asia where biogas technology is developed.

I checked the stock pages. Beane stocks had traded at 90 cents the day before. I phoned Bungee. There were 100,000 shares bid at 95 cents and only 30,000 shares offered at $1.00.

"You won't believe this," Bungee said. "There's talk that Holstein is planning to bring over 50 Chinese, Indians, and Pakistanis to Canada to train domestic farmers about energy self-sufficiency. He wants to bring them over as part of a special immigration package. Every applicant for immigration to Canada gets special status and almost immediate entry if he or she can invest $150,000 in a thriving enterprise," Bungee, now an immigration expert, told me.

"This, by the way, hasn't been confirmed. Oh yeah, did you know that Holstein has relatives who have been in Hong Kong banking for 100 years?" Bungee said. I groaned. I was impressed with Holstein's ability to spread it on thick.

"The governments of China, India, and Pakistan feel good about exporting technology to more economically advanced countries like Canada and the U.S. This sort of thing makes everybody feel that Asian countries, other than Japan, Singapore, and Hong Kong, are contributing. Holstein will get the red carpet treatment in Asia. He is making them look good in North America. This is going to be one of those international friendship deals. I can't believe this is happening," Bungee said. I couldn't either.

I multiplied 50 immigrant investors by $150,000 per investment to get a potential revenue source of $7.5 million for B.H. Beane's coffers. Jack then phoned me. He was excited about more hot news. Jack had just heard that Holstein was negotiating a $1 million government grant to develop B.H. Beane International's biogas technology," he said.

"Jack, how many people know about this?" I asked. Jack told me just a handful of people knew. I asked Jack if he was now officially listed as an insider of the company.

"Holstein says I can visit him anytime. In fact, I just saw him yesterday. I wanted him to confirm that the Beane stock is a solid buy," said Jack.

"Think of it this way," I said. "You don't talk to Holstein every day. He has meetings every day. You really don't know anybody who goes to these special closed door meetings. So how do you know that only a few people know about this government grant?" I asked. Jack was upset with me.

I then bought another 10,000 shares at $1.45 anyway. Why not? The guy was telling the world he was recruiting investors from Third World countries and negotiating for government grants. Even if it wasn't true, other investors would believe it and

Jack Asks Naive Beginner Questions

"Are you sure this B.H. Beane stock will get us a pot of gold?" Jack asked a thoughtful Rampaging Bull.

RAMPAGING BULLS: Outfox Promoters At Their Game On Any Penny Stock Market

puff up the share prices. I now had 35,000 shares worth $50,750 which I had purchased for about $38,750. I felt good—like a man about to be inducted into the One-Percent-Know-It-Alls held in high regard by Oswaldo.

MONDAY, MARCH 23 — the plot thickens

The next day the newspaper carried a photo of Holstein, the director of international trade for the region, and the mayor of the city. The mayor said: "We are always pleased when our economy diversifies. We are especially pleased to be part of the worldwide reformation and revolution in renewable energy. We look forward to learning more about this technology with our friends from Pakistan, India, Taiwan, Singapore, and China," the mayor said.

The director of international trade said: "We will do everything in our power to help local entrepreneurs diversify our economy. Mr. Bob Holstein is an excellent example of a businessperson who is finding unique ways to bridge differences in the world and make new friends. Mr. Holstein will be helped in his efforts by our trade missions in India, Pakistan, Singapore, Taiwan, and China. This wonderful exchange of technology will benefit our countries."

Jack had picked up a real insider tip about the expected government grant for Beane International.

Jack phoned proudly: "We had excellent advance information. By the way, Holstein says he would be more than happy to meet with you when he gets back from his pilgrimage to the Asian heads of state." He and Holstein were now apparently close and dear friends.

I then checked with Bungee who told me that B.H. Beane International was going to move through the $2 barrier in minutes, two days ahead of Holstein's prediction at the gala. B.H. Beane International, according to pundits in the 12 St. Bar & Grill, was going well over $5 a share and maybe as high as $10. Holstein was predicting a $20 stock.

I started multiplying 35,000 shares by $20 and started dreaming of an early retirement. Jack was already telling me how he was going to be worth one million dollars.

"I'm going to buy a house, a sports car, take a vacation, and put the rest of my earnings in Treasury Bills," Jack said.

We were hooked. We were confident. We were brilliant young investors who had found our pot of gold. We were brilliant One-Percenters!

THURSDAY, MARCH 26 — everybody's pal

The local newspaper, which by now was feeding all its B.H. Beane International stories to various news wire services, published yet another story about Holstein's reception in Taiwan. The newspaper said Taiwanese farmers wanted to be part of the biogas experiment.

North American farmers were all amazed at what might happen. "It's hard to believe that 500 cows can generate enough dung to produce all the energy for one farm," a Bill Gatesby of Acme, Montana said. "Yup. It's the miracle we've all been waiting for," he said.

A second newspaper story quoted the director of a farm organization in Saskatchewan, a David Mykamu. He was lobbying government for subsidies to help farmers increase their cattle and/or pig herds. Mykamu's argument for this subsidy program was far fetched but it did create big news:

■ Every farmer could become energy self-sufficient using Beane's new technology if he or she developed a large enough herd.

■ If cattle and pig herds increased dramatically this might force beef and pork prices lower. Lower commodity prices wouldn't matter to farmers, since farm energy costs would decrease more.

■ Lower commodity prices would help consumers and reduce imports.

■ Farmers could still make a profit if beef and pork prices were lower because the North American farmer could then compete more effectively in subsidized international markets. The national government could even eliminate other subsidies, argued My-kamu. It was a compelling argument that created even more excitement for B.H. Beane International.

MONDAY, MARCH 30 — lobbying starts

Four days later the local newspaper ran two stories for and against Mykamu's plan. There was even a wire photo of Holstein, Pakistani V.I.P.s, and a villager who had been using biogas diges-ters successfully for 30 years. Holstein received praise for deve-loping friendship and trade between Pakistan, Canada, and the United States.

The company's spokespersons also announced that the govern-ment of Pakistan had accepted in principle B.H. Beane Interna-tional's offer to recruit biogas technologists. The government of Pakistan would get stock options and warrants for its support. A group of Pakistani professionals would get an opportunity to make a fortune in the New World as shareholders and employees of a new growth company.

B.H. Beane International stock reached $2.50 the next day. This was a major breakthrough on a penny stock market since the average price of a share was well under $1. Everybody said so.

I phoned Bungee. He was ecstatic. He was now as rich as David, Vic, Jack, and I. I asked Bungee two questions. How much money did B.H. Beane International have in the bank? Who was going to produce this patented and highly sophisticated biogas digester designed by B.H. Beane geniuses who had yet to be identified? The answers: B.H. Beane International had less than $100,000 in the bank which would hardly pay for Holstein's bribes and hotel bills in Asia. But a plan was in motion, he told me, to raise additional capital. Several brokerage firms planned to raise more money to complement the immigrant investors.

"B.H. Beane International will be swimming in money. And don't worry about who is going to produce the digester. It works in Pakistan doesn't it?" Bungee said.

"Who told you that several brokerage firms have committed to raise money?" I asked. Bungee said Holstein had mentioned this during a meeting with brokers at his firm. Bungee told me to relax because Holstein, even if he didn't know much else, is an expert on convincing people to give him money.

Jack said the same thing when I phoned him with questions. "It works in China doesn't it?" Jack said. I was surrounded by experts.

WEDNESDAY, APRIL 1 — April Fool's Day

I phoned Milan Monday morning to confirm what I had heard. He then proceeded to tell me the same thing more or less. "It works in Taiwan doesn't it?" Milan said.

I had to conclude that this digester, which creates an airtight atmosphere for dung to ferment and produce methane gas, must be the wave of the future. North American farms are being squeezed by high energy prices, low commodity prices, and a severe decline in land prices. This makes it unattractive to sell out and impossible to borrow money for expansion. I envisioned thousands of North American farmers scooping fresh cow and pig dung to deposit into super duper high technology biogas digesters. At least I thought I could see all this happening. The idea couldn't be a prank I told myself.

APRIL 6 to APRIL 10 — all quiet

The price of the stock was holding steady at $2.60. I couldn't figure out what was happening. Holstein was out of town and nobody appeared to be guarding the fort? Was Holstein going to start unloading stock? I had a panic attack. Then an announcement came.

The announcement came on the radio, courtesy of the news wire services. The story in short told us that the Asians were eager to promote biogas digesters!

At least 50 potential immigrants to Canada from Taiwan, China, Singapore, India, and Pakistan were being processed thanks to some very fast work by Asian governments. These people, some of whom were being bankrolled by their government, were prepared to invest $150,000 each for the privilege of being on B.H. Beane International's support team. Each of them would get 100,000 shares at $1.50 each, warrants to buy an additional 100,000 shares at $5 per share within two years, and a monthly salary of $2,000. This was Holstein's signal to the market that the share price was going over $5 now that the company was flush with cash. Several immigrants per month would come to Canada according to news reports to join B.H. Beane International's team across North America. Cash flow each month could top $900,000.

"You know what this means," Oswaldo said. "This means that Holstein will have enough money to take the share price as high as he wants. I'm sure he's working out a plan to seduce the really big money. This is excellent," Oswaldo said just before he told me he bought 50,000 shares of B.H. Beane International at $3 for his clients.

I had no idea what "big money" he was talking about. All I knew was that my 35,000 shares were now worth $105,000 at $3 per share and I was happy. Jack phoned and reminded me his 40,000 shares were worth over $120,000 at $3 per share. We decided to have lunch together and figure out what to say to Bob Holstein when we met him .

"We should do the dance of joy," I said to Jack. He laughed.

"I think we have found a pot of gold," said Jack. "I feel like — like I got some magical beans from a stranger on the side of the road. They really did grow into a beanstalk leading to the Giant's gold," he told me.

I laughed. "That's good Jack. We're in a fairy tale."

About two months had gone by since Jack had spilled his drink on his trousers because he had bumped into Bob Holstein. And now Jack was already thinking of himself as a man of destiny, discussing the significance of classic fairy tales, and wanting to buy me lunch.

WEEK OF APRIL 13 to APRIL 24 — bad news

A press release from the Big Three automakers—General Motors, Ford, and Chrysler—denied these companies had discussed the development of a methane engine with anyone. The

Big Three automakers did not mention B.H. Beane International by name. The release said recent rumours about a methane gas engine were totally "spurious". I looked the word up in the dictionary. I was not encouraged. The press release went on to say that the internal combustion engine using petroleum gas was here to stay because petroleum gas is available, relatively inexpensive, and more efficient than methane gas—at least for now.

A few press people wrote interpretive stories that were negative to B.H. Beane International. This stirred the pot. Nothing happened. Most people don't want to believe anything negative. There was no news or reaction from anyone at B.H. Beane.

Bob Holstein had just disappeared. Reporters couldn't find him for a comment. There was only silence. Investors and brokers were all wondering what happened. Interest in B.H. Beane International stock was on hold—but solid. The quote remained a steady $2.60 bid and $2.75 offer.

Some brokers claimed that this was a typical and common thing in any stock promotion. The promoters, they said, usually had to get things organized once share prices reached certain resistance levels. Brokers, at the larger firms, said B.H. Beane was an excellent candidate for "shorting". There was no revenue; no money had been raised; and financial fundamentals warranted a share price of five cents instead of $2.60.

Milan phoned to wonder out loud: "Suppose Holstein is really a Criminal Incompetent? Suppose he scooped the money and ran? Suppose there is no biogas digester?"

Bungee phoned to wonder out loud: "Suppose the company drops back to 30 cents per share?"

Oswaldo phoned to wonder out loud: "So? What do you think?" None of them said anything about selling—yet.

A few other brokers were "overheard" telling their clients to collect a little profit by selling some B.H. Beane International at $2 or more. These investors had bought at 50 cents, 90 cents, and so on. "Why be greedy?" their brokers told them.

Bungee phoned back a couple days later: "It wouldn't hurt to collect some profits," he said being the psychic that he is.

Then the weirdest thing happened. A couple of brokers starting spreading the rumour that Canada Immigration was not happy with Holstein's plan to recruit 50 bright Asian scientists. The reason for the anger was simple. Holstein, apparently, had not discussed his plan with immigration before he announced it. The immigration people were jealous, miffed, and angry.

Bungee phoned: "This pisses me off. I don't know who to believe. An unsubstantiated rumour is making the rounds 'on the street'. I've tried to get in touch with immigration authorities but they say that they 'are not at liberty to discuss the situation'. For God's sake. Everybody is going to believe this rumour because immigration authorities in Canada and the U.S. are recognized as cranky people."

There was also an eerie silence "on the street" because two bad news stories had gone unchallenged. This wasn't your ordinary type of silence. I had experienced this silence before in my professional career. This was "The-Silence-Before-Panic".

A few reckless short sellers had been active against B.H. Beane International all the way up. Short sales finally peaked at 150,000 shares by April 15 at prices ranging from $1.50 to $2.60 just before the immigration rumour made the rounds.

Now that The-Silence-Before-Panic had fallen on "the street", a few last minute short sellers tried to muscle their way in before the share price started to drop. Short selling is allowed only in a rising market. It sounds more complicated than it is. The stock exchange wants to prevent trouble makers from creating a selling stampede by short selling weak stocks which have already dropped in price.

A short sale allows a trader to borrow shares from his brokerage firm and sell them with the expectation the share price will drop soon after. The trader will then buy the shares back at lower prices and return them to the brokerage firm. The goal, of course, is to pocket the difference thanks to all the suckers who over-valued the stock. Since Holstein was almost a missing person, the short sellers were excited and waited for the stock to drop.

"Suppose B.H. Beane International can't raise one cent from immigrants?" Jack asked me April 17. The share price then held steady for the next several days until the immigration rumours got around. Then the bid dropped by 30 cents to $2.30.

The share price then dropped again to $2.10 on a small trade of about 15,000 shares. The price dropped to $2. The price dropped to $1.75. The price dropped to $1.50. The drop in price was coming on moderate buying and selling. Most people, it seemed, were reluctant to sell and were waiting for Holstein to bring "reality" back to the share price so it could "deservedly" trade at $2.60 or even higher. There was no word from Holstein's offices.

The short sellers were happy. But the rest of the "investors" were terrified. With every trade a few more people sold more and more shares. Jack and I agreed that the whole B.H. Beane International promotion may have been a scam.

"I think the beanstalk has stopped growing," said Jack. I asked Jack if he had ever heard of the South Seas Bubble? That was the stock promotion started by Britain's King George in 1719 when he gave exclusive trading rights in the Pacific Ocean to the South Seas Company. The promoters had a field day on that one. The South Seas Company was going to pay for the national debt, make everybody rich, distribute magical beans, and provide for every-one's old age. The problem started when the South Seas Company promoters convinced King George to prevent other companies from going public and raising money! Talk about greed. All the investors who had leveraged and margined themselves in other stocks suddenly had cash flow problems. They started selling the South Seas Company, which was the hottest stock at the time, to pay other debts. The entire economy went into a tailspin.

"I never heard that story," said Jack.

"Most people haven't," I said.

Most of the selling was coming from people who had bought in early at under 50 cents and were happy to collect a profit by selling at 90 cents to $1.50. Some of the selling was also coming from people who had bought at $2.60, panicked, and decided to cut their losses.

"Jack, nobody wants this stock. Investors are bidding at lower and lower prices," I whined. This scared me because I was starting to act like 99% of the people in time of crisis.

Holstein's spokespersons finally issued a murky press release which said he was expected back from Asia in a few days, that he would have some announcements, and that "everything is under control".

"What does 'everything is under control' supposed to mean?" Jack asked me. I had no idea. The price dropped to 90 cents following the "reassuring" press release from Holstein.

"The minute somebody says there is 'no reason to panic' then almost everybody thinks there is a reason to panic. What is wrong with the public relations people in Holstein's office anyway?" Jack asked.

The stock bottomed out at 80 cents Thursday morning April 23. B.H.Beane International Inc. stock had dropped $1.80 per share in a week. The stock dropped on sales of just 600,000 shares in five days. Nobody could actually believe the stock was going to drop completely out of sight. Seller resistance set in at 80 cents.

"For God's sake. We haven't even heard from Holstein and everybody is selling. This is crazy," Jack, the newly crowned expert on crowd psychology, said.

By Friday afternoon a few short sellers bought B.H. Beane International at 80 cents to cover their positions. The offer to sell was 90. The "word on the street" was that investors were angry and and resisting all offers to sell under $1 per share. "Conventional wisdom" said Holstein should get a chance to speak before everybody unloaded the stock.

"This Holstein guy must be a student of Howard Hughes," said Oswaldo.

Milan tried to get in touch with Holstein. Oswaldo tried to reach Holstein. Bungee didn't try to get Holstein because everyone else in his firm was already trying to reach Holstein. Jack, the man who had discovered the hen who lays golden eggs, tried to get in touch with Holstein. No broker could get in touch with any of Holstein's brokers, representatives, or spokespersons. Every single one of Holstein's stock brokers were either sick, on holiday, or out of town that day. It was strange. How do known supporters of the biggest stock promotion on the street suddenly disappear for a day? Was it a UFO kidnapping? The situation was totally out of control. Nobody at Holstein's offices could comment.

Then finally one of the depressed brokers on the street snagged one of Holstein's people coming out of the toilet at the 12 St. Bar and Grill. It took about five minutes for other key brokers to find out by cellular phone. As you can imagine, there was an emergency meeting with Holstein's representative at the 12 St. Bar and Grill in the downtown business section. The "word on the street" spread so fast that at least 50 brokers showed up to find out what the "hell" Holstein was doing. Three of the brokers were mine— Oswaldo, Bungee, and Milan. The bar tab that one day topped $5,000. When share prices decline, bar tabs go up. The results of the meeting were "inconclusive".

Jack "just happened" to be at the 12 St. Bar and Grill. He told me he had to find out what the "hell" was going on. Jack told me that Milan had soaked up five beers in an hour.

"He was swearing the whole time. All he could say was that this was the last stock promotion he was ever going to get involved with. I felt sorry for Milan because he had encouraged 40 of his clients to buy at $1.75 to $2.50. He had been sure the stock was going to $5 quickly," Jack told me later.

The only people who were smiling were the ones who had shorted the stock. They were talking about finishing the job Monday, Tuesday, and Wednesday by buying stock to cover their positions.

"What a bunch of jerks," said Jack. "You should have seen the short sellers. They were all sitting in a small group at The 12 St. Bar and Grill smiling, looking thoughtful, and highly intelligent. They looked as if they had eaten something tasty—like medium rare roast beef," said Jack.

"Roast Bull," I replied.

One of the shorters, Archie Beerbum, had explained to Jack that anyone buying a stock on a penny market at over $1 per share was looking for trouble. When the stock tops 50 cents and starts moving to $1 it's time to start looking for ways to sell, not buy.

Archie, a 50-year-old chain smoking member of the Reformed Skeptics Society, told Jack that an "investor" should never buy a stock from a promoter he doesn't know.

"An investor should never buy a stock at a price higher than the market average on a penny stock market. You have to expect a sharp and almost instant decline in share price if the bidding gets as high as $2," said Archie.

Jack told me he felt like punching Archie in the nose. That's when Jack and I decided to sell some shares to take some profits.

WEDNESDAY, APRIL 22 — We Take Profits

On Wednesday morning both Jack and I offered about 10,000 shares each for $1.10. This was good because the bid was still 90 cents.

"I think we are doing the right thing," said Jack.

"I think we should scoop some profit," I said. We both convinced ourselves that we were Careful Traders because we had, after all, made a profit on the shares we were about to sell. In fact, Jack reminded me that we were about to make an "excellent" profit on the shares.

"I don't know about you, but if I sell my 10,000 shares at $1.10 I'll earn over 300% on my money," Jack said proudly.

Then something strange happened. It was incredible. The stock of B.H. Beane International started going up from the moment we offered, and sold, our shares at $1.10.

■ There were bids for 20,000 shares at $1.20.

■ Then there were bids for 50,000 shares at $1.50. The sellers held firm and demanded at least $1.60 per share.

■ Then there were bids for 150,000 shares at $1.70.

■ Then there were several bids for a total of 100,000 shares for $1.75

■ Then the bid went to $1.80 for 100,000 shares.

■ Then the bids moved to $2 for another 100,000 shares. Some bids were filled. But it looked as if the share owners were holding out for a higher price at every step. Nobody knew who was pushing the bids up so quickly. The bid on B.H. Beane International stock hit $2.50 during the middle of lunch.

Many people had decided to sell early Monday morning because they had no idea what was going on. Some had made a big profit at $1.10 because they had bought early at 30 cents to 50 cents like Jack and I had done. Other investors were irritated. They had bought at $2 or higher and had decided to cut their losses by selling from $1.30 up. Others decided this buying spree was some sort of fluke which should be taken advantage of before it dried up—again.

The shorters were also buying before the share price increased higher than they had sold it. The short sellers didn't know what was going to happen next. Everytime they made a bid somebody came along and increased the bid.

The shorters knew they were in trouble. The shorters had fully expected to be the only people in the market Monday buying up B.H. Beane International at lower prices. The shorters had, for some strange reason, believed Holstein wasn't strong enough to take this stock back up. They had suddenly discovered that their equations were wrong. Somebody with lots of staying power was buying B.H. Beane International stock. The stock had regained its old high of $2.60 by 2 p.m. and held firm until closing. The shorters were in a frenzy.

Jack phoned me after lunch. He told me he had sold another 5,000 shares at $1.95 because he got carried away. Jack was, however, unhappy. It's hard to understand why Jack, who had pocketed $20,000 at a profit of 500% that day, should be unhappy. Greed can make a person crazy.

"God! I don't understand what the hell is going on. How can B.H. Beane International move from 90 cents to $2.50 in one day. Where did buying for 750,000 shares come from?" Jack asked.

"Where are you?" I asked Jack.

"At the 12 St. Bar and Grill. You should see the shorters. Talk about depressed. Archie had five beers in an hour while telling everyone that he would never short sell a stock again.

"I told Archie that nobody should short a stock on a penny stock market if they didn't know the promoter," Jack laughed. Archie, Jack said, looked him in the eye and then told him that "the stock market is a constant learning process".

"Then Archie bought me a beer," Jack said. "Milan, however, was looking happy. He ordered a medium rare roast beef, an expensive bottle of wine, tipped the servers, and smiled at everybody. Milan kept repeating that he was lucky to be alive. He said that he would hedge his involvement in any future stock promotion," Jack laughed.

We paused for a moment on the phone. The idea of hedging our future involvement was new to us. We both knew that we were very lucky guys. We were still winners in this stock promotion. We couldn't admit, however, that we had been suckered into selling a stock just before it dramatically increased in price.

"Oh yeah! I almost forgot. I found out that Holstein had completed a private placement to Asian scientists between $1 and $2 and had crossed a few hundred thousand shares to somebody else between 90 cents and $1.60," said Jack. There was so much to learn.

11 | I Meet The Rampaging Bull

. . . And Get A Good Meal

THURSDAY, APRIL 23 — The Bull is back

Everybody was buzzing the next day. Holstein was back.

His spokesperson Dave Diddle told the media that Holstein would make a statement at 11:15 the next morning. Diddle, the manager of a local public relations firm, predicted good news from Holstein.

"I think investors who have shown faith in B.H. Beane International are about to be rewarded," said Diddle.

The share price peaked at $2.75 that day. This, as you might guess, encouraged everyone to go drinking after work to see if they could collect more gossip. The bar tab was enormous at the 12 St. Bar and Grill owned by Gus Pitas. Gus, an investor in B.H. Beane International, decided to offer Happy Hour prices all night to keep everyone happy.

"Hey, these are my people," said Gus. Everybody clapped Gus on the back while he collected almost $5,000 in bar tabs from brokers during the five hour drinking binge.

FRIDAY, APRIL 24 — The Bull Speaks

Thoroughly hungover brokers traded heavily from the opening bell at 7:30 a.m. The stock exchange administrators had their morning coffee and then halted trading in B.H. Beane International around 9:30 a.m. The price of B.H. Beane International was frozen at $2.95. The share price had climbed quickly from $2.75 to $2.95 on a volume of 200,000 shares in only two hours of early morning trading.

Bungee said the shorters panicked. They knew they would have to buy back their shares for a higher price than they sold them. They recognized the entire two weeks of silence had lulled them into a false confidence. They thought Holstein had lost control; that the whole deal was a fantasy.

"The shorters are having another bad day at the 12 St. Bar and Grill," Jack said. Every broker involved in trading the stock had the office television tuned into Holstein's press conference. The whole thing looked like a U.S. presidential press conference. Diddle introduced Holstein; Holstein walked to the podium as cameras flashed; and Holstein paused before speaking. He looked indignant as he took a puff on his cigar—slowly and unhurried.

"First and foremost, I want to assure everyone that Beane International is doing well. Some of our investors should be ashamed of themselves. I am hurt. There was no need for some automakers to criticize our efforts to develop a methane gas engine. Do they still have the vision that inspired Henry Ford? I think not. I never said which automobile company was discussing the development of a methane engine with us. We are discussing the methane engine with a major company. This does not affect the finances of B.H. Beane International. The methane engine for tractors and combines is part of our long term strategy—I just wish Henry Ford were alive today to see the lack of vision in the North American auto industry. I think Henry Ford would be on our side, maybe even on our board of directors," Holstein said with passion.

"I am shocked at how disloyal investors can be. I was in Asia putting this deal together. I had to concentrate. And some people had the nerve to think the deal has fallen through. Come on!

"B.H. Beane International is in business. The stock has recently traded at $2.95—an all time high for B.H. Beane International," Holstein said proudly.

"This should teach investors to have more faith in B.H. Beane International. Constantinople was not built in a day," he laughed. "We now know that our biogas digester can produce fertilizer and methane gas. Farmers will save a lot of money. We are currently negotiating with several farm co-operatives throughout North America to market surplus fertilizer from farmers or ranchers at a reduced rate. We are helping North American farmers become more efficient. You'll be hearing more on this shortly. The important thing is that co-operatives throughout North America will be on our team," Holstein said.

"We have identified the Asian experts who will be joining our team in North America over the next three years. We are proud of this accomplishment. We have moved quickly, had tremendous support everywhere we went, and believe we have recruited the best minds in Asia. These new immigrants will come to Canada at a rate of about three per month. We will set them up in field offices throughout North America.

"Yes, we have had a small miscommunication with our friends at Canada Immigration. We have negotiated a solution. We have filled out all the correct forms. That's why we only want to bring in three immigrants per month so we can work closely with Canada Immigration to process our people carefully," Holstein said.

"We are real; B.H. Beane International is real; and the biogas digester works brilliantly. You will be meeting our engineering team in the next few months. You will all be invited to product demonstrations," Holstein finished with gusto.

Trading in B.H. Beane International shares resumed almost immediately. I phoned Oswaldo. He was laughing. The price of B.H. Beane International stock had passed the $3.25 mark and was moving up. The shorters, for the most part, were now getting a severe spanking. It was month end when all accounts at brokerage firms have to be settled. The shorters were required to return borrowed shares if they weren't properly "covered" by collateral. Holstein had also arranged a "stock sweep". He had asked all his friends and associates to ask their brokerage firm to give them their shares. The brokerage firms then had fewer shares to lend for

The Rampaging Bull Explains "The Ditch"

"I'm in Asia negotiating agreements and a few people
have the nerve to think the deal has fallen through. This
deal is for real. Constantinople wasn't built in a day.
Trust me," The Rampaging Bull said to the media.

RAMPAGING BULLS: Outfox Promoters At Their Game On Any Penny Stock Market

short selling. The panic by shorters trying to buy back the stock and an excited general public trying to get in on the action pushed the stock to $3.25 in one hour.

"Oops. I lied. The price is now $4," Oswaldo said. "More than 200,000 shares traded in the hour after Holstein made his announcement. B.H. Beane International is about to make a one day trading record on the exchange. This is amazing," Oswaldo said.

Jack phoned me. "Holstein says he is ready to meet any friend of mine. How about that? I actually got through to him," Jack said. He was laughing about how we had almost prematurely sold our golden eggs.

"I didn't tell you that I sold 10,000 shares at $2.00 to grab another $20,000," Jack told me. "I have only 25,000 shares of the original 50,000 which I bought between 30 cents and 75 cents," he said. My heart went out to Jack. The man was suffering because he had earned only 300% to 500% on his investment.

"Well, Jack. I sold 10,000 at $1.95. I have only 15,000 shares left," I said. We both laughed. We knew we had panicked. Milan said many of the original investors who had bought at 30 cents to $1 were now gone. Holstein had exchanged these smaller, and unstable, investors with heavier rollers who had bought between $1 to $3. The bigger investors expected a higher share price because Holstein has international connections, a good story, ability, and broker support. Holstein had also dealt the cynics and shorters a terrifying blow by forcing them to buy the stock back at higher prices. Holstein had kept B.H. Beane International share prices low just long enough to cross shares to several large investors and his specially selected immigrant advisers at $1 to $2. The buying spree that pushed the stock above $4 came from the general public, from short sellers, and from Holstein himself trying to keep everyone excited.

"The B.H. Beane International share price will be stable between $4 and $5 for awhile. Everybody is now waiting for the share price to move to $6 before even thinking about selling," Milan said.

"The shorters and the general public played into Holstein's hand. This was a stunning performance. This whole exercise was a test of wills. Holstein has won the first round. Who knows what will happen next. Holstein did a classic manoeuvre," Milan said. I didn't dare tell Milan I was one of the cowards who had unloaded his cheap shares and that I didn't fully understand this classic manoeuvre.

I was lucky I was still in the game. I promised myself I would manage my last 15,000 shares of Beane stocks better. Jack and I had missed the chance to buy more shares at prices as low as 90 cents during the Holstein induced panic. We weren't sure if Holstein was a Criminal Incompetent who would disappear with the money or if he was a Rampaging Bull ably promoting his stock. We now knew, at least, that Holstein was committed for an extended promotion.

FRIDAY, APRIL 27 — We meet the Bull

B.H. Beane International opened trading Friday morning at $5 on strong demand. Bungee thought the surge in buying had something to do with investors thinking Asian immigrants would exercise their $5 per share options as soon as the share price topped $5.

When Jack picked me up at my office he was in a great mood. We were off, he said, to meet the giant at the end of the Beane stock. We both laughed. We were about to meet The Rampaging Bull—Bob Holstein. Holstein had asked us to meet him in his office so he could drive us to La Chez Dolce—a fancy French/ Italian/Mozambique restaurant.

When we walked into the office we noticed *The Secretary*. She was a five-foot eleven-inch blonde with a figure that demanded attention. We said hello. She said, "Jack, how nice to see you again." Jack looked proud. Jack introduced me to Candace, *The Secretary*. We were five minutes early. We were still waiting 20 minutes later enjoying the leather sofa and reading *Scientific*

World, Engineer Digest, and *Architectural Review*. I can't understand why waiting rooms always have magazines that no ordinary person reads.

Candace's entire job involved taking messages non-stop from people asking to speak to Holstein. She told almost every person that he was out of the office, that he would return soon, and that he or one of his associates would phone back. She thanked everyone for phoning. She also told five people that B.H. Beane International had no announcements. Candace smiled at us.

"Everybody is phoning Mr. Holstein. Some people are just pushy and I have to tell stories," Candace explained. Then Holstein came out in a rush; he was talking on his cellular phone.

"Vito! How are you! You bet. It's big. Don't worry, you're in!" said Holstein. Then he looked up and saw us.

"Jack! Jack. How are you—and your pants?" Holstein smiled at us both. When Holstein grabbed my hand I thought he was going to rip it off. Holstein, a small man, was behaving like a politician trying to show that he is dynamic and worthy of support. There was one other strange thing about Holstein—his head is big. He is no ordinary Taurus.

"I'm sorry I'm late. You know how it is. Rush, Rush. It isn't easy building a company that has caught the public eye. Everybody wants a piece of you. It's incredible," Holstein said as he led us to the elevator. Holstein asked Candace to phone ahead to tell the maitre de at La Chez Dolce that we would be late.

Holstein laughed a lot. He asked many questions. I couldn't ask him a single question on the way to the restaurant. In less than 10 minutes he had asked me a dozen questions about women, sports, cars, the meaning of life, joy, my future, and whether I liked his new fancy-schmanzy expensive four cylinder import. I didn't really answer any of his questions too directly. I told Holstein that foreign cars mean fewer jobs for North Americans.

"Besides, I love my car. The eight cylinder 305 Chevy engine, which I have, is one of the finest engines ever made."

"Did you know that a Russian American working for Ford invented the 305 engine. Ford turned down his ideas even though Ford's eight cylinder engine wasn't as good. So naturally GM grabbed the engine and made the Russian American rich," I said. Holstein just looked at me. He wasn't sure what to say.

"I personally think any engine with less than eight cylinders isn't worth driving," I said. Holstein laughed loudly. Jack was looking nervous.

I wasn't sure what Holstein wanted from us. I figured if I acted cranky he wouldn't ask too much from us. I knew he was looking for some weakness. Were we easily impressed? Were we greedy? Did we love money? Were we dishonest? Could Holstein seduce us?

I noticed that Holstein was always playing with his gold looking watch—not to show off, but more as a way to release tension. Holstein asked what we thought about B.H. Beane International. Jack started to say something. I kicked his shin under the table. Jack shut up.

"Well, to tell you the truth I don't know very much about your company. The press really doesn't explain much. Do you have handouts which explain what you are doing in greater detail," I asked.

"Sure. No problem. We have so much material it is hard to keep track. B.H. Beane International has an amazing future. We are excited. We can't contain ourselves. But there is a lot of work ahead of us," Holstein said. I asked about financing. I couldn't understand how he could launch such an ambitious initiative without much money in the corporate treasury.

"That is a very good question. Many people have asked me that. You must understand that we wouldn't have come this far if we weren't sure we could complete a major financing. I haven't really discussed this in public," Holstein lowered his voice.

"We are about to begin negotiations with a half dozen pension funds in the United States that work closely with major brokerage firms. We have an inside track thanks to certain key brokers who are excited about our stock," Holstein said. He was going to start negotiations in a few weeks when he cleaned up his backlog of paperwork after his Asian trip.

"But it isn't as if we are out of money. We have a prototype, we have engineers, we have patents, we have public and farm support, we have government support, and we have international support. My God, I can't begin to list the people who are behind us. You may have noticed that our stock is holding steady at $5. I think you can figure out that our management team is now personally very well off today," laughed Holstein.

Jack tried to change the topic. I kicked him again.

"Well, that's why I'm asking. Why hasn't the company raised any money? What you have is yours, not the company's," I asked.

Holstein was looking at me. He held my eye firmly. He was fighting me. I stood my ground. I think he was trying to decide if he should continue being our friend or whether he should become a harsh disciplinarian.

"I am amazed at how the stock rebounded so quickly from 90 cents to $5. It's a miracle. And yet the company didn't put one penny in its coffers, sell one biogas disgester, or arrange a single contract," I said pushing things to the limit.

"Well . . ." Holstein said calmly while his eyes narrowed slightly. "I think our plan to recruit 50 bright technicians and scientists who will invest in the company is incredible if I don't say so myself," Holstein challenged me.

"That means you'll have a product to sell—soon," I pushed.

Holstein laughed. He was losing the initiative. I was grilling him for a change. It made him uncomfortable.

"Yes and no. We are recruiting our team slowly. We need time to set everything up. We might have 20 to 30 technicians in place to help American and Canadian farmers during the next year or so. This gives us time to set up a manufacturing plant.

"You might as well know that we have arranged to have some of the biogas digesters produced for us until we get our own plant up and running. It's still hush, hush. If this unnamed company does well, we'll give them the contract, do a share exchange, and acquire their operation. It's good for them and it's good for us. We are in the middle of a recession. This manufacturing company needs our business and we need their plant capacity. They won't charge us anything to produce the prototypes if we give them the production contract. It's all a bit complex," Holstein smiled at me.

Jack was looking at me closely. I was feeling unsure of how to follow up. Jack was, for the first time, looking pleased. This was news—*Big News*. The biogas digester was going to be produced soon. Holstein was looking warmly at Jack. Jack was looking warmly at Holstein. I was looking at both of them less than warmly. I decided to kick Jack in the shins. It made me feel better.

Holstein ordered consomme flavoured with Madeira; spinach leaves garnished with apple, goat cheese, and walnuts; saddle of fresh lamb; a chocolate cake; and a glass of red Burgundy. There isn't any point telling you what Jack and I ordered because our psychological profile isn't important to you. I'm only sharing this with you because Holstein has expensive tastes and you should know about them.

"Are you happy with the price of the stock. You have to admit $5 sounds great doesn't it. I sure hope you didn't sell your shares," Holstein said. We nodded as if we were the most loyal of investors. Holstein smiled. He knew we were lying. He also told us that the price of the stock was going to $15 much earlier than he had predicted.

Holstein told us not to sell our stock—especially during the next month. The price of the stock was going to remain steady at $5. He was about to begin negotiations in New York for a major financing. He was also finishing off all the paperwork associated with his Asian trip.

"The stock won't be going up or down the next month. You may have noticed how irritated the short sellers are. They lost money selling short at $2.60. Now the stock is $5. They don't know what is going to happen. They are watching to see what I do before they commit themselves again. This means, of course, they aren't sure if they should buy or sell. Some of the short sellers went long from $3 to $5 because they now think the stock will go higher. I think I might knock the share price down for a week or two. I want them on edge," winked Holstein.

"I like to call this 'My Whipsaw'. The shorters lost money when they sold short and now some of them will lose money when they bought long. There's poetry in there somewhere. It makes me feel good," Holstein said.

I was getting just a bit nervous. I couldn't figure out how Holstein had so much power in the market. He, apparently, could support the share price of this company even though the share float was increasing.

"Managing a stock promotion is like playing a chess game," Holstein said. "A master chess player can predict what is going to happen at least a half dozen moves ahead; an advanced chess player can predict four moves ahead; an intermediate player can predict two moves ahead; and a beginning chess player doesn't know his next move even if he studies the board for an hour," Holstein said.

"I don't want to promote our abilities. We predicted almost every thing that has happened up to now. We know what we are doing. Most people, on the other hand, don't know what they don't know. I think you will agree that we have the confidence of investors, the agricultural community, the government, and brokers. Yet it all seemed touch and go just a few days ago, didn't it?" he said. We nodded our heads.

Then Holstein did something incredible. He shouted the word, "Ayeeeeeee" and moved his hands into a martial arts stance. "We are the Ninja warriors of promotion," he said. The waiter looked at us confused. Jack and I looked at each other. This guy was starting to get to us—not to mention, scare us. Holstein smiled and reassured us that he wasn't crazy. He said that he just wanted to show us a move which a B.H. Beane International investor showed him over lunch recently in Singapore. Holstein then explained to us patiently that there hasn't been a penny stock company in memory that got the interest of foreign governments as fast as B.H. Beane International.

"The Asians are excited. They want to be part of something big. B.H. Beane International might even export biogas digesters back to Asia within two years," Holstein said proudly.

"Listen fellas. I am going to make you an offer you *can* refuse," he laughed. "I'll be negotiating with several New York brokerage firms and pension funds about investing in B.H. Beane International. As long as I keep the price of the stock around $5 I'm safe. Skittish investors will sell their shares to collect profits when B.H. Beane International moves from $6 to $8 per share. I have to show buying strength when I talk to the New York money. That is why I want you to look deep into your heart and consider my proposal to you.

"Here's the deal. We're friends. I want each of you to buy 5,000 shares between $6 to $7. Hey, it's only about $30,000. I'll give you 1,000 shares each under the table as a Frequent Buyer bonus. We'll all get rich. Think of it as a $7,000 token of my appreciation and deep abiding friendship. I also want you to hold all the shares until the price tops $10. Then I don't care what you do," Holstein said.

I gulped. Jack gulped. This was heavy. I knew something like this was going to happen. Holstein was asking Jack and me to invest almost every cent we had earned in this promotion to help him take the stock price higher.

"Isn't that illegal or something?" Jack asked. Holstein laughed heartily. "Everything is illegal these days. What's wrong with an incentive plan for buying stocks? I can't see anything wrong with that. Think of my offer as a treat for Frequent Buyers. One hand feeds the other. That's all. Just don't go around advertising our deal," he said while lighting his cigar and unbuttoning his belt buckle.

Holstein explained that pension funds and brokers in New York played hardball. They were going to test his financial

"Here's the deal. I want each of you to buy 5,000 shares of B.H. Beane stock between $6 and $7. I'll give you each 1,000 free shares as a Frequent Buyer bonus. We'll all get rich," The Rampaging Bull said to Jack and me.

RAMPAGING BULLS: Outfox Promoters At Their Game On Any Penny Stock Market

strength by short selling B.H. Beane International stock at $5 when he started negotiating with them.

"The short selling spree by the big money won't last long. They'll toy with me. If I can hold the line and maybe even bid up the share price then they'll be happy."

"The New York money will try to pick up as many shares as possible at the lowest price possible. We will try to sell them as many shares at the highest possible price."

"The negotiations are all friendly. If I can't keep the price up, then they win and pay less per share. If I can keep the price up, then I win and they pay more per share. In some strange way, they want me to win. If I can show muscle, then they will feel safe about investing $5 million at $7 or $8. Will they lose money by short selling B.H. Beane International if I take the price higher? Hell no! If they invest $5 million, they will have more than enough shares to cover their short position for as long as they want to have a short position. At some point in the future, the share price might drop below the price they sold short. They'll make money on their short sales then. But I know I can get the share price to $25 within three years. Everyone will want a piece of my action," Holstein said soberly. For one split second, Holstein wasn't acting. He was explaining his strategy.

Holstein explained he was planning to move the stock as high as $8 during his negotiations with the New York money to show his power. But, said Holstein, some local investors would sell their shares at $6 to $8 to lock in their profits.

"I need a few friends like you to help me absorb the sudden selling binge. This shouldn't last more than a couple weeks. This will encourage the New York bankers to invest money with us. Then you can sell your $6 stock between $10 and $15. Investors all over the world will be excited about what we are doing. It's cool," he said.

I didn't think it was so cool. I had made about $40,000 and Jack had made about $45,000 on Holstein's promotion so far. We were being offered a $7,000 bribe as a hedge against losing

$30,000 or more on a hunch that B.H. Beane International would go to $10 or more per share.

"I think it's a lot for us to think about. How do we know you aren't going to unload your shares on us at $7," I said. Holstein laughed. The man had a deep and hearty laugh. He enjoyed laughing.

"Think about it? How many penny stock promoters do you know who have taken their stock to $5 and held it there? Good God. I've already made a bucket load. I can hold the stock at $5 myself until hell freezes. My goal is to take this baby to $25 a share, raise millions, and build a great agricultural corporation," he said.

Holstein said that we should consider his offer; that the offer was open if we bought between $6 to $7; that we wouldn't lose a cent of our investment as long as we were under his protection; and that we each might pocket $60,000 or more if we sold our 6,000 shares at $10 or more.

Holstein excused himself, told the waiter to put the lunch on his tab, and then disappeared. Well, he didn't disappear immediately. He bumped into a man eating pasta at a table on the way out. Holstein apologized, handed the man a card, and then disappeared. Jack and I just looked at each other.

"Do you get the feeling we are now in the big leagues," Jack asked me. I said that we are probably small fry looking for a pan to get cooked in.

"Did you understand everything Holstein said?" I asked.

"Sure," said Jack, The Professional Trader. "He wants us to buy high priced shares to convince others to buy even higher priced shares. It's simple," said Jack.

"Are we going to do what Holstein wants because we are greedy?" I asked. Jack nodded. We felt a rush of excitement. Greed does that to people.

NEXT DAY — My brokers had the same lunch

Jack and I were a bit disappointed when we phoned our brokers Oswaldo, Milan, and Bungee. Jack and I weren't as special as we thought. All three of our brokers told us everything Holstein had told us just 24 hours earlier—with one minor exception. The brokers did not mention anything about a Frequent Buyer program. We didn't ask them about it either.

FRIDAY, MAY 8 — something happens

B.H. Beane International stock had not moved one cent up or down since Holstein had beaten back the short sellers in April. In fact, buying and selling was sparse. Barely 20,000 shares per day traded between $4.50 and $5.25. Jack and I thought Holstein was behind most of the buying and selling to keep the market for the stock active.

Milan, Oswaldo, and Bungee had absolutely nothing to report during the entire two week period. Everything was quiet. Everyone assumed Holstein was in deep discussions with important money people—which, by the way, was true.

The newspaper announced Dr. Benjamin de Poplar, a retired congressman from Kansas, was going to be the first farmer to install the B.H. Beane International biogas digester. The news article said the retired congressman would receive a prototype biogas digester within one week. This announcement brought a flurry of buying that pushed the stock up to $5.50.

MONDAY, MAY 11 — Holstein visits N.Y.

Everybody was talking about Holstein's deal with the New York money. The market, as usual, responded positively to this rumoured initiative with moderate trading as the price of the stock inched to $5.75.

Jack phoned to ask what we should do. I had no idea. Bungee, Oswaldo, and Milan agreed that Holstein had positioned himself very well. Many people wanted to buy at $6 or more. The short sellers were very quiet. Everything was stable. There was, obviously, joy in the B.H. Beane International offices which, we heard, were being re-decorated to emphasize the new status of the company.

MONDAY, MAY 18 — It was New Jersey

Bungee phoned to tell me that Holstein had gone to New Jersey, not New York.

"It's a more informal atmosphere in New Jersey," Bungee said. I had no idea what he meant by that.

"What does that mean? The hotel rooms are cheaper, is that it?" I asked. Bungee didn't want to discuss it. Bungee just said that he thought B.H. Beane International might be an excellent buy at $6 if Holstein makes the deal with the pension fund. I agreed with him.

TUESDAY, MAY 19 — The share price wavers

The share price wavered back and forth from $5 to $6.

WEDNESDAY, MAY 20 — More increases

The share price wavered between $5.50 and $6.50.

THURSDAY, MAY 21 — The share price drops

The share price wavered between $5 and $5.50.

MAY 22 TO MAY 30 — More wavering

The share price actually dipped below $4 Friday before it rebounded to $5.50. Most of Monday through Wednesday was a replay of the week before as the stock closed at $6.25. The price wasn't $8 but the share price had staying power. Holstein had predicted everything accurately.

MONDAY, JUNE 1 — We buy more shares

B.H. Beane International stock moved to $6.50. Jack and I each bought 5,000 shares of B.H. Beane International which almost cleaned out our bank account. We phoned B.H. Beane International offices and left a message for Holstein. We told Candace we had bought B.H. Beane International and we expected to see him on his return. We both crossed our fingers.

TUESDAY, JUNE 2 — They announce the deal

A very short notice in *The Wall Street Journal* reported that General Trust of Southern Jersey Pension Fund was considering B.H. Beane International because the pension fund had interests in agriculture throughout America. Further information was pending.

"I have a feeling," Jack said.

WEDNESDAY, JUNE 3 — Cash pours in

The financial press reported the story. In fact, the story appeared in almost every major North American newspaper. Why not? B.H. Beane International, a penny stock, was getting a $5 million cash infusion from General Trust of Southern Jersey Pension Fund. The details of the investment were confidential. Jack, Bungee, Oswaldo, Milan, Vic, and Dave all phoned me—at different times of course.

"Great," they said.

I said that there is every possibility the stock might go to $15—as if I knew! They all agreed—as if they knew! Bungee said that Beane could get $10 million by the end of the year if contributions from the pension fund, immigrants, other investors, and government materialize. Bungee said that B.H. Beane International would easily qualify for listing on the National Association of Securities Dealers Automated Quotations—NASDAQ.

"If B.H. Beane International keeps its nose clean for a couple of years a listing on the Toronto Stock Exchange, the American Stock Exchange, or the New York Stock Exchange is certain," Bungee enthused.

I was multiplying my 20,000 shares plus my 1,000 free shares by $15 to estimate my potential windfall. I tried not to think about Jack and his 30,000 plus 1,000 free shares.

JUNE 5 TO SEPTEMBER 23 — Bonus time

B.H. Beane International share prices started increasing almost immediately from $6.75—but not smoothly. Nobody knew what was going to happen. Jack and I were familiar with this pattern by now—but not as familiar as we needed to be. The share price always wavered, dropped, and rose again on a press release or interview with Holstein in a continuous cycle. Jack and were starting to get whiplash from being on the roller coaster too long.

One of Holstein's assistants, Lucio Gutterman called us. He said he was delegated to deliver our special bonus. We waited a month. We phoned. Lucio said the paperwork was done. Holstein only had to sign the paperwork when he was next in town. Five weeks had gone by. I was irritated.

Then Lucio phoned to tell us that Holstein wanted us to deliver a copy of our brokerage statements for the last two months. He needed proof we had bought and still owned the shares. By the time we delivered the statements and got confirmation from Holstein's people, three months had past since we had bought B.H. Beane International at $6.50. Jack and I had still not received our special bonus. Bungee laughed when I told him.

"You too?," I asked.

"No comment," Bungee said.

Apparently, Milan, Oswaldo, Dave, and Vic were *all* waiting for their Frequent Buyer shares from Holstein. We were in a circus.

I finally received my shares from Holstein by registered mail—four months after my original purchase. I guess I should be happy. Holstein could have conveniently ignored our deal. The note accompanying the 1,000 share certificate thanked me for being part of the team and waiting so patiently. Holstein had signed the note. Everybody else got their special bonus as well. We were all happy—for two days.

12 | Faked Out Again

. . . I Could Have Made A Fortune

FRIDAY, SEPTEMBER 25 — More tricks

Jack and I *should* have been prepared for almost any trick Holstein could dream up. Unfortunately we still hadn't graduated from the Holstein school of stock manipulation.

We thought Holstein wouldn't ever put his stock promotion at risk. We shouldn't have assumed anything. Sherlock Holmes never assumed anything and was able to beat his arch enemy, the diabolical malignant narcissistic Dr. Moriarity. Nayland Smith and Dr. Petrie never assumed anything and were able to beat their arch enemy, the sinister malignant narcissistic Dr. Fu Manchu. Jack and I, as you might guess, were just beginning to grasp the dark truths behind people like Bob Holstein. That is why he could trick us one last time.

B.H. Beane International shares finally traded at $10. Everything Holstein had promised, happened. Most investors, especially those who had bought early, were very pleased and expected even more.

Holstein had created a tremendous amount of interest in B.H. Beane International because he had raised money from immigrants, the government, pension funds, and brokerage firms. The typical investor could only conclude that more knowledgeable people than he or she had blessed this stock.

Jack and I, instead of selling at a tremendous profit, decided to let our greed take over. We waited for the stock to go to $20 just like Holstein had predicted.

I imagined Holstein's conversations with reluctant investors as being even more compelling than those he had with us.

The local press, displaying some courage, suggested Beane shares might be over-priced. Beane spokesperson Dave Diddle came out swinging and threatened to sue the newspapers and reporters. A few brokers, however, told their clients to collect profits. Most investors shrugged these negative ideas off. Jack and I should have picked up on this advance warning. But we didn't.

MONDAY, SEPTEMBER 28—The rumour

The rumour started in the 12 St. Bar & Grill. Gus, the manager, told Jack the whole thing started almost by accident before it turned into front page news two days later.

Five brokers were sitting at one table laughing, drinking, telling tall tales, and moving into unconsciousness. One broker, a Holstein associate who begged me not to use his name in this story, had too much to drink. In fact, the broker was drunk and talking gibberish.

This broker, who we'll call Joe, suddenly blurted something about global warming, flatulence, and extinction.

"We can't increase cattle herds too much. Cattle emit gases which might extinguish life as we know it," said Joe the stockbroker and part time scientist. Nobody at the table knew or cared anything about global warming. However, everybody at the table was tuned into anything that might sound like bad news. Everyone stopped talking and became conscious instantly. Joe tried to laugh it off. Everyone begged Joe to spill his story. Joe, according to Gus, even tried to leave but was forcibly restrained by the other brokers and browbeaten into telling what he knew.

Joe finally confessed. Joe, broker and budding scientist, told us about a geochemical research study which claimed dinosaurs had killed themselves off. Apparently, dinosaurs had produced enough methane gas through flatulence and dung to warm the atmosphere, change the environment, and cause their own extinction.

Everybody just sat there. You could have dropped a pin on the carpet and heard it. When Joyce, The Server, showed up to ask about refills she was startled and worried. She later told me that for one split second she thought everyone had food poisoning.

"If this dinosaur thing is true," whispered Joe ". . . there's a chance that cows, sheep, and pigs might kill us all off with their flatulence!"

Everybody was fidgeting and thinking about selling their Beane shares and buying toilet and plumbing company shares. The questions started slowly. Further questioning revealed that geochemists had found fossilized dinosaur dung which contained signs of bacteria and algae. This meant, according to Joe, that dinosaurs had digested their food, like cows, through fermentation.

"The flatulence, and the dung, would have contained methane gas. Methane gas is a greenhouse gas like carbon monoxide which animals and smoke stacks emit. These gases trap solar heat in the atmosphere. This warms the planet and screws up the environment. Even a small change in the earth's temperature can create havoc with all forms of life," said Joe.

Joe, naturally, begged his broker friends to keep their big mouths shut; but he knew that he was in deep dung.

TUESDAY, SEPTEMBER 29 — Trading halted

The rumour took about an hour to make the rounds the next morning in every brokerage firm. Nobody really knew the implications for B.H. Beane International. Yet almost everybody suddenly decided, as newly aroused Diligent Traders with well researched information, to take some profits. The selling stampede was terrifying. Selling was so intense that Beane stocks dropped $3 that morning. Holstein asked the Stock Exchange to suspend trading until his team could figure out what was happening.

The local newspaper had a field day with the story. The news story quoted scientists who agreed with the premise that methane gas from cows could warm the atmosphere, destroy life, and end the "highly evolved civilization that man has created". Other scientists claimed pollution from industries was a far bigger enemy than cows, sheep, or pigs. All of the scientists were sympathetic to the theory that dinosaurs had created enough methane gas to make themselves extinct partly because many scientists can smell a future funding opportunity immediately. No scientist, however, wanted to go out on a limb and claim that dinosaur flatulence killed the dinosaurs.

"I'm not sure who the old farts are—the scientists or the dinosaurs," Holstein was widely quoted as having said.

WEDNESDAY, SEPTEMBER 30—More news

Holstein's managers, in a press release, denounced the idea that cows, pigs, and sheep could ruin the atmosphere. The press release said the flatulence story was a plot by oil companies trying to discredit renewable energy.

"Cows, sheep, and pigs will be around long after people have killed themselves. Major industrial polluters should look at their own operations before blaming innocent animals. We will destroy our 'highly evolved civilization' ourselves," the release said.

FRIDAY, OCTOBER 2—Press conference

Holstein finally invited the press to his offices for a briefing with three scientists from a highly respected think tank and local celebrity Dr. J.R. Van Guilder. Holstein said that B.H. Beane International management could not be held responsible for every decline in B.H. Beane International share prices because of investor panic. The company fundamentals, he said, were sound.

"We are looking into the recent rumour connecting cows with human extinction. For now it all sounds like bullshit," Holstein said while looking the assembled journalists in the eye, man to man.

"Beane International is always being discounted by short sellers. These cynics don't believe a company like ours can succeed. These people hate success. These people are barnacles on the heart of society," Holstein said angrily.

The three scientists said that "extensive volcanic eruptions and other factors that increased carbon dioxide levels were probably behind global warming during the age of the dinosaurs".

"In short, gentlemen, dinosaurs and cows are not the cause of global warming. Pollution from factories and other sources is the cause of our nightmare," said Dr. J.R. Van Guilder.

Trading resumed. Investors were not confident. The share price declined from $7 to $6. In the next few days trading in Beane stocks was sluggish as bids dried up and selling continued. Holstein kept silent.

Jack phoned me. "Well," he asked. "What should we do?" I had no idea what to do. The question, as usual, was the same: is this the day we kiss our capital gains goodbye as they turn into worthless stock?

"Why don't we hedge?" I said using a great new word we had discovered as being important to our success. "Let's keep some of our position. I'll sell 10,000 shares and keep 11,000. You sell 20,000 shares and keep 11,000 shares. How's that. If it goes into the sewer we've still made money since we did buy some shares at very low prices. If the share price goes up we'll still make money, but not as much as we might have had we kept all our shares," I said.

Jack, Bungee, Milan, and Oswaldo agreed with our initiative since Holstein had made no further announcement. We were starting to behave like real traders, like professionals. Jack and I sold some stock between $4 and $5. We felt lucky. In fact, we felt brilliant as we pocketed lots of money.

WEDNESDAY, OCTOBER 9—Stock bottoms

A week later, B.H. Beane International shares hit a low of $3. We did not know what was going on, as usual, because Holstein had again disappeared.

Candace, *The Secretary*, had developed some excellent stories about Holstein's whereabouts whenever we phoned:

■ He's getting his passport photo taken.

■ He's in a long distance phone conversation with the president of Pakistan, Taiwan, India, and Australia.

■ He's meeting his board.

■ He's spending the day at the agricultural college.

■ He's out for lunch. This was the most popular excuse between 10 a.m. and 3 p.m.

The Secretary was good, *very* good. Every executive dreams about hiring a beautiful liar to keep people at bay. Everyone seemed convinced that B.H. Beane International was going no where. Fear was on the march again. And then, as you might imagine, a strange thing happened. Holstein appeared at the 12 St. Bar & Grill for lunch with a few brokers.

Bungee phoned me almost out of breath. "Nuts! I think Holstein pulled another stunt. He was just overheard telling some brokers that the whole town is full of "shitheads and idiots" who don't know anything about the stock market or global warming. Holstein said he is going to buy 500,000 shares to move the share price over $10," said Bungee.

"Do you get the weird and twisted feeling that Holstein created this flatulence controversy?" asked Jack.

"Everybody hates conspiracy theories. But I think conspiracies are as common as grass. All great thinkers and writers believe in conspiracies. They aren't Naive Beginners," I said.

Oswaldo phoned. "You don't suppose this whole thing was designed to encourage all the people with free bonus shares to sell at outrageously low prices which Holstein had previously picked out?" he said.

Bungee agreed that Holstein might have concocted the flatulence story to get everybody to sell low. Holstein had shorted his own stock as it increased in price from $7 to $10 during the previous promotional buying binge.

We were beginning to understand, perhaps for the first time, the depth of Holstein's psychological manipulations. We had received our bonus shares just before share prices dropped. That was fishy. Holstein knew we would panic at bad news and unload our shares for a much lower price—a price Holstein had picked for us a long time ago. That's exactly what we did because we wanted to lock in some of our profits. Our brokers Bungee, Oswaldo, or Milan couldn't decide on what to do.

Two days later we discovered that Holstein had crossed several hundred thousand shares to unnamed offshore buyers.

"You might now consider buying B.H. Beane International," Milan laughed on the phone. Milan wasn't laughing at us. Milan was laughing at himself because he had sold his shares, like we had, at less than $5 per share.

"I think the stock is going to move back up. Holstein is probably doing all the buying. I've noticed that all the heavy buying is coming from small brokerage firms recognized as agents for offshore buyers," Milan said.

Within a week the buying frenzy by shorters and Holstein had pushed the stock to about $8. Many short sellers were buying shares before the price went over $10 again.

News stories started appearing in weekly, daily, and monthly newspapers about anti-renewable energy forces conspiring to destroy B.H. Beane International. Local farm newspapers portrayed farmers who used biogas digesters as local heroes because oil and gas companies had been "gouging farmers for years". A few newspapers, especially some of the tabloids, sponsored contests which included biogas digesters as a major prize.

"It's about time farmers start getting self-reliant," one editorial writer enthused.

The recruiting of farmers to test the biogas digester was working beyond B.H. Beane's expectations. Every farmer in North America knew about renewable energy, cowshit, methane gas, dinosaurs, the potential for a methane gas engine, and so on.

B.H. Beane International announced that several agricultural implement companies were evaluating the methane gas engine for combines and tractors. More than 50,000 farmers had already applied to be part of the experimental group. Everybody was excited. Holstein appeared on TV networks such as CNN, ABC, NBC, CBS, CBC, CTV, A&E, Global, MTV, ESPN, and TSN because the flatulence controversy had intrigued everyone.

"This is real life, real drama," Holstein told TSN. "I believe in the biogas digester so much that I'm going to retail it for about

$1,000 instead of the $3,500 my marketing people tell me is the appropriate retail price," Holstein said.

"B.H. Beane International will, after all, receive a 15% royalty from every farmer for every dollar of energy produced. We will offer service, support, and technological innovation. We have created a new utility. We want every farmer to have the biogas digester. That's why we are selling it at an affordable price. We even have a low interest leasing plan," Holstein said.

The Fine News Network's program *Money Month* estimated that B.H. Beane International Inc. could earn $1 billion if one million farmers bought the biogas digester and a further $350 million a year in annual royalties.

Big Money magazine had Holstein on the cover with a story titled, "B.H. Beane International: Is it real or is it B.S.?"

Watch Your Cash magazine had Holstein on the cover with the headline, "B.S. Is Us, Holstein!"

Holstein was even interviewed by CNN's Larry Queen, NBC's David Keyman, CTV's Dina Penny, NBC's Jane Joni, ABC's Donaldhue, CTV's Shirlee, and ABC's Jessy Michaelangelo. Keyman, on his late night show, wanted to know if he could install the biogas digester in his backyard and turn bird droppings into energy.

THURSDAY, OCTOBER 15—Big news

B.H. Beane International spokespersons announced that 500 farmers had been chosen, from the more than 75,000 farmers who had finally applied, to receive free biogas digesters immediately. The 500 lucky farmers were also going to receive a two-hour training video and 40 hours of on-site training from B.H. Beane International's Asian experts. This was front page business news throughout middle America.

The Des Moines Register proclaimed: "B.H. Beane International uses Apple Computer marketing strategy." In fact, several newspapers compared the B.H. Beane International marketing effort with that of Apple Computers when it first promoted the Macintosh computer. B.H. Beane International stock hit $13.

Within days another announcement trumpeted B.H. Beane International's negotiations with the town councils of Buffalo, New York; Buffalo, South Dakota; Red Deer, Alberta; and Moose Jaw, Saskatchewan about building a manufacturing plant. Each of these towns, according to Holstein, met the requirements needed by B.H. Beane International. The towns and cities were small enough to appreciate B.H. Beane International's contributions and were centrally located in middle America and/or Canada. The current manufacturer of B.H. Beane International's experimental prototype biogas digester was being retained as the manufacturer for some production. The idea, of course, was to save transport costs and provide employment. The stock moved to $15 on that news.

The Kansas City Star, where Colonel Theodore Roosevelt wrote articles before becoming U.S. president, announced that the Farm-Aid concert to help the agricultural community was to feature Willie Waylon, Jennings Nelson, and Elvis Hisself (a real last name) in concert with the new friend of the farmer, Bob Holstein, as master of ceremonies. The stock moved from $15 to $17 on this news.

The share price increases in B.H. Beane International stock didn't come in one big wave. There were several minor price declines and increases all the way up. Many inexperienced shorters would invariably short sell when things got quiet and buy long when things heated up. Nobody really knew how strong Holstein really was. That's why the discounters, or the shorters, got burned so often. That's also why fewer and fewer professionals shorted B.H. Beane International at the dizzying $17 per share.

Bungee explained, however, that there were a few powerful professional discounters who were so courageous that they kept shorting B.H. Beane International fearlessly at every step. I could not imagine who would short B.H. Beane International at a time when the price of the stock seemed to be going to the moon.

FRIDAY, NOVEMBER 20—all quiet on the front

Bob Holstein was being promoted by absolutely everyone when the stock price hit $18. In fact, demand for B.H. Beane

The Rampaging Bull Gets Respect
By Helping The Needy

"The Rampaging Bull is so famous there's no way this stock is going into the toilet," Jack said to me during a charity fund raiser for financially troubled farmers.

RAMPAGING BULLS: Outfox Promoters At Their Game On Any Penny Stock Market

International stock was so strong everyone believed the price could increase for ever. The trading was being managed professionally by market makers at three brokerage firms. Everything was under control. There was no pressure. There was joy and anticipation of future capital gains and revenues.

The Farm Aid Concert was a tremendous success for farmers and Holstein. His face appeared on TV screens throughout North America. Jack and I decided to spend Saturday afternoon drinking beer and watching Holstein's promotional stunts. Holstein looked in charge while smoking his cigar on the big stage.

"Holstein is so famous, there's no way that the Beane stock is going into the toilet," said Jack after three beers. I forgave Jack because I know what alcohol can do to Naive Beginners.

A week later, the Vice-President of the United States said, at a small fair in Kansas, that self-reliance was an American ideal; that time had come for farmers to focus on self-reliance; and that B.H. Beane International's ideas could help America. Strong words.

Jack and I watched these developments carefully. Bungee, Milan, and Oswaldo thought anything could happen. The price could go to $30 or it could go to $4. Everything hinged on how the farm community responded to the biogas digester—among other things.

13

Fighting Back

... Farmers Don't Lie

Jack and I couldn't figure out why everyone was getting so excited about B.H. Beane International stock. The company didn't have revenue, profits, or even a fully tested product. The whole thing was premature. Something had to be wrong.

That is when Jack and I decided to put into practice exactly what we had distilled from this adventure. We decided to complete our own version of a due diligence investigation. The two of us decided to do five things: visit a "real" farmer to see what he or she thought about the biogas digester; read all we could about biogas technology; meet the inventors of the biogas digester; search out all public information filed by the company; and visit Holstein's offices at least one more time.

Desmond Icon is a dairy farmer who lives less than a three hour drive from the city. Icon was one of 500 farmers who accepted the biogas digester for testing. We were introduced to him by a friend of a friend. I promised Icon that we wouldn't reveal his name to Holstein if we found something negative.

Holstein had said: "If there is something wrong with the first 500 biogas digesters we can fix the problem easily. We can't do that with 1,000,000 biogas digesters on the market. We will make sure everything works and works well."

Icon's farm essentially had everything—a loving wife, three cranky teenage children, debt, lots of land, and enough cows to provide milk for a small third world country.

Icon was always smiling. Icon couldn't say enough good things about the biogas digester.

"This thing is great," said Icon over breakfast. "I think the biogas digester is going to take over the world. We are already producing methane gas to power heaters in the barns and the water heater in the house." There was something about Icon's eagerness that made it difficult for me to believe him. Farmers are not known to be eager promoters.

"Mr. Icon, have you been paid to recommend this product?" I asked. Icon laughed. His face turned red.

"Absolutely not," he said very quickly. I knew I was onto something. I asked Icon to give us a tour of the farm. I noticed Icon's sons—Jacob, Nick, and Epfrem fixing a tractor tire.

"Nick! Who collects the cow manure?" I asked. Nick laughed. I don't know what made me ask that question. Nick laughed some more. Then I knew Nick and his brothers, Jacob and Epfrem, were the ones delegated to collect cow manure. All three of them, I guessed, hated collecting cow dung. Epfrem and Jacob didn't say anything, but they looked cranky as if they thought the biogas digester was a waste of time.

"It's a bit tricky collecting cow dung. It takes time. You have to collect it when fresh. There's more moisture," Nick said. Collecting cow dung sounded messy.

"If your dad wasn't forcing you to do this, would you?" I asked the three of them. They didn't say anything while looking at their father for direction. Jack and I suddenly knew that the biogas digester had a major hurdle to overcome—market acceptance. We were pleased with ourselves on our drive home.

"Even if the biogas digester works, which we doubt, will people want to spend time collecting cowshit, dogshit, pigshit, or sheepshit to produce methane gas?" Jack asked me.

"Why not? When people are flat broke they'll *eat* cowshit," I said as an expert on depressions and recessions.

We visited Holstein's office the next day. Candace was guarding the fort. Candace, friendly but firm, explained that Holstein was currently on a two week trip to New York, Japan, India, and

Singapore. When we asked about the inventors, Candace smiled. The inventors, she said, were on the same trip with Holstein.

"I'm not at liberty to divulge any information about anyone to anyone," she smiled at us. I couldn't help thinking that she was an excellent secretary. I was glum. But Jack was smiling as we walked out. We both waved goodbye to Candace. She winked at us. The doors on the elevator closed. Then Jack held up the magazines from the waiting room.

"You took the magazines—*Scientific World, Engineer Digest,* and *Third World Review,*" I said amazed.

"I think I know who the inventors are. Look at the subscription labels," Jack said. The name on the label read: Dr. J.R. Van Guilder. The address was a post office box which was also the mailing address for B.H. Beane International. I didn't get it.

Jack then explained that J.R. Van Guilder was the man who had praised Holstein during the Victims Of World Hatred and Sexual Harassment banquet and the man who had criticized the global-warming-caused-by-flatulence theory to the press.

"Don't you get it? J.R. Van Guilder is a scientist, an engineer. He is, for some reason, receiving magazines at B.H. Beane offices. Is he working for the company? I'll bet he knows who the developers of the biogas digester are. In fact, it might be him," Jack said.

"All we have to do is check if J.R. Van Guilder is on a business trip. If he is on a business trip I think we have our man. It's elementary my dear Watson," Jack, the detective, said.

We needed just one phone call to J.R. Van Guilder's office at the university. The engineering department secretary, after we begged and lied, told us that J.R. Van Guilder was on a two week business trip overseas. Then she hung up on us. Jack and I were feeling like Sherlock Holmes. We agreed to put the squeeze on J.R. Van Guilder when he got back. We were determined to find out everything he knew about the biogas digester.

The material from the stock exchange revealed a number of things. Holstein and his board of directors had so many stock options that they could flood the market with their shares for years. We also discovered that Holstein had not filed his insider trading reports for the last quarter; that B.H. Beane International had yet to receive one dollar in revenues; and that independent auditors had offered "qualified" but friendly opinions on the company's books. This information wasn't sinister although it was interesting.

NOVEMBER 23 TO DECEMBER 23 — Trouble

Jack and I started asking more questions. We were turning into private eyes. We now understood that there are two ways to make money—on the way up and on the way down. We wanted to short the stock if there was something wrong with B.H. Beane International. As you might guess Jack and I were insecure about shorting Holstein's stock. Shorting a stock at $17 isn't an easy thing to do if the stock increases to $20 per share. That is why we were in J.R. Van Guilder's office the day he got back from his Asian trip with Holstein. You won't believe what we did. Jack pretended he was a farmer who didn't like the biogas digester because it wasn't working well. Jack even dressed the part with a cap, boots, and a jacket that said "John Deere is great". Van Guilder's secretary wasn't around. So Jack just walked in.

"Dr. Van Guilder. How are you? My name is David Lupinsky. I'm a farmer. I think the digester doesn't work," said Jack. Van Guilder almost fell out of his chair. Van Guilder said he didn't know what Jack was talking about.

"Holstein asked me to talk to you about the problems I'm having," Jack said. J.R. Van Guilder didn't say a word. His lower lip dropped.

"It's like this professor. The biogas digester won't work when it gets cold. In fact, just the other day the temperature dropped below zero in my area. The digester won't ferment properly," Jack said. J.R. Van Guilder looked trapped. His face was red.

"That can't be," said J.R. Van Guilder. "We have designed the digester . . ." then he stopped talking. Jack looked excited—like a cat face to face with a mouse. Jack had uncovered the brains behind the digester.

"You of all people should know there is a problem with the digester!" Jack went on boldly. J.R. Van Guilder tried to make excuses. Van Guilder said he was only a consultant to Holstein.

That's when I walked into his office with the magazines Jack had scooped from Holstein's waiting room. I introduced myself as Jack's older brother and asked Van Guilder why magazines in the B.H. Beane offices were addressed to him.

"Holstein ordered material for research—for fun," said J.R. Van Guilder.

"The digester won't work in cold weather, will it?" I asked. I forgot to tell you, dear reader, that Jack and I phoned Nick Icon, Desmond's good humoured son, to confirm how well the biogas digester worked. Nick, out of hearing distance from his father, said the biogas digester performed poorly when the weather was cold. J.R. Van Guilder laughed; turned red; and got angry.

"You guys aren't farmers. Who the hell are you?" he shouted. Jack, looking outraged, told Van Guilder he would tell everybody that Van Guilder had stolen the biogas digester designs and never added a single innovation to them.

"Boys. Boys. Take it easy. The biogas digester needs work. There is no doubt about that. There's no need to get excited. We are working hard to perfect the damn thing," Van Guilder said.

"Holstein jumped the gun by promoting the stock prematurely, didn't he?" I asked. J.R. Van Guilder, recognizing he was on thin ice, didn't say anything. He was polite, firm, and escorted us out the door with his sincere university-professor-knows-all-look.

We recognized that we had made a direct hit on the B.H. Beane empire. The biogas digesters were going to become front page news when the weather got colder. Holstein would exploit this imperfection in the product to start a selling spree. We decided to beat him to it. We phoned Bungee immediately, from the university cafeteria pay phone, to open a short account to complement our long account. Bungee got irritated at us.

"You are going to lose a fortune," he said.

"Here's how it is. I want you to sell 5,000 shares for my short account and sell 7,000 shares for Jack's short account. You can also unload 20% of our Beane stocks while you are at it," I said.

I now had 17,000 shares in my long accounts and Jack had 25,000 shares in his long accounts with Bungee, Milan, and Oswaldo. We had more than enough shares to cover our short account with Bungee if the share price increased. If the share price declined from $17, we would make money in our short accounts and start a steady sale of our long accounts.

We were proud about hedging our bet. The concept was exciting. We realized that we had managed our greed. We also understood that we had moved up into a more sophisticated class of trading. We had completed a major due diligence effort that included one trip to a farm where we spent time with three teenage kids; a visit to the terrified inventor; a careful reading of information filed at the stock exchange; and a review of our strategies.

"If the price goes up, you are going to be sorry," warned Bungee. Jack and I laughed. We were being arrogant. We knew we couldn't tell Bungee what we had learned immediately. The stock didn't go up. The stock didn't go down. The stock stayed where it was for one week. Then people started selling the stock "to lock in profits". The B.H. Beane International share price dropped to about $14 in two weeks of steady trading. There was no panic selling because Holstein had beaten back the threat from short sellers at least a half dozen times in the past. Everybody believed he could do it again. Everybody said so. Jack and I, however, were celebrating because we felt something big was going to happen largely because of our research.

While we were waiting for the bottom to drop out of the stock we started selling off the B.H. Beane International shares in our long account. I sold 3,000 shares at $13 and Jack sold 6,000 shares at $12.50. Jack took me to a fast food restaurant for lunch where we celebrated with a low fat hamburger, a low fat muffin, a low fat milkshake, and a diet cola. No fancy restaurants for Diligent Traders like us.

After our diet lunch we phoned our brokers and stepped up our attack on B.H. Beane International. The share price dropped again by the afternoon. We each sold another 5,000 shares from our long account. The next day we told our brokers to sell our remaining long positions. Our three brokers asked if we knew something they didn't know. Jack and I told them. Why shouldn't we? Jack and I had both agreed to share our findings with our brokers as soon as possible. They were, after all, supposed to be on our side. We also decided to start our own rumour. A selling spree of B.H. Beane stock would force the price lower and give us a bigger profit in our short accounts. We didn't mention, in case you are interested, Van Guilder or Icon to our brokers.

I then did something really crazy. I told Oswaldo to short sell 5,000 B.H. Beane shares at $11 because Holstein had managed to temporarily push the stock price back up. I had enough money in my cash account to cover the short sale. The stock eventually dropped in heavy trading to $10.50. I was starting to feel like a professional who can predict the market. I wasn't nervous because even if the stock turned up I could easily cover my short positions. I would lose some of my profits. So what. The odds were good.

We later discovered that Bungee and Milan had actually visited Holstein to tell him they were considering short selling his stock. They wanted to hear Holstein's side of the story.

The demand for B.H. Beane shares was, however, strong. One should never underestimate the power of a Rampaging Bull. The bids were so strong for the next several days that the price of the stock rebounded to $14.50 per share. Jack and I were calm about the whole thing. Our short positions were covered with cash profits we had earned earlier. We had more than enough money in our cash account to settle the short account if share prices increased dramatically. The word on the street for the week was "indecision". Christmas was just a week away and interest in the stock markets was always weak just before the holidays. Yet Holstein

My Brokers Challenge the Rampaging Bull

"We're thinking of 'short selling' your stock. What are you going to do about it?" Bungee said to The Rampaging Bull while Milan waited for a reply.

RAMPAGING BULLS: Outfox Promoters At Their Game On Any Penny Stock Market

had apparently sparked another buying flurry to stabilize the stock. Holstein was lucky. The weather was unusually warm throughout North America which allowed the digester to work late into the year. Jack and I decided that we would not settle our short accounts at a loss. We would ride the adventure out.

Then it happened—two days before Christmas. All the newspapers ran a story about a David Walmeer, a farmer in Idaho, who said his biogas digester wasn't working at moderately cold temperatures. The newspaper carried a reaction from a B.H. Beane International spokesperson who said that "the company would correct any technical problem". The silence on the street was similar to when we first found out about the extinction through flatulence theory.

Many people decided to sell some of their B.H. Beane International shares as a Christmas gift to themselves. The stock dropped $8 on a trading volume of 500,000 December 23 and 24. Jack and I both went to church. Jack and I were having a great Christmas— our short account was making money. Jack and I did manage to dress like Santa Claus to deliver a small truck load of food to the local food bank. We also sent a large cheque to the Salvation Army and the United Nations hunger relief. Jack and I felt we had to give meaning to our almost crazy adventure in the stock market. We even sent Holstein a holiday card.

B.H. Beane International, as you might imagine, put up a valiant fight against short sellers. B.H. Beane International's vast army of supporters, many of whom had invested big money or been bribed, started promoting the company more aggressively.

Holstein appeared on the national television show, *America In The Morning*, to say he was recalling all 500 biogas digesters. His engineers could correct any technical errors.

"But Mr. Holstein," the interviewer asked. "We know the digester will work in the spring. Do we have to wait another year before we discover the digester will work in cold weather?"

Holstein laughed and explained that the digesters would be tested in cold weather conditions in his laboratories which, for some reason, were still at a secret location—possibly on the planet Krypton. Jack and I were toying with the idea of revealing that J.R. Van Guilder was the brains behind the whole operation. We kept our mouth shut.

The stock price finally bottomed out at about $7 before the end of the year. All the people who had held on expecting Holstein to perform a miracle were in for a surprise. It seemed that Holstein wasn't going to rush into promoting the share price until he was ready—apparently in the spring just as everyone had feared. Jack and I were sure that Holstein would launch a tremendous campaign in the spring. He had enough money in his war chest to move the stock to $20 all over again.

JANUARY 1 TO MARCH 23 — All quiet

I should tell you we think Holstein may have anticipated everything that happened—especially the reports of the biogas digester's inability to function in cold weather. We think Holstein just wanted to take the winter off and go for a holiday. I don't have any real hard evidence. Jack said he went to the 12 St. Bar & Grill early in January where he saw Holstein holding court, buying everyone drinks, laughing loudly, and being everyone's best friend. Jack says that Holstein waved at him.

"Hiya Jack," Holstein said to Jack as if they were old school chums. "I'm going to Hawaii with my wife for a well deserved vacation," Holstein said. Jack says Holstein told everyone that efforts to correct technical problems with the biogas digester were moving along well.

"I can use the break. Everybody knows I'll be back in the spring raring to go. I think the share price will top $30," Holstein said. A few brokers, said Jack, tried to pin Holstein down about what went wrong. Holstein laughed. He told everyone that if they no longer believed in B.H. Beane International he would buy their shares back—at a discount of course. Holstein was grinning when he said that, says Jack.

"We never promised anyone a rose garden. We said the price of the stock would be in God's hands. Besides, Alexandria wasn't built in one day," Holstein said. "If everybody is patient with me they will make a killing in the spring. What can I tell you? I'm not a God. I just look like one," laughed Holstein as he waved at Joyce, The Server, to put the next round of drinks on his tab. Jack says everybody groaned because Holstein was intentionally being evasive—and proud of doing it well.

Bungee, Milan, and Oswaldo, who weren't at the 12 St. Bar & Grill that day, but who heard everything, speculated that Holstein was running the B.H. Beane International stock promotion like a typical gold mining stock.

"A gold mining stock is heavily promoted in the spring when drilling, testing, and assaying are being done. Nobody knows what the results will be so the stock can be promoted beyond what it is worth. When the results do come in, the share price usually declines, the winners collect their money, and the promoter flies south for his winter holidays," Bungee said.

"I think Holstein is starting a new Beane promotion in the spring. He can promote B.H. Beane International all spring, summer, and fall. Who knows what will happen to the biogas digester next winter? We'll have to wait, won't we?" said Bungee.

The farm community, as you might expect, was divided on how to react to B.H. Beane International. The 500 test farmers were calm; were hopeful about the coming improvements which apparently called for special insulation; and looked forward to continuing their experiment in the spring.

FINALE

Our Beane and Rampaging Bull story is essentially over. I can summarize what eventually happened to Beane International. Holstein did launch another B.H. Beane International promotion on March 8 at the Victims Of World Hatred and Sexual Harassment dinner. Professor J.R. Van Guilder was again master of ceremonies. None of us were there, but we heard all about it.

Vic, Dave, Bungee, Milan, Oswaldo, Jack, and I each bought 5,000 shares of B.H. Beane International trading steadily at $4 in anticipation of Holstein's promotion. We wanted to play this stock

Jack Adopts The Rampaging Bull's Style As Part Of His Marketing Strategy

"We're pals," Jack said. "If everybody is patient with us while they use prices falling in the spring, What can I do with a bull in a China shop," Jack replied. "It's the Rampaging Bull who keeps us the investors happy and in the market."

"We're pals. I want to offer you a small token of my appreciation. You get Happy Hour prices anytime you come in," Jack said to the Rampaging Bull while my brokers, Bungee and Oswaldo, sipped beer.

RAMPAGING BULLS: Outfox Promoters At Their Game On Any Penny Stock Market one more season. We watched the stock rock and roll for most of the spring and summer during the second year as the share price reached $20. We then replayed, with many improvements, everything we had done the year before. The seven of us were by now very informed traders.

Holstein, as you might imagine, earned another fortune as the stock moved up and down all year with a few variations on his tricks for new bunch of Naive Beginners. In fact, Holstein ran the promotion for three full years with the share price topping $25 in year three. We share some of the details in the next two chapters.

Jack, by the way, opened a small deli bar with the money he earned on Holstein's promotions. He named his new watering hole Jack's Bean Stock Bar & Grill. The operation was an instant success because Jack had learned the fine art of promotion thanks to our experiences in the stock market. Jack invited Holstein to the grand opening of his restaurant and told everyone Holstein taught him everything he knows. Holstein was pleased with this public expression of thanks which, by the way, was sincere.

"We're pals. I want to offer you a small token of my affection. From now on, I'm telling my staff that they are to offer you Happy Hour prices anytime you come in," said Jack. Holstein laughed out loud. He loves it when people learn to do business his way. This little exchange between Jack and Holstein became something of a legend in the local brokerage industry. Every broker now respects Jack's brassy attitude. All of us understand why Holstein eats regularly at Jack's Bean Stock Bar.

"I taught Jack everything he knows about the stock market. Jack even named the bar in honour of a deal we did once," Holstein likes to tell everyone.

Jack is convinced his bar and grill is popular because brokers think he knows something about the market that they don't.

"You see," Jack likes to tell me, "I know how The Rampaging Bull thinks. They don't."

14 Personality And Set Up

... At Least He Tries

If Holstein had treated Van Guilder with respect and followed through on his promises then we wouldn't have ever discovered the mysteries of a great promotion.

Thank God there is no honour among thieves.

After our confrontation with Van Guilder in his office we tried to make it up to him. We felt bad. At first he wouldn't talk to us because he thought, and rightly so, that Jack and I were a couple of "weasels".

"Special situations call for special solutions," I said to Van Guilder. I remember him looking at us with his face all screwed up as if he had just finished eating a whole lemon. Then the *Holy Spirit* moved Van Guilder to speak to us. I think Van Guilder realized that Jack and I were the only people he could trust with his pain. Holstein had promised Van Guilder the moon—options, free trading shares, cash, and God knows what. Holstein, according to Van Guilder, kept delaying delivery of shares, cheques, and cash because he didn't want Van Guilder to unload his shares in the market. Van Guilder always laughed when he mentioned this.

"Holstein knew that I knew the whole story. Holstein believed, and he was right up to a point, that I would unload my shares to collect a profit. So he double crossed me. What was good for him was not good for me," said Van Guilder.

By the time Van Guilder got the shares, the promotion was essentially over. Unfortunately, Van Guilder had participated in a scheme to defraud thousands of people with a phony product.

Could Van Guilder, a university professor, whine to friends and family about his partner in crime? Heck no! Since Jack and I essentially knew the whole story the three of us shared a special bond. So it isn't surprising that Van Guilder eventually used us as his therapy group.

I know it all sounds somewhat crazy if you have never experienced something like this. Yet it all makes sense to anyone who has ever been defrauded, hustled, swindled, conned, hoodwinked, and scammed. Trust me.

"You won't believe what he's doing now," Van Guilder would complain to Jack over the phone. The two of us would hang out, drink coffee, play amateur psychologist, and listen to Van Guilder discuss Holstein's personality and his latest scheme.

We've already mentioned some of these ideas in earlier chapters so we'll try not to repeat ourselves. We will, however, fine tune our understanding of Holstein as a Rampaging Bull in this chapter. Jack and I liked to hear all the gossip even though the promotion was essentially over. We realized, through Van Guilder's rambling, that Holstein's "malignant" personality is ideally suited to manage a stock promotion.

▪ A. THE PERSONALITY

1. Fearful and Greedy

Van Guilder said everyone involved with B.H. Beane International, including Holstein, knew the development of a product which can ferment animal waste into methane gas in cold weather would take longer and cost more money than Holstein was allocating.

"For God's sake. What's to figure out? You people are scientists—right? You can put it together in six months?" Holstein told his research team of three engineers led by Van Guilder. When Van Guilder told him he was being unfair, Holstein only laughed.

"It's my management style. You'll want millions of dollars and take your time if I don't push you. You need discipline. You are lazy supine bastards," Holstein once said to his research team.

"I've never seen a guy so tight with money. Holstein often delayed paying the bills, argued about expenses, got other people to buy him lunch, and sometimes even picked fights to avoid paying debts. Yet he had to have the top of the line limousine because, as he reminded us, it was good for business," Van Guilder said.

"We started paying the bills out of our own savings rather than go to Holstein," said Van Guilder.

2. Angry Rage

"There wasn't a day when he wasn't criticizing someone. I could never figure out if he was acting or if he was truly angry," Van Guilder said.

"Sometimes he'd scream at someone and then start laughing as if he'd just used a management technique he picked up at a pretentious business seminar," said Van Guilder.

3. Vain and Critical

"Nobody could ever do anything right in Holstein's eyes," Van Guilder said. "Holstein always had to improve everything even if he didn't know what he was talking about. It was, and is, incredible. I think he believes he is infallible. I kept telling him he could join any number of religious organizations which believe they have a direct fax line to God," said Van Guilder.

"A promoter like Holstein, himself vain and critical thanks to a troubled childhood that includes physical or mental abuse, often deals with people he can dominate. He prefers the fearful and greedy to the vain, angry, and critical like himself," said Jack, a budding *New Age* psychologist.

"That is why Holstein has the utmost contempt for anybody who wants to be his friend even though he hides his emotions well. Holstein pleases others when he needs them—not before. He is then charming. His tolerance is low for anyone who won't give him money or do his bidding," I said.

"What's the point of competing. There's only room for one boss. That's me," Holstein used to tell Van Guilder.

4. Courageous and Blunt

"Holstein is tenacious, independent, a self starter, and seemingly attentive to detail. When you first meet him he laughs, brags, drops names, tells dirty jokes, and looks for weakness. If you are a Naive Beginner you may think he is a daring and charming man. You soon discover, however, that you are in the presence of a man who uses every technique in the book to draw you out," Van Guilder said.

Holstein immediately wants to convert any so-called "new friendship" into advantage. If a person shows weakness, Holstein invariably behaves as bluntly as he can to put a person on the defensive. If the behaviour works, then the weak person will become a servant.

Holstein, as The Rampaging Bull, pushes the limits of acceptable behaviour with everyone as part of this technique. Most people with typical family backgrounds do not understand how to cope with or diagnose this type of person. The fearful and greedy mistake Holstein's arrogance for ability; anger for determination; cunning for charm; and his inability to feel as strength.

5. Deepest Need

"I think Holstein is torn by conflicting needs — greed versus the need to be important and loved," said Van Guilder while flipping through a book by a noted psychologist.

"Holstein's involvement in the Farm-Aid Concert and The Victims Of World Hatred and Sexual Harassment Society was a natural evolution in a Rampaging Bull's life. Once the malignant narcissistic or criminal incompetent steals enough money he or she may compensate for his or her criminal behaviour by becoming a philanthropist," Jack said.

6. Our Conclusions

The Rampaging Bull is a man who can win in the short term. The Rampaging Bull usually loses in the longer term because he overrates himself. He will lose even when his company or organization matures and produces real products unless he does one of two things:

■ The Rampaging Bull must *sell* his now successful company and promote something new if he isn't in the mood to retire with his millions hidden offshore somewhere.

■ The Rampaging Bull must *attract* a cadre of professional managers who can control his narcissism, reduce his influence on staff, and keep morale high.

Any other corporate strategy by The Rampaging Bull will eventually lead him and his associates to total financial and personal disaster. That is why a highly intelligent Rampaging Bull such as Holstein sticks to promoting. He is like a shark. If the Rampaging Bull stops promoting he dies. He intuitively knows, at least most of the time, that he is a poor manager of people. Holstein knows that if he organized a real team to produce and market a real product he would eventually fail. The whole process of production and day to day drudgery is boring to his frenzied mind constantly dreaming of new schemes.

■ B. THE SET UP

1. The Principle

The master promoter must find a "shell" listed on a penny stock market or elsewhere, buy most of the outstanding shares inexpensively, and assign appropriate stock options to himself and the board of directors. Options to buy inexpensive shares sometime in the future are a major incentive for the insiders and a concern for traders and investors who are afraid the insiders will flood the market with their shares at inappropriate times.

"Stick with me and you'll get rich peeling off shares to suckers—er—buyers (heh, heh, heh) whenever you need cash," Holstein told Van Guilder.

2. The Small Investors

Holstein had no problem establishing a share price between 50 cents and $2. The small investors, puffed up with their self importance as friends of Holstein, bought stock because they believed what they heard.

"Yet Holstein was always too busy to talk to small investors when the share price topped $2 or $3," said Van Guilder.

3. The Shell

Holstein started developing the B.H. Beane International promotion almost a full year before he finally made his ideas known publicly at the dinner Jack attended. Holstein wanted a company listed on a penny stock market which was essentially a "shell". A shell company has no assets other than the value of having gone through the time consuming paperwork required for listing on a stock exchange. This sort of company has been "packaged" for the highest bidder, preferably a master promoter.

Holstein could have gone through the more arduous task of starting his own shell company and getting it listed on a penny stock exchange. But he didn't for several compelling reasons.

"Find me a nice clean shell somewhere," Holstein told stockbrokers.

i. Advantages/Disadvantages Of Buying Existing Shell

■ An existing shell usually has free trading shares instead of "escrow" shares which are prohibited from being traded freely up to three years to protect investors. An existing shell has probably been around for sometime and perhaps been in a previous promotion that went awry.

■ An existing shell should be carefully reviewed for any liabilities because of previous promoters.

■ An existing shell probably has no money.

■ An existing shell has many investors who are stuck with worthless shares for which they paid a lot of money. These investors have few expectations about making money on this stock. These investors might be eager to sell their shares to recoup as much of their money as possible. This means that these shares can be bought back by the promoter at lower prices than a newly formed shell which has many investors with big expectations.

■ Some existing shareholders, however, might not sell until the share price increases dramatically. This can be helpful in the early stages of a promotion. There is less premature profit taking.

■ The original insiders or owners of an existing shell will often sell at a "cheap" price because they are tired of listing fees, tax filings, legal filings, and criticism from cranky investors.

■ The remaining investors of an existing shell, once they discover that a new promotion is about to begin, will help promote the company to others. They want to sell their shares at a profit.

■ Many existing shareholders may have died. The actual number of shareholders may be much less than the statistics show. This can help a good promotion.

ii. Advantages/Disadvantages Of Creating New Shell

■ A new shell company listed on a penny stock market has at least 300 greedy investors eager for something to happen. Getting control of these shares for a moderate price to launch a powerful promotion is very difficult.

■ Most of the shares owned by the officially sanctioned insiders are escrowed for at least one to three years. These shares can't be used in a bigtime stock manipulation. Many stock exchanges are tightening up escrow rules by linking release of escrowed shares to performance and earnings rather than to how much money is spent on a project.

■ The stock exchange, lawyers, securities commissions, and accountants can drag out the listing procedure for a new penny stock a long time while billing large fees.

■ A new shell will likely have a couple hundred thousand dollars in the bank as the result of an initial public offering between 10 cents to 50 cents.

4. Holstein's Shell

Holstein found B.H. Beane International, then known by another name, through a mutual acquaintance. The company, recovering from a poorly conceived stock promotion, was barely able to pay its listing fees on the stock exchange. There were 1.4 million shares trading freely among many investors and three million shares, about to come out of escrow, owned by insiders.

Holstein encouraged 30 of his greediest associates to invest $5,000 each. He raised $150,000 to buy this shell which investors believed, and correctly, would give them a return of 1,000%. The money was deposited in a bank under the partnership name.

"I've told all my investors that we are going to develop a prototype of the digester within six months. You better get on it. You can do it. I have full confidence in your ability," Holstein told Van Guilder whenever Van Guilder doubted his abilities.

Holstein offered the existing insiders of the public shell company $45,000, or 1.5 cents per share, for almost all three million shares in escrow. This is much less than the cost of listing a company on the stock exchange. The insiders accepted this offer because they could keep their free trading shares to sell during Holstein's promotion which would give them a huge profit.

Holstein then proceeded, starting late in the summer and without fanfare, to buy free trading shares on the open market from two cents to six cents. This wasn't hard to do. Holstein was patient. He bid up a two cent stock to five cents and then let the price fall back to two cents by withdrawing his bid. Most people eventually sold their shares next time the bid went to five cents.

This is not an overnight process. Stubborn investors were suspicious. Holstein bought about 600,000 free trading shares for $30,000 at an average price of about five cents. The partnership account had about $75,000 left from the original $150,000 raised to buy the shell. The stock reached eight cents a share when Holstein completed this buying spree.

Holstein convinced a few brokers from his previous promotions to help him raise $100,000. He sold 1,000,000 treasury shares at 10 cents to some well heeled risk takers according to the press releases. Holstein, however, bought the shares through his various trading accounts. This increased the total share float of the company from 4.4 to 5.4 million shares. Holstein and his associates now held 4.6 million of the 5.4 million shares and about 500,000 share options which they could buy at 30 cents.

This entire process took until the end of November.

Holstein then proceeded to buy more stock in the company's name. Holstein managed to buy back, in an even more patient campaign, about 400,000 shares at an average of 12 cents per share during January and February. This is legal. Public companies are usually allowed to buy 10% of their total outstanding shares each year. Since B.H. Beane International had 5.4 million outstanding shares, this allowed Holstein to scoop as many as 540,000 shares in the company's name. The 400,000 shares cost the company another $48,000. This left $52,000 in the corporate bank account and $75,000 in the private partnership account which was more than enough to start a strong promotion. Holstein and his team now owned about five million shares, all in a pooling agreement, of the 5.4 million outstanding shares—all of which were free trading by now. The pooling agreement essentially called for all the shares to be pooled and kept under the control of a third party. Holstein sold the shares when he deemed it appropriate.

Holstein, of course, was satisfied with this share ownership structure. He knew the last 400,000 shares would be hard to buy for less than 50 cents because they belonged to investors looking for action.

Holstein also offered the North American sales rights for the biogas digester, which he and his team owned, to B.H. Beane International. Holstein and his team received 10 million shares at 20 cents each for a supposed value of about two million dollars. This exchange of product rights for shares, all of which couldn't be bought or sold for at least three years, was already being evaluated by the securities commission. In short, Holstein knew that he and his insiders owned as many shares as they needed for an excellent promotion.

Holstein was finally ready to do the work God had ordained for him—to promote. To take over complete control of a shell on a mid-sized penny stock market in North America had cost Holstein $100,000 and his associates about $150,000 in cold hard cash. This might be considered somewhat expensive.

Yet Holstein and his 30 key associates had a lot to show for their money. Holstein and his associates owned a company which was positioned for an excellent promotion; owned the rights to a "wonderful" new product; owned almost all the free trading shares; had $52,000 in the public company's bank account; had old shareholders excited and ready to talk it up; had brokers expectant because they knew Holstein had invested his money and would be leading the promotion; and had a solid base price of 12 to 15 cents per share before Holstein started the promotion. There was also about $75,000 left in the private partnership's bank account to set up the various offshore and domestic brokerage accounts needed to develop the promotion. We discuss this in the next chapter. This wasn't bad for a company whose stock was worthless and trading at two cents, when it traded, less than a year earlier.

"I hope you have the prototype ready. The promotion is starting in four days," Holstein finally told Van Guilder.

"I was in a state of panic when Holstein told me that," said Van Guilder. "He was going to start the promotion without having a fully perfected product. I didn't walk away because I believed we could develop the product—and I still believe that this product has a future in North America," Van Guilder added.

"I noticed you were stressed during the World Hatred and Sexual Harassment dinner," said Jack.

"You were there!" said a surprised Van Guilder.

It's amazing how small the world really is.

15 | The Hook And The Sting

. . . Continue Inside Bull's Pen

When B.H. Beane International shares traded at 15 cents all the insiders celebrated according to Van Guilder. Who wouldn't?

A two cent stock was now trading at 15 cents after a year of careful nurturing. Rumours of a great future were already swirling through the financial community.

"We are going to have a good time," Holstein told his insiders according to Van Guilder.

"Say what you want about Holstein, but he knows how to hook people with panache. He's still doing it well," said Van Guilder.

Jack and I both liked these new words. *Hook. Panache.*

We could argue that the word "hook" may be the most important word for stock traders to remember. Here are some conclusions we made after our discussions with Van Guilder and our own experiences in the stock market.

■ A. THE HOOK

1. The Broad Outline

■ A hot deal must be worthy, big, and thrill people into believing the product or process will change the world or that the mineral deposit is "world class"—a phrase used by everybody to pump up the importance of anything even when it is not necessary.

■ Important people and the press must lend support either directly by saying kind things or indirectly by not being critical. This is easy when libel and slander laws are so strong they turn everyone into sycophants.

Holstein, recognizing the realities of life, had written letters to ambassadors in several countries; had discussions with several farm groups; had developed a product based on models found in Asian villages; had applied for government grants; had worked out an immigration/investor plan in detail; and had recruited the first 100 farmers to test the biogas digester.

■ Important people must be recruited for the team by offering them options, warrants, cash, and free trading shares.

"I think my special incentive fees will cost me $200,000 in cash and shares over the next couple years," Holstein said.

Holstein understood that the expense of getting important people on side as spokespersons would pay off handsomely in the future when his critics acted up. Holstein's "impartial" observers would cancel out critics, confuse the issues, and allow him to promote the stock successfully.

A national farm co-operative manager, for instance, had recruited 10 farmers to test the biogas digester. The farmers and the manager all received Frequent Buyer shares. In short, a few farmers stood to earn some serious money if they recruited neighbours, local farm groups, and the local press.

Holstein also had given stock options to three national journalists with drinking problems and major debts; had made contributions to campaigns of several political leaders; had joined the local ruling political party; had become active in the 4H Club as an adviser to young farmers; was a recognized leader of Victims Of World Hatred and Sexual Harassment; and was organizing a fund raising concert for destitute farmers.

■ The promotional effort must not unveil all the company's achievements, perceived achievements, or hoped for achievements at once. The only way to get people excited when they become bored is to unveil new and exciting news. If the promoter runs out of news, the stock promotion will falter and fail.

■ A Rampaging Bull will not diversify his company because this is the equivalent of admitting defeat.

■ The promoter must unveil bad news about the company at appropriate times to force the stock prices lower. This allows the promoter and insiders to buy back shares at lower prices to restart the promotion. The goal of this seemingly self-destructive process is to accumulate personal and corporate wealth and finance an even stronger promotion. The Master Promoter must have the nerve and willingness to create several stock selling panics. Without this, there can be no successful stock promotion.

This process also encourages small investors to sell to richer investors. Richer investors sell to pension funds. Pension funds sell to new and thrilled investors or they get stuck "holding the bag". The goal of stock promotions is to attract the richest people.

"Holstein always called his big investors 'My people'," said Van Guilder.

■ The promoter must not laugh or speak too loudly. The preferred stance is to speak in serious and low tones except for rare social events when the promoter shows himself to be a "regular guy".

■ The promoter will hint at "secret knowledge" or "secret influential friends" regularly.

■ The Master Promoter will befriend the weak, greedy, and foolish when he starts a promotion. The weak are favoured as investors because they can be controlled and manipulated to tell others—especially if they believe the information is confidential.

■ The wealthy investor who is usually in on the confidence game wants The Rampaging Bull to manipulate poorer investors but not wealthy investors like himself. That is why wealthy investors and The Rampaging Bull pretend to be best friends.

■ The company story must be believable but not perfect. Some weakness in a story encourages people to believe even more. Nobody believes everything is perfect. A great stock promotion must have some problem that can be corrected in time.

■ A stock promotion, however, based on a story which assumes a mass audience is "completely" stupid will fail. There must be elements of truth in every lie.

■ The Rampaging Bull will tell as many people as possible about the stock and predict various price levels during the early stages of the promotion. This develops confidence among investors that The Rampaging Bull is in control. This allows The Rampaging Bull to remind the initial skeptics, especially rich ones, that they missed an opportunity to make even more money.

When Holstein told us the stock was about to increase to 35 cents, 50 cents, $1, $1.50, $2.50, and $3.50 he was sincere. Holstein was ready after a year of preparation.

Holstein knew that the dozen people he spoke to at the Victims Of World Hatred And Sexual Harassment dinner would talk to several hundred people. Holstein understood the fine art of the whisper. Holstein made several other appearances, according to Van Guilder, at important functions where he spilled several drinks on unsuspecting people.

Jack and I estimated that over 2,000 potential investors kept an eye on Holstein and B.H. Beane International stock in those early days of the promotion. Holstein knew he could get everybody excited by moving the stock up gently but firmly—like any good seducer.

■ The investors must believe there is a groundswell of public opinion in favour of this stock. This should happen as a seemingly natural phenomenon that encourages people to believe in the popularity of a stock even more.

■ The Master Promoter will use the money raised to control the share float, promote share prices, and attract others to invest.

■ A Rampaging Bull must not be seen using the money raised for the company's project for his personal living expenses even though he may actually do this.

■ The Master Promoter will encourage several powerful backers to provide a backstop for the stock price below which it will not drop at each stage of the promotion. The stronger the financial backing, the higher the share price can be promoted.

■ Beginning promoters rarely, if ever, have access to powerful financial backers because they have no track record. A promoter's track record is everything. A promoter without a track record cannot develop an extended promotion unless he or she is lucky or unless he or she has a genuinely popular product.

■ A Master Promoter will try to limit the sale of stock through fear, abuse, promises, bribes, and feigned friendship.

■ The Rampaging Bull will short sell his stock at a ratio of two to one. The promoter will try to sell for his short account two shares for each share sold by others as the share price increases as part of a buying wave. This allows The Rampaging Bull to accumulate enough money to bid the stock price up again when independent buying dries up and the share price falters. That is why the Rampaging Bull tries to limit the sale of stock by others; tries to keep short sellers out of the game as long as possible; and encourages as many people as possible to buy.

■ The Master Promoter, unlike the beginning promoter, will not depend on stockbrokers to get investors to buy and sell. The Master Promoter will convince people to buy with intimidation, incentives, or just plain hype. The Master Promoter encourages his clients to buy stocks with favoured brokers who in turn get their clients to buy. A weak promoter will depend on brokers to a higher degree, offer brokers fewer new clients, command less respect, and eventually fail to develop a great promotion.

■ The Master Promoter will always leave out important information in every conversation, press release, and prospectus. This is the equivalent of lying, but can never be proven as lying.

■ The Rampaging Bull or Master Promoter will always try to make investors believe there is no time left to buy.

■ The Master Promoter will cultivate greedy people in every field of activity because they are predictable.

■ The Master Promoter always has his sights set on scooping the money of the rich rather than the poor. The poor must be part of a promotion to offer the semblance of mass interest in a stock promotion and attract the rich. The weaker promoter, who is less aware, is more interested in the poor because he believes he cannot develop an extended stock promotion to attract the rich.

■ If the poor make money with a Rampaging Bull they will invariably tell everyone which enhances The Rampaging Bull's public image as a "Man Of The People". If the rich lose money, they will rarely tell anyone. They want to protect their image. This gives The Rampaging Bull another chance to repeat his efforts with other rich people.

■ If the poor lose money, they will invariably tell everyone and make it impossible for a weak promoter to work in the same town again. Therefore, the only promoter who can win repeatedly is the Rampaging Bull. Weaker promoters have few chances to ply their trade in any community.

2. Creating The Hook, Backstop, and Ditch

When Van Guilder started talking about The Backstop and The Ditch we really got excited. The Backstop and The Ditch are vital components to getting investors hooked on a stock. The industry usually refers to these two initiatives as "wash trading"—the simultaneous buying and selling of a security without beneficial change in ownership by one or more persons acting together.

I'll be honest with you. Jack, Van Guilder, and I hate the phrase "wash trading" because it doesn't describe what's happening accurately. So we'll dispense with the phrase wash trading in favour of more colourful and useful language like The Backstop and The Ditch.

But first, we have to describe the four types of brokerage accounts which a Rampaging Bull can use to develop The Backstop and The Ditch.

i. The Market Maintenance Account

Holstein opened a "Box Account" or the "Market Maintenance" account at a brokerage firm actively involved with penny stocks. Holstein placed 200,000 of his investors' pooled shares and $20,000 of his private partnership's remaining $75,000 into this account. This account, in Holstein's name or a key associate's name, buys B.H. Beane International stock when the price is low and sells when the price is high.

This account has two major functions:

▇ to finance all the "incentives" for the investors and promoters who toe the line including cash, ski trips, fine dinners, and so on.

▇ to maintain an orderly market and provide "liquidity".

ii. The Short Sale Account

Holstein opened a short account in another city with a brokerage firm actively involved in penny stocks and willing to offer flexible terms. The location of the city is important. If the promotion is taking place in the "west", then this account might be opened in the "east" and vice versa. When the share price declines the promoter can always blame "short sellers" in some distant city as trouble-makers.

Holstein opened a short account, in a corporate name or in the name of an easily controlled associate, with approximately $40,000 from his private partnership's remaining $55,000.

He used the account to short sell B.H. Beane International shares when the independent buying was pushing the stock price up. When the independent buying dried up the share price declined. Holstein would buy back lower priced shares, settle his account with the brokerage firm, and turn a profit.

He used the profit, in the short term, to buy back shares at lower prices and create the illusion of a new demand. Holstein just kept the profits when the promotion finally wound down. That's why Holstein publicly promoted and secretly shorted the stock all the way up to $20.

Holstein had to do these two seemingly contradictory and manipulative tactics to create adequate financial reserves at each step of the promotion. Holstein could never have developed a $20 share price had *he* not shorted his *own* stock! Profits from short sales allowed him to pump up the share price every time profit takers and other short sellers forced the share price to decline. Holstein's buying binge aroused renewed interest and buying from other traders.

Holstein's short account, by the way, was almost an endless source of cash. Since Holstein, the company, and other insiders owned millions of shares, this short account could theoretically sell or buy millions of shares on credit. If the Beane shares increased in price as Holstein sold the shares for his short account, he could transfer an appropriate number of additional shares to this short account as collateral to cover the short sale and keep the brokerage firm happy. Holstein would then of course have to wait until the share price fell dramatically before settling this account to turn a profit.

Holstein's short account was a potential gold mine for him over the length of the promotion because he would be selling in a rising market and buying in a falling market. The short account complemented the market maintenance account. The profits, of course, in the long term made Holstein and his partnership extremely rich.

iii. The Personal Account

Holstein opened his personal account with a rookie broker to show off. The rookie stockbroker always likes to brag about having important clients. Holstein would only buy B.H. Beane International stock in this account. Everyone, thanks to the loose-lipped rookie broker, eventually heard about Holstein's complete confidence in B.H. Beane International.

Holstein may have opened several "personal accounts".

"The whole thing made me sick. The young stupid brokers would run around telling everyone about Holstein's integrity and faith in the stock," said Van Guilder.

iv. The Offshore Account

Holstein also opened an account with an offshore branch of a large domestic brokerage firm. The offshore offices of this domestic brokerage firm were in a country which does not get foreign aid or other considerations from either Canada or the United States. This is important. Nothing can be confidential in a country which depends on foreign aid or economic support from a larger country. The offshore brokerage account should not, however, be confused with an offshore bank account. These are two different although often complementary things.

The offshore account provided four services:

■ Allowed Holstein to develop The Backstop which we will explain shortly.

■ Allowed Holstein to develop The Ditch which we will explain shortly.

■ Transferred shares to the short account, discussed earlier, when necessary.

■ Helped avoid capital gains.

This offshore brokerage account was held in the name of a "dummy" company wholly-owned by Holstein and described as an international marketing company. This supposed international marketing company had an arrangement with B.H. Beane International to develop and market its products world-wide, to offer technical assistance, and to find investors. The supposed international marketing company offered these services in exchange for "only" 300,000 shares. This agreement, by the way, was promoted as a major breakthrough for B.H. Beane International. Everyone assumed that this "dummy" company was managed by serious businessmen instead of Holstein's offshore flunkies.

"The press, repeating what Holstein said, told everyone that the agreement with the offshore company was a major coup. I think the press and investors must have had a lobotomy just before Holstein completed this deal," said Van Guilder.

This offshore company was completely controlled and owned by Holstein who had given himself 300,000 free Beane stocks which may have been subject to trade restrictions for a short period. This offshore account, however, actually helped the investors' cause during the three year promotion. Holstein used the offshore account to establish The Backstop and The Ditch to hook investors.

Holstein's offshore marketing company opened an account with the offshore branch of an unnamed domestic brokerage firm. This offshore branch of the domestic brokerage firm then opened several accounts in its name at other domestic brokerage firms to trade shares for Holstein. This made it impossible for anyone to figure out who was buying or selling and easy to set up The Backstop or The Ditch.

"The professionals call these accounts 'jitney accounts'. The word jitney actually refers to a small bus which carries passengers on a regular route for a small fare. I guess that describes what happens when one brokerage firm asks a second brokerage firm to buy and sell stocks for it," said Van Guilder.

"Holstein liked to use a pay phone whenever he phoned his offshore broker. He didn't want to leave any clues for securities regulators. The guy thought of everything," said Van Guilder.

You should have seen Jack. His mouth was hanging open.

"I can't believe this. This is slick," he said. I knew what Jack was thinking. I frowned at him. There was no way Jack and I were going to do something like this.

"Forget it," I said.

v. The Backstop

"Holstein set up many Backstops to create the illusion of demand. Here's how he did it," said Van Guilder.

Let's assume there are no bids or offers for the stock; that Holstein is the only person selling or buying; that Tom is the local broker who manages Holstein's maintenance account; and that Gonzalez is a broker on some tropical island who manages Holstein's offshore account.

Holstein did not deposit money with Gonzalez. Holstein deposited the 300,000 shares he received for his offshore marketing company and another few hundred thousand shares of his own. These shares were all trading at about 15 cents. Holstein showed good faith in Gonzalez' eyes. The offshore account was worth $45,000 to $100,000. As the share price increased Holstein sold shares to collect profits. Gonzalez gave Holstein a credit line to buy low priced shares. The whole thing was a money machine as long as Holstein kept the promotion going—which he did.

As the independent buying wave weakened, Holstein also sold B.H. Beane International stock for his short account. Holstein

198 ——————————————————— RAMPAGING BULLS

knew that once an independent buying wave dried up, the stock price would decline.

Holstein made money in his market maintenance account and offshore accounts by selling shares as the share price increased; by selling and shorting at the crest of a buying wave; and by buying back shares for his short and maintenance account when the share prices dropped. Jack and I were somewhat confused.

"You guys need an example," Van Guilder said.

Suppose Holstein tells Gonzalez to bid 10,000 shares at 20 cents through the domestic offices of his offshore brokerage office. Holstein tells Tom, who manages his maintenance account, to offer Beane stock at 30 cents. No trade takes place.

Holstein tells Gonzalez to bid another 10,000 shares at 30 cents for his offshore account through the domestic offices of a second brokerage firm. Holstein tells Tom to sell 3,000 shares at 30 cents from his maintenance account and to offer 5,000 shares at 35 cents.

Holstein tells Gonzalez to bid 10,000 shares at 35 cents through the domestic offices of a third brokerage firm. Holstein tells Tom, who manages his maintenance account, to sell 5,000 shares at 35 cents and to offer 5,000 shares at 40 cents.

Holstein tells Gonzalez, who manages his offshore account, to bid 10,000 shares at 40 cents through the domestic offices of a fourth brokerage firm. Holstein tells Tom, who manages his maintenance account, to sell 5,000 shares at 40 cents and to offer 5,000 shares at 45 cents.

This scenario could go on indefinitely as The Rampaging Bull bids up his stock through various brokerage accounts to whatever price he wants *by selling the shares to himself.* The Rampaging Bull, however, doesn't want to do all the buying. The Rampaging Bull will do this stunt after an extended series of public pronouncements similar to when he first met Jack at the Victims Of World Hatred And Sexual Harassment dinner.

"Try to visualize how the greedy average investor will react to all this. Will the average investor get excited when the stock price moves from 20 cents to 50 cents on buying from five brokerage accounts all secretly managed by The Rampaging Bull's offshore broker?" Van Guilder asked

"Heck yes!" Jack said.

"Nobody knows that all five buyers are the same person. The typical investor only knows that something is happening, that this is the chance of a lifetime, and that the stock might go to the moon," said Van Guilder.

The Backstop, added Van Guilder, must be established at every stage of the promotion when buying looks like it might dry up. The Backstop must progressively become more sophisticated and powerful as the share price increases. The Backstop encourages investors to believe that demand for stock is widespread and that investors won't get stuck with worthless stock.

The Backstop must also be complemented by news releases that show strength and support from consumers, investors, government, the press, and so on. The propaganda, however, must have some semblance of truth.

Holstein, at this early stage of the promotion, had fun. He developed an extensive network of farmers, politicians, and V.I.P.'s to say positive things about the biogas digester. This network came through for him beautifully. Who could resist the lure of joining the biogas revolution with so many experts.

The propaganda frenzy, unseen manipulation, and steady growth in the share price created several independent buying waves throughout the three year promotion. The short, maintenance, and offshore accounts all earned enough money to continue the promotion over a long period that finally attracted the rich and powerful to take a chance.

If you think carefully about all this you'll see it is analogous to what most governments did during the past 50 years as part of their "Keynesian Economics" strategy. Governments, following the ideas of John Maynard Keynes, tried to create the illusion of demand by spending borrowed money. You and I were supposed to be impressed, spend our money, and keep the economy growing! This idea worked sometimes and failed other times. The reason this strategy failed so often is simple. Many government leaders were, to put it simply, poor promoters who failed to "cash in" or set aside enough money during the boom to pay the bills in the next recession. Government only created more and more burdensome debt which everyone in the world will be paying off for the next 100 years. Is this hard to believe?

Keynes, as a speculator and not an economist, increased the King's College, Cambridge endowment fund tenfold. Keynes correctly predicted time after time which stocks would attract frenzied herd-like speculators. Couldn't Keynes' economic ideas for curing depression, which dominated almost every post-World War II government, have been nothing more than rearranged ideas from his experience as a speculator. Keynes was encouraging government to manipulate the economy like promoters manipulate the stock market. This may explain why many political leaders have learned to manipulate rather than lead by example.

vi. The Ditch

Holstein could set up The Ditch as easily as The Backstop. The Ditch, the flipside of the Backstop, encourages investors to panic. Here's how it works:

Let's assume Beane shares peak at $8.25; that Holstein has sold much of his holdings to excited investors eager to own a piece of the action; that Holstein has made substantial profits; and that Holstein now wants to regain control of the share float.

Let's also assume that independent buying starts to dry up; that there are not many buyers for the stock offered at $8.25; and that Holstein is the only one buying and selling. And finally, let's assume Holstein has had extended negotiations with a large pension fund which wants to get in on the action at $6 or less.

Holstein tells Gonzalez, who manages his offshore account, to bid 5,000 shares of B.H. Beane International at $7.50. Holstein tells Tom, who manages his maintenance account, to offer 100,000 shares at $7.75. This makes everyone nervous. The only thing anyone sees is a demand for 5,000 shares and an offer of 100,000 shares. A few investors will get very nervous and offer a few of their own shares for sale, just to be safe, at $7.75 instead of $8.25.

Holstein tells Tom, who manages his maintenance account, to offer 50,000 shares at $7.50. Holstein tells Gonzalez, who manages his offshore account, to buy 5,000 shares of B.H. Beane International at $7.50 and bid 5,000 shares at $7—a drop of 50 cents.

Holstein tells Tom, who manages his maintenance account, to offer 50,000 shares at $7. Holstein tells Gonzalez, who manages his offshore account, to buy 5,000 shares at $7 and bid 5,000 shares at $6.50—another decline of 50 cents.

Once this happens you can expect a state of panic to sweep over many investors who expected their $8 stock to increase. Panic stricken investors, eager to lock in profits or limit losses, might ditch their shares at $6, $5.75, $5.50, $4.50 and so on to create a downward spiral. This allows Holstein and his pension fund client to buy lower priced shares for as long as they want.

The Rampaging Bull might also arrange to cross some shares to the pension fund through his own broker. A "cross" is just the sale of a pre-arranged amount of shares at a pre-arranged price by a broker from one client to another client. If a cross is taking place when the share price has declined this may be good or bad news.

Good news: The Rampaging Bull is cash rich again and will promote the stock and develop the company.

Bad news: The Rampaging Bull is cashing out just before he lets the share price drop. Who knows what the promoter will do? That is why there are selling sprees.

Once the stock gets as low as The Rampaging Bull wants, the Rampaging Bull starts buying stock from the panic stricken while telling them that the price of the stock will go back up. The Ditch allows The Rampaging Bull to buy back stock for less than he originally sold the stock. The Rampaging Bull will only create The Ditch when he needs to sell shares at an attractive price to rich and influential investors. They are necessary to make the final leg of the promotion a success.

vii. What Holstein May Have Done

Holstein arranged at least four Ditches and Crosses.

The first cross was arranged at around $3 per share after Holstein knocked the share price back from $5. About 40 mid-level investors, convinced that Holstein had clout, bought the $3 shares. These 40 investors bought the entire box account or maintenance account of 200,000 free trading shares at $3 per share. This gave gave B.H. Beane International another $600,000 to manipulate the share price and develop the company. This money, as you might guess, gave Holstein considerable financial clout and ability to manoeuvre the stock to $8 through a well orchestrated series of Backstops and Ditches.

The second major financing was completed at $5 after Holstein's Ditch brought the price down from $8 to $5. Holstein arranged a private placement with a New Jersey pension fund which included one million escrowed shares at $5 per share and 300,000 free trading shares at $5 per share from the company's and/or Holstein's accounts. Holstein and B.H. Beane also granted 100,000 share options at $3 per share to the top pension fund managers and gave 20,000 shares under the table as a "gift" to the pension fund managers. This scenario guaranteed B.H. Beane International the following positive results:

■ Everyone in North America heard that a pension fund believed and invested in B.H. Beane International.

■ The company raised an additional $6.5 million dollars to complement the $600,000 from the sale of shares in the box or maintenance account.

■ The share float was now 6.4 million shares not counting Holstein's 10 million escrowed shares. Of the 6.4 million shares one million were escrowed shares owned by a pension fund at $5 per share; 200,000 were free trading shares owned by 40 mid-level investors waiting for their $3 shares to move to $10 and beyond; 300,000 were free trading shares owned by a pension fund which would probably not sell these shares for a long time as "investors"; 2.5 million were free trading shares owned by Holstein, the company, and a few insiders; 300,000 were free trading shares owned by an offshore marketing company as far as anyone knew; and 1.5 million were owned by other investors who had bought at an average price of about $2.50.

■ B.H. Beane International had also raised about $900,000 dollars from a half dozen Asian immigrants. They had come to Canada as part of the special immigration program requiring each of them to invest $150,000 in a viable Canadian business. This increased the share float by another 600,000 shares to seven million shares.

■ B.H. Beane International now had financial clout with more than $7.7 million in the bank. This financial clout, used in conjunction with all the manoeuvres we have discussed, gave Holstein's prediction for a $20 share credibility.

Why wouldn't investors believe him? If Holstein was prepared to invest the money he had raised into manipulating the share price then there was no reason why the share price couldn't increase beyond $20.

viii. Corrections And Shakedowns

When the share price declines dramatically as shares are crossed to rich investors or to The Rampaging Bull, this is described as being a "correction", as in "the market is correcting".

This is supposed to mean that the free market is working at random to find a realistic price for the stock. The truth, of course, is that there is no such thing as a correction, in the classic sense of the word, for a penny stock and for some senior stocks. The promoter is either trying to buy back inexpensive shares to keep the promotion going or the promoter is collecting his profits before taking a vacation.

The more appropriate term for this whole process is "shakeout" as in, "it's time to shake out all the puppies." In a promotion operated by a less powerful promoter the shake-out or correction may actually mean that the promotion is over. The insiders may actually be selling off their shares to collect as much profit as they can. That's why it is vital that you know the intentions and abilities of the promoter.

ix. Short Selling In Tandem With Promoter

We've already said a smart short seller should not sell shares for his short account during the early stages of a big promotion.

But there is one trick that Master Traders can try if they buy in early and heavily. Let's assume a Master Trader buys as many as 20,000 to 100,000 shares of B.H. Beane International stock during the early stages of the promotion between 35 cents and $1.50 per share because he knows Holstein means business.

Here's what The Master Trader can do:

Let's assume that the trader opens a Long Account "A" in his wife's name and deposits 50,000 shares purchased at an average price of 75 cents. Let's assume that the trader also opens a Short Account B at another brokerage firm in his mother's birth name.

As the share price increases, The Master Trader is aware that The Rampaging Bull can hold the share price and perhaps increase it even higher. This Master Trader, as you might guess, wants to encourage other investors and The Rampaging Bull to promote the price of the stock higher, sooner. So what does he do? The Master Trader short sells some shares. Let's assume The Master Trader "waves a red flag" in front of The Rampaging Bull like any good matador by short selling 2,000 shares per day for three weeks from $5 per share and higher. Even this nominal amount of short selling can get true believers very upset—especially if it happens early in a promotion. The Master Trader expects this anger to work in his favour. As you know, traders short sell when they no longer have faith in a promoter's ability to hold the price of the stock. The traders believe that they can buy the shares back at lower prices, return the shares they borrowed from the brokerage firm, and pocket the difference.

Holstein, as only a true promoter can, encourages his investors to fight back and bid up prices. This forces short sellers to buy stock at prices higher than they sold. The idea of course is to discourage the short sellers from creating a panic which can lead to a downward spiral in the share price. The frenzied buying activity naturally helps push the stock to new heights. So who wins? The Master Trader.

The Master Trader will sell as many as 30,000 shares from his Long Account "A" for an excellent profit to an eager buying public bidding up share prices. The Master Trader will also keep at least 20,000 shares in his Long Account "A" to cover his Short Account "B" for as long as it takes the share price to drop below the price he sold short the stock. The Master Trader knows the share price will eventually experience a "correction". He will buy back shares at prices lower than he sold them to make a profit.

For this manoeuvre to take place successfully there must be a Rampaging Bull involved in the action, not a lower level promoter. The promoter must have the ability to marshal his buyers to take the share price higher. Investors must also believe a foolish beginner is daring to short stock in the early stages of the game.

x. Limiting Stock Sales

Holstein went to great effort to discourage his friends and supporters from selling their shares.

"You should have seen him spread it on thick with everybody. He tried to tie up their shares. In fact, he spent half his time trying to convince investors to order up stock and put it in a safety deposit box," said Van Guilder.

Holstein convinced his investors not to sell their shares five ways:

■ **Threats**—You might think that threats won't work. Well, threats do work. Holstein kept track of every transaction because he had brokers in most brokerage firms keeping tabs on what was happening. Holstein would remind his big investors, when he found out they were selling shares, that they would lose any future considerations in his promotions.

■ **Escrow**—Holstein escrowed stocks or delayed delivery of shares as long as possible.

■ **Ordering Up**—Holstein convinced his friends to keep their stocks in their safety deposit boxes. This made it difficult for his friends to sell their stocks and difficult for short sellers to borrow stock from brokerage firms.

■ **Retirement Savings Plans**—Holstein encouraged many of his investors to buy shares in their retirement savings plans which are protected against capital gains taxation. These shares, by law, are not allowed to be lent to short sellers.

■ **Bribes**—Holstein bribed friends and associates with options and cash to invest and not sell.

■ B. The Sting

The Rampaging Bull knows when the promotion is over.

The game is over when he runs out of investors, especially big pension funds, to buy his stock. The well prepared Rampaging Bull must always be long gone and fully prepared to blame others when the share price eventually declines and collapses.

"I'll know when it's time for a vacation," Holstein liked to say. He recognized his promotion was coming to an end when farmers starting complaining about the biogas digester's performance in cold weather.

Holstein, because he is a sophisticated con man, did not just walk away from the promotion. Holstein developed plausible excuses to explain why the biogas digester wasn't working. The excuses were accepted by investors, the public, the press, the farm community, and the government because they wanted to believe. Holstein also offered a plausible solution to the problem.

This, of course, gave Holstein time to plan his next step.

Holstein could have acquired a new product for a new promotion; could have sold the rights of the biogas digester to a larger corporation; or could have sold his interests in the company to a more dedicated team. Holstein chose to hire more researchers to fix technical problems and appoint a new chief operating officer to take the blame when things went wrong.

"We were somewhat naive," Holstein liked to say.

"Not to worry. We'll work out all the technical problems. But I must tell you that all those cynical short sellers have really hurt us. They are fat pigs and sleazy bastards," he added.

The Rampaging Bull Understands "The Sting"

"What do you mean 'where am I?' I'm doing my laundry," The Rampaging Bull said to a friend back home.

RAMPAGING BULLS: Outfox Promoters At Their Game On Any Penny Stock Market

The share price declined steadily after that because everyone recognized the promotion was over. Careful Traders, Professional Traders, Diligent Traders, and Master Traders who understood his strategy made money. Most investors, especially Naive Beginners, lost some money because they misunderstood The Ditch and The Backstop. Yet Holstein retained enough of a public image that he didn't have to leave town in disgrace. In fact, Holstein was considered a hero and treated as such by many people. Nobody really hated Holstein except some people who had come into the promotion late. Almost everybody had ample opportunity to sell their positions over an extended period.

"Hey, it isn't my fault if people are too greedy to sell in time," Holstein said.

Holstein, with more free time, hung out with old associates and friends in the local pub. Stockbrokers continually pleaded with him to start another promotion. Holstein laughed, bought drinks for everyone, told tall tales, and made jokes about gullible people in the company of his best friends and associates. He promised everyone he would take care of them next time.

Everything was back to normal especially when Holstein went on vacation to some Caribbean island. Bungee said that Holstein still managed to stay in regular touch with his people but never told them on what island he was vacationing.

"He was always talking about the weather being so hot and sticky he had to send out laundry four times a week," said Bungee.

"I think he was in the Twilight Zone," said Van Guilder.

The Criminal Incompetent

16

. . . Guernsey Tries His Hand

Jack and I decided to try our luck with other promoters.

I laugh about this now. Jack and I thought we could diversify our risk by finding another hot promotion. The joke, of course, was on us. The two of us had yet to learn that *we didn't know what we didn't know.*

Jack and I asked Bungee, Milan, and Oswaldo to "find us a hot promotion with a hot promoter". They laughed at us.

"A great promotion doesn't drop out of the sky every day," Oswaldo said. Milan suggested we talk to Bill Guernsey. He had managed at least one excellent promotion which peaked at $3 per share.

"What do you know about this guy?" Jack, the professional stock trader, asked.

"Enough to make some money; not enough to make a fortune," Milan said.

Guernsey was promoting Black Box Enterprises which had worked out a deal with a group of disgruntled former employees of Sony, Hitachi, Mitsubishi, RCA, Xerox, and Canon. They wanted to develop a high technology company with a manufacturing plant in Sonora, Mexico; research offices in Buffalo, New York; and a head office in the Grand Cayman Islands.

The concept was at best semi-legit. Some investors liked the deal. Jack and I decided to listen to this incredible story because the stock had increased from 20 cents to 50 cents. The rumours on the street predicted a $3 per share within two months. Jack and I both agreed that the whole scenario could be as hot as Holstein's promotion.

Milan, being the eager broker that he was, arranged a meeting for us with the head promoter, manager, and president Bill Guernsey. We expected to see a "Rampaging Bull" — a man with expensive suits, neatly trimmed hair, a firm handshake, and an easy charm.

Guernsey, to our surprise, was wearing a plaid suit popular with car salesmen and was smoking, judging from the smell, a French cigarette. The offices, unlike Holstein's spotless environment, featured an arborite coffee table, ashtrays which needed cleaning, and the latest issue of *Sports Illustrated* and *Casino News*. The art on the walls included shrink wrapped posters of James Dean, Sylvester Stallone, and Arnold Schwarzenegger. The posters were all supposedly signed by the stars themselves.

"Maria loved the gift. Thanks," signed, Arnold S.

"Let's do it again," signed, Sly.

"Your bike is tops," signed, James.

You didn't have to be a rocket scientist to know that James Dean could never have signed the poster since the copyright on the poster was dated 1975. We all know that James Dean died at 5:59 p.m. on Sept. 30, 1955 near Cholane, California while driving a Porsche. Trivia is important.

"Hey, fellas. Come on in," Guernsey said. "Milan said you were going to come by. I understand you are excited about our stock," laughed Guernsey. Jack and I looked at each other.

We said we were interested, not excited. Guernsey told us he understood our reservations while he poured us a coffee.

"I'll be honest with you. I'm serious about that. I wouldn't even be talking to you guys if Milan hadn't said you were straight shooters. We are in the middle of very delicate negotiations," Guernsey said.

"We are negotiating with a group of scientists that have developed revolutionary improvements for the standard fax, VCR, and TV. It's hard to believe. These experts, who went to school together, work all over the world for several major organizations whose names I don't want to mention. You can guess what happened. They got disillusioned. Everything they developed was owned by the companies they worked for. They eventually couldn't take it anymore. They wanted a piece of the action. They are now prepared to build a manufacturing plant in Sonora, Mexico. Free trade between Canada, the U.S., and Mexico will help these guys sell a lot of units. In fact, they already have an option on a vacant plant. We hope to develop nothing less than several new fax, VCR, and TV products. They will sell for half the price of any other brand name. This is big.

"Our sales network of existing appliance dealers will be part owners of the entire operation. We will have the strongest warranty in the business. Imagine if you could buy a TV, fax, or VCR with a four year *unlimited* warranty at *half the retail price* of any other brand name. Consumers will love it," Guernsey said.

I would like to describe every nuance of this deal to you. But let's face it. It isn't necessary. If you want more details stay in touch. Here are the highlights we uncovered during that period.

■ Smoke and Mirror Products Inc., an offshore company registered in the Grand Cayman Islands, owned the world distribution rights and manufacturing rights to the product line.

■ The Canadian public company, Black Box Enterprises, was negotiating to buy Canadian distribution rights for "only" $500,000 and a 20% royalty fee payable to Smoke and Mirror Products Inc.

■ Black Box Enterprises was raising $800,000 from established distributors who wanted the Canadian marketing and sales rights.

"We have everyone just about signed up," said Guernsey.

■ Each distributor would receive six things in return for a $25,000 investment in Black Box Enterprises: a few shares in the offshore production company, Smoke and Mirror Products Inc.; shares in the Canadian public company, Black Box Enterprises which owns the Canadian distribution rights; a chance to retail very competitive high technology products at low prices; a chance to earn capital gains if Black Box shares goes up; a chance for tax free earnings since revenues due the offshore company stay offshore and are tax free; and a chance to make money when the offshore company sells distribution rights to dealers in other countries.

■ The offshore company was supposed to make it hard for large appliance manufacturers to sue for patent infringements—if any.

■ Black Box Enterprises had 2.5 million shares outstanding. One million shares were in escrow and owned by insiders like Guernsey. About 1.5 million were free trading shares, of which Guernsey and his team owned 60%.

■ Guernsey rounded up the appropriate number of distributors to invest $800,000 in Black Box Enterprises at 20 cents per share. The share float increased by another four million shares. The distributors, Guernsey explained, would probably hold their shares as "true believers". They expected the stock to make them fabulously wealthy over the next few years.

■ The offshore company, Smoke and Mirror Products Inc., would support the Black Box Enterprises share price with the $500,000 paid by Canadian distributors. Guernsey was excited. We were amazed.

"Think about the impact we'll have on the share price if Smoke and Mirrors commits at least $150,000 to the Black Box stock promotion. A solid Black Box share price, which we will achieve, can help us raise even more money to develop the manufacturing plant. The more money Black Box Enterprises can raise, the more we can develop the plant in Mexico," Guernsey said.

"The balance of the money raised from distributors, the other $350,000, will pay for the initial manufacturing capacity in Mexico. The Mexican government is eager to offer special concessions to get the plant functioning," Guernsey said.

"I hope this deal is easy to understand," Guernsey said.

"The way I understand it, the investor gets a piece of everything," I said. Guernsey laughed. "We are not greedy," he said.

Then Guernsey said something we had heard before. He told us that the stock was trading at 50 cents, would increase to 60 cents by the end of the week, would increase to 75 cents in three weeks, and would increase to $1.50 within two months. We would, according to our careful calculations, double our money within two months if we paid 75 cents or less for our stock.

"We fully expect the share price to reach $3.50 by the end of the year," Guernsey said. "Geez," I said. I noticed Jack was already day dreaming about another fortune. Something very strange happens when you find a hot stock. Your brain, which normally has problems handling basic arithmetic, can suddenly handle complex calculus.

Guernsey noticed that Jack and I were interested in his James Dean poster on the way out.

"Somebody pulled a prank and signed the James Dean poster," Guernsey said politely. Jack and I smiled. Guernsey noticed everything. The truth is that Jack and I were still inexperienced. We should have known better than to invest in a company being promoted by a man who displays a fake James Dean signature poster in his waiting room. Live and learn.

Jack and I delayed buying shares until we reviewed the stock's trading charts. The share price climbed to 75 cents from 30 cents just as Guernsey had predicted. Jack and I then each bought 25,000 shares of Black Box Enterprises between 80 cents and $1—a price that was high for a typical penny stock.

The releases were works of art. The local newspaper even printed some of them. One of the releases said Guernsey and his associates, Lou Dickerson, Bill Miata, and Dave Cougare, were on their way to a major convention of appliance dealers in New Orleans; that 30 major retailers had already invested; that the company was working closely with the Science Council; that the Mexican government was offering red carpet treatment; that the products were ahead of their time; and that Sony, Hitachi, and RCA had sent industrial spies to snoop around.

The industrial espionage angle was thought provoking.

Wouldn't you react positively if you thought that a major corporation was jealous? Nobody, of course, ever saw representatives of these major corporations snooping because nobody at these corporations had ever heard of Black Box Enterprises as we discovered later.

Jack and I paid another visit to Guernsey's offices because Guernsey had invited us to see the newly-arrived VCR.

"It's a beauty," Guernsey said.

Jack and I were happy. This was exciting. We were going to see "the product" immediately. The most exasperating aspect of the B.H. Beane International promotion was the constant delay in getting a product demonstration. Guernsey took us into the back room to see the VCR. The name plate on the case said *Black Box —the future belongs to us*.

"This Black Box is a beauty. It can do everything. It's a miracle," said Guernsey. "Let me put in a video cassette. See. The TV picture is beautiful," said Guernsey as Sylvester Stallone's movie Rambo started playing. I had to admit that the VCR worked, that the brand name on the case did say *Black Box*, and that it was a beautiful looking product.

"How do we know that this is a new improved product instead of black casing on someone else's patented electronic equipment," I asked. Guernsey laughed.

"You don't," he said. Guernsey also said, during the conversation, that the "proof will be in the pudding"; "that everyone is a Doubting Thomas"; "that Benedict Arnold had many relatives"; and that "we might consider buying another stock if we didn't believe him."

Then Guernsey suddenly went into another office and brought out someone named Jake Q. Dunbar. Dunbar had apparently spent 10 years with a major high technology appliance company, which I won't mention because he is suing them. Dunbar developed revolutionary products for this unnamed conglomerate until he got disillusioned because he was never offered a piece of the

The Criminal Incompetent Tries His Luck

**"Jack! This 'Black Box' can do everything. It's a miracle,"
said Guernsey, The Criminal Incompetent, to Jack.**

RAMPAGING BULLS: Outfox Promoters At Their Game On Any Penny Stock Market

action. Dunbar showed us memorabilia from his life at the un-named major corporation. Jack and I were impressed. We decided that Dunbar was the real thing.

Less than two days after our meeting at Black Box Enterprises the stock started to climb from $1 to $1.25. Buying was steady. Bungee, Oswaldo, and Milan all thought that the promotion might be a strong one, although they didn't think it would be as strong as Holstein's effort. Bungee said he was certain Guernsey was using the money he had raised from distributors to prop up the stock price.

Bungee had some compelling evidence because the trading in Black Box was "thin" and peculiar. There might be a bid for 10,000 Black Box shares at 60 cents and an offer to sell 10,000 shares at 65 cents. The bid to buy 10,000 shares might move up to 65 cents while the offer to sell 10,000 shares might move to 70 cents. The price of the stock seemed to increase five cents on every trade.

"Guernsey is doing all the selling and buying," said Bungee.

Milan phoned to tell us that Guernsey had made a deal with five stockbrokers to help him promote the stock. The deal, appar-ently offered to Milan until he declined, included an option to buy 20,000 shares at $1; 10,000 shares at $1.75; 10,000 shares at $2; and 30,000 shares at $3. Each broker, as you might guess, con-vinced clients to buy shares priced between $1 and $3.

"I might have accepted Guernsey's offer if it wasn't illegal," said Milan.

"If Guernsey convinces the brokers to promote, a $3 share price is very possible," said Milan.

"Milan, do you think Guernsey will offer this deal to Bungee or Oswaldo?" I asked. Milan laughed and said that Oswaldo would never even talk to Guernsey.

"Bungee can be a weasel. You better ask him," said Milan.

I phoned Bungee's office and left a cryptic message. My message read: "Do not accept offer of fame and fortune from bull. Stop. You are being tested." You should have heard Bungee yell at me when he phoned back. When the dust settled, however, Bungee admitted that Guernsey had made a tempting approach. Suffice it to say that Bungee declined Guernsey's offer—or so he said.

A few professional traders also made it known that they doubted Guernsey's ability to promote or develop the deal. None of the professional traders shorted the stock between $1.25 and $1.75. The professional discounters wanted to evaluate Guernsey's style. If Guernsey looked weak promoting the stock to $2, the short sellers knew he would have an impossible time promoting the stock to $3. This would encourage the short sellers to move in.

The share price did in fact stumble along from $1.25 to $2. This was considered an achievement since few penny stocks trade that high. The professional discounters didn't care about Guernsey's achievement. The professionals shorted the stock because they didn't think Guernsey could keep up his promotional effort or develop the company.

Guernsey then urged all his people to buy as many shares as possible to catch the short sellers in a squeeze. The idea, as you remember, is to promote the share price higher than the share price at which short sellers sold. Guernsey encouraged his supporters to keep buying until the end of the month when many short sellers would be required to settle their uncovered short positions. That's exactly what Guernsey managed to do.

The share price moved from $2 to $2.50 by the end of the month. A few short sellers took a loss at the higher prices because they had to settle their accounts. The small buying spree by short sellers pushed the share price to $2.75.

Jack and I were happy. In fact, we were about to sell some shares to pocket a small profit. Guernsey had actually beaten back the short sellers in a show of strength. This convinced many people that Guernsey could be another Bob Holstein. Many investors decided to jump on board. In fact, there was a small buying spree by several traders who thought Guernsey had the right stuff to be a Rampaging Bull. Then something strange happened.

Even though there was a buying spree, the share price did not increase. The share price dropped a few cents. Milan phoned.

"I think Guernsey is unloading stock on all the new buyers," said Milan.

"Nuts," I said.

Milan thought Guernsey was a big fake. Guernsey had over-estimated his market support and was offering too many shares for sale. The press asked Guernsey why there was so much action in the market. "Black Box Enterprises is as solid as a rock," Guernsey said.

The professional traders quickly re-evaluated their position on Guernsey. The professional traders started to unload and short more stock. The traders recognized that larger and larger trading volumes without a corresponding increase in price was a sign that Guernsey or some other insider was unloading stock.

The share price dropped to $1.75. The share price started dropping so quickly that it was almost eerie. Oswaldo described the share price drop as an excellent example of "gravity" in action on the stock market.

"If there is nothing to hold up the price, the law of gravity must assert itself," Oswaldo the physicist said. Guernsey told the press: "The whole market is down. We are experiencing a correction."

"I don't know what investors want. We are building the Mexican plant; production will begin shortly; and the products are excellent," Guernsey said.

The share price continued its freefall. Jack and I managed to each sell 10,000 shares at 75 cents before the stock exchange halted trading in the stock "to protect investors and clarify the situation".

The stock exchange, the securities commission, and the police investigated the promotion and charged Guernsey with fraud. Guernsey had disappeared by then.

Jack and I had each lost about $28,000 in this promotion. We still held on to the pathetic hope that Black Box Enterprises might recover. We weren't holding our breath about this.

"Double Nuts," said Jack.

"Damn," said Bungee.

"I knew it," said Milan.

"What a bunch of bubbleheads," said Oswaldo.

Jack and I realized that Guernsey just wasn't secure enough in his abilities to develop the Black Box Enterprises promotion like Holstein had been with B.H. Beane International.

"It's obvious that Guernsey didn't believe in the products. He probably didn't even believe the products worked. In fact, when the truth comes out we'll probably discover that the short sellers spooked Guernsey into taking the money and running," said Jack.

"Guernsey is an incompetent in business; but an excellent criminal. Black Box Enterprises was just another 'bubble stock'—a quick share price increase and a quick share price decrease," Jack told me over a garlic pizza in his bar.

■ EPILOGUE ON GUERNSEY

The truth came out slowly over the next few months during gossip sessions at the 12 St. Bar and Grill. Here's the scoop:

■ There really were several disgruntled former employees from major high technology companies who had visions of producing their products. Unfortunately, Guernsey didn't think they really could manufacture anything although he never told them what he really thought. These unfortunate scientists and technicians are still trying to raise money to develop their products even though everyone has lost faith in their judgement.

■ Guernsey could have used the hundreds of thousands of dollars in the offshore account, raised from distributors, to prop up and promote the share price of Black Box Enterprises to well over $5. However, Guernsey didn't think he could convince pension funds, mutual funds, drug lords, and others to provide the required financing to help promote the stock to $20.

■ Guernsey knew that to develop viable manufacturing, distribution, and marketing for a new high technology company required at least two to three years. This required more money than was available in the offshore account or was possible to raise locally from brokers. Guernsey recognized that he was not enough of a salesman to convince offshore and foreign investors to put up money for a *new* electronics firm without the support of at least *one major* electronics firm.

■ Guernsey's insecurity about being able to develop the company encouraged him to stop thinking about the long term. He focused on the short term which included unloading shares from the offshore account on unsuspecting and excited investors.

■ Guernsey propped up the share price for a short period, but resented spending the money from his offshore account on a share promotion he just didn't believe in.

■ "Guernsey didn't know how to create a team of diligent, hard working people because he was too preoccupied with his personal needs and trivialities. Guernsey was not as bright, cunning, and dedicated as a Rampaging Bull should be. Guernsey is the typical con man running from himself because he is weak and incompetent," Oswaldo said.

■ Guernsey had also pulled a simple but effective con on several brokers just before he left town. Guernsey had deposited 30,000 Black Box shares with each of the five brokers who had accepted his deal to promote the stock. When the share price reached $2 to $2.50 these accounts were worth a lot of money. Guernsey then asked each broker to let him buy an additional 20,000 Black Box shares on credit. Only Guernsey knew that he would be buying shares from his own offshore accounts. *These secret offshore accounts were listed under various assumed names.* He promised the brokers that he would pay for the 20,000 extra shares in a "few days".

Guernsey paid for each of the five 20,000 share purchases with a cheque from an offshore bank. He knew the cheque would clear in about two weeks. The brokerage firm used the 30,000 shares in

Guernsey's long account as collateral. The cheque, as you might guess, never cleared and Guernsey disappeared with another $250,000 in hard cold cash courtesy of five trusting brokers. By the time brokerage firms tried to sell the shares they held as collateral, trading in the stock had been halted.

The truth, of course, is that Jack and I could have made a bundle on this deal if we hadn't been greedy and asleep at the wheel. We could have sold our shares at over $2 and made a tidy bundle. Instead, we got stuck with a load of worthless shares.

Bungee phoned.

"I really must thank you and Jack for helping me to recognize Guernsey for what he is. I could be under investigation like the brokers who agreed to help Guernsey promote Black Box Enterprises. You are starting to understand the stock market. Good work," said Bungee.

We didn't know if we should laugh or cry. Jack and I didn't have the heart to tell Bungee our whole ill fated story which cost us a bundle. We had bought the Black Box shares from Milan. But Bungee was right. Jack and I were getting a little smarter.

17 | Minor Achiever

. . . Honest Guys Can Win

Bungee kept thanking us for saving his career.

"I am going to find some ethical people in the stock market for you guys," said Bungee. I laughed.

"I think you'll have a hard time. Truly ethical people represent less than one percent of the population. They typically live in remote areas; are rarely busybodies interested in power; and are very self-reliant. This definition disqualifies almost everybody I know," I said overstating my case to make an impact.

"Are we being cranky today?" asked Bungee. I couldn't tell Bungee I was still upset about the Black Box affair.

"Excuse Meeeee," I said.

"Geez," Bungee said just before he hung up on me. Bungee phoned a half hour later.

"I want you to meet Dave 'Big City' Jersey of Minor Achievement Co. Ltd. and Wilt 'Whiplash' Charolais of Godot Inc. They're both honest guys," Bungee said. When I phoned Jack to announce our meetings with Jersey and Charolais, he laughed.

"Let's try to lose less than $20,000 this time. Guys with cattle breed names make me nervous," Jack said. Jack and I decided to drive out to the hotel owned by Minor Achievement to meet the main players and see the property. It was only a few hours away by car. We learned the importance of visiting the main office because of our experiences with Guernsey and Black Box Enterprises. Mind you, we probably would never have flown to Sonora, Mexico unless we were looking for a holiday.

Bungee, however, was right this time. The manager of Minor Achievement Inc. was honest. He was so honest it made me nervous. Minor Achievement had offices in an attractive three-star 75-room hotel, named the Bull & Bear, in the Canadian Rockies. Minor Achievement owned the hotel and 30 acres in a very picturesque British Columbia valley near the Trans-Canada Highway. The hotel was built to cater to wealthy and pretentious European tourists and business people. The place had an "Alpine-old-wood" feeling. The office decor included lithographs of British Pubs such as The Dorking Beacon, Pope's Head Alley, Ram Jam Inn, Romping Donkey, The Red Rooster, and The Rampaging Bull.

"I like the lithograph of The Rampaging Bull," I said. Jersey said it was one of his favourites. I begged Jersey to sell it to me. He told me he knew the artist and would order one for me. "Big City" Jersey was enthusiastic about his company's opportunities.

"This company is going places," he said as he poured us a coffee. Jersey showed us several recent newspaper clippings which praised the company and 'Big City' Jersey. The news stories said Jersey was innovative, gutsy, and competent.

I asked him for the most recent annual report, the quarterly report, and an explanation of some expenses in the reports. Minor Achievement was profitable, had made a $50,000 profit during the past quarter, and was about to announce an increase in profit from two cents per share a year earlier. Jersey was scouting for another hotel and the stock was trading at 30 cents.

"It's going to take a while to build up critical mass so you can earn large profits," I said. Jersey said that the hotel business was generally undergoing a transition from large expensive chain hotels to more intimate or affordable operations.

"Minor Achievement will buy, merge, or takeover at least a half dozen properties over the next 10 years to cater to this specialized market," said Jersey. "We are developing a terrific team of managers, trained at major hotel chains, who are looking to find their fortune."

"Who is your stock promoter," I asked. Jersey laughed.

"We don't actually have a promoter. We have a stock broker, Dave Bingham-Birmingham, who keeps an eye on the share price to make sure nothing unusual happens. We believe our product is strong enough to attract all the investors we will ever need," Jersey said confidently. Jack was nodding his head eloquently.

"What about dividends?" Jack asked.

"It's premature for dividends."

"I guess your share price will be stable since you have real earnings," said Jack. Jersey said that he would never allow the share price to be on a rollercoaster because it just wasn't the company's style.

I got depressed. Jersey didn't sound like he was willing to hire a hot promoter. Jersey said 600 shareholders owned 10 million shares; the shares were all free trading; the land and buildings were almost worth more than the current total share value of $4 million; and trading was moderate.

"Every major hotel chain wants to buy this operation. The share price will increase when the annual report cames out. Earnings will increase every year," said Jersey. Jack and I believed this.

Jersey took us to the hotel's pub, called The Bear's Pit. The pub, half full with upscale types of people, had genuine oak panels, a dart board, a waitress in a peasant dress, and neon signs promoting beer which nobody serves. Jersey ordered beer in large mugs for us. Then he left.

You've noticed, I'm sure, that Minor Achievement seems like a straightforward deal. This stock, unless we missed something, might achieve substantial increases in share prices over the next five years. For this to happen, the managers must develop more hotel properties, maintain a positive cash flow, and develop a powerful marketing program.

Jack and I bought 10,000 shares just for fun. There was a small chance the stock might go up when the annual report came out. We knew that Dave Bingham-Birmingham was a strong enough broker to encourage the price to move up at least another 30 cents—but no more.

We knew that Dave Bingham-Birmingham specialized in making money on Minor Achievement deals like this one. Bingham-Birmingham's strategy called for his best clients to buy shares at 15 to 25 cents; his less valuable clients to buy shares at 30 to 40 cents; and everybody else to buy until the share price topped off at 50 to 70 cents. Bingham-Birmingham's best clients would sell from 40 to 50 cents on the way up or on the way down. There was always a chance that the stock would become a darling of the industry. Share prices, unfortunately, almost always levelled off at around 35 cents to 55 cents. Bingham-Birmingham didn't have the street smarts to seduce the "Big Money" into any of his deals.

The whole promotion usually took six months to one year. The company would have revenues and good possibilities. Investors would not complain too loudly because they never lost much money.

"Big City" Jersey's company was real. Yet greedy traders or promoters would not buy these shares because there was very little immediate opportunity for serious capital gains. In fact, Jersey's somewhat false pride at not wanting a major promoter made me nervous. Jersey didn't understand that he needed a promoter. Without a strong promoter his company couldn't move the share price high enough to raise the necessary capital and expand. On the other hand, Jersey could have just been doing a good job of covering up his inability to recruit a promoter.

Minor Achievement Inc. was a candidate for a good mid-level promoter, but not a Rampaging Bull. The good mid-level promoter could have promoted the stock price higher and raised money through a private placement to buy another small hotel. This flurry of activity by a mid-level promoter would have pumped up the share price by another 75 cents to $1.50 thanks to investors excited about the company buying another hotel.

Bingham-Birmingham, who is an example of a broker in every community in the world, didn't really qualify as a dedicated promoter. He is more of broker who, while being supportive, doesn't love the company enough to dedicate time to get things done. We just hoped "Big City" Jersey would figure this out.

"Hotels are too real and too easy to evaluate. There is no sizzle even if the company has earnings and chance to do well in the future," Jack said. "There is no mystery, no fantasy, no miracle. There are only rooms with an upper limit on how much you can charge for them," he added.

There are many companies like Minor Achievement Inc. which may be producing and marketing energy, fad products, and labour saving devices. Most of these companies in their initial stage of development have enough money to produce a product at a profit in the local market. The Minor Achievers, however, just can't raise enough money to complete a major production run, a national marketing effort, or national distribution.

"The problem is obvious. Minor Achievers never have enough money to pay for everything—production, marketing, packaging, advertising, bribes to distributors, payoffs to brokers and promoters, and fees to regulatory agencies. Everybody seems to forget the cost of developing a market can be enormous and often more than the costs of production," Jack said.

"All traders are greedy and impatient. They want instant returns. The manager usually has to convince investors that financial returns will be enormous within months," I said.

"These Minor Achievers need big investors who can help build or buy several hotels. The company can then be promoted nationally. This company is not for us right now," I said.

Two weeks later, Minor Achievement reported profits of $300,000 or three cents per share, a 50% increase over the year before which is admirable in any business. Everybody knew the increase in occupancy from 50% to 70% boosted earnings. Future earnings increases would be smaller since the number of rooms are limited. The bank told everyone it would loan the company substantial amounts if private investors invested an equal amount. The local newspapers lavished praise in a story headlined "Minor

The Naive Beginner Becomes Diligent

"Sure, there's a business, assets, and earnings. There's some beef . . . but there's no sizzle," Jack The Diligent Trader said to me.

RAMPAGING BULLS: Outfox Promoters At Their Game On Any Penny Stock Market

Achievement To Expand". The share price moved to 70 cents on the strength of local buying.

Jack and I sold our 10,000 shares when the share price declined to 60 cents for a small profit before the share price levelled off at 55 cents. Jack and I knew the price was not going higher because there was no promoter. The bank's offer, we believed, would still be there one year from now. The press releases, while favourable, had a small town mentality. Jack and I considered ourselves lucky when we sold at a 30 cent per share profit.

Minor Achievement might do well over the next five years. Jack and I, however, want to do well in five months.

Bungee phoned. "Hey, we did O.K. with Minor Achievement," he said. I agreed. Jack and I each made about $3,000 on the deal.

"Jersey really is an honest guy," I said.

Bungee was pleased that we were pleased. We had evaluated the company correctly. I realized we weren't just looking for honest guys in the stock market. We were looking for someone who offered more than just honesty. We were looking for somebody who combined courage, benevolence, technique, and honesty. We were, in short, expecting a lot and would therefore have to work harder to find it.

Waiting For Godot

18

. . . Time To Get Real Job

Our next stop was Godot Inc.

Wilt "Whiplash" Charolais of Godot Inc. and his five associates were honest, hopeful, and depressed. The management team included engineer John Z. Marjoribanks, accountant Milton Polinsky, financial consultant Reginald Ransfulry, designer Tony A.A. Cowper, and technician Leone Sextus. All of them seemed to have a good background.

I think Bungee wanted us to meet these guys because we could never again accuse him of only introducing us to dishonest people. We had a problem finding the management team because they were out of their office a lot. When I finally reached Charolais on the phone, he seemed very pleased that I showed an interest.

"Why don't you drop by anytime? I have an idea. Join us for lunch—say around 11:30 a.m. in The Last Tango Bar. It's a small out of the way place. Our whole board of directors will be there. We'd love to meet you," said Charolais. What could I say?

Bungee had promoted this company as a great buy at two to four cents a share.

"As soon as the company gets financed the stock is going to $2," Bungee told us. Jack thought this story was worth checking.

When I finally found The Last Tango Bar I didn't want to go in. The bar looked like a combination motorcycle club and food bank. There were actual bars on the windows to protect the place against late night visitors. Two intoxicated old men, even though it was still morning, were sitting on the front step discussing the merits of whiskey and rye.

When Jack and I walked toward the men I had some loose change ready as an offering if they asked for money. They asked. I gave. It's important to make friends in a strange neighbourhood.

When I walked into the bar I could barely see because it was so dark. Six men were sitting at a table with paperwork spread all over the place. I smiled and waved. They waved. Charolais was a big man. He pulled a chair over for me and welcomed me to the group.

"I'm Charolais. You must be Bungee's friends. Meet John, Milt, Reg, Leone, and Tony. This is the board of directors for Godot Inc.," he said. We shook hands. These people seemed to be exactly what they appeared to be—regular guys.

Charolais waved at the waiter who brought a round of draft beers. I wasn't sure how early the bar opened but it seemed to me that the board of directors was getting an early start on the day's festivities. Charolais drank his beer in three gulps. Big guys can do things like that. The waiter brought him another.

"I hope you don't mind the informal atmosphere. We get more done in an informal atmosphere. Our offices are right next door," said Charolais. He explained that Godot Inc. owned the patent on three revolutionary products which improved pump efficiency.

"Our prototype is excellent. It works like a charm. All our potential customers are excited about the product. The government thinks our pump improvements are excellent. Several brokers have expressed an interest in financing this deal. Several major manufacturers are seriously thinking of incorporating our product in their operations," Charolais said.

"We are going to change modern industry as we know it. Imagine if only a handful of companies throughout the world buy our product at prices ranging from $30,000 to $50,000. We will have a multimillion dollar company," he said.

You, as a Diligent Trader, are probably interested in knowing more about the nature of these pump improvements. Relax. It isn't important. The Charolais team said they needed $300,000 to launch a limited production run. They thought I was there to write them a cheque. I'm not sure what Bungee told them, but from the looks of things Bungee had said more than he should.

We had to listen to the whole epic story associated with this revolutionary deal. We had no choice. We will spare you the ordeal. One of the directors, Tony to be exact, was drunk by 1 p.m. when everyone decided to show us the prototype of the pump. Charolais and Tony started showing off a little bit. I don't know if they were just having fun or being serious.

"Has the multi-national sent us the *million dollar* cheque yet?" Charolais said to Tony while looking at me in the eye. Tony laughed and snorted in his beer.

The corporate offices, in the warehouse district, featured an old sofa, two desks, a phone sitting on a chair, one computer, a rug that needed vacuuming, seven chairs, a large table, and two filing cabinets. Three men in overalls were working on a machine that looked like a pump. Charolais explained the dynamics of this product. I don't know much about pumps, but I do know when a company is in deep trouble. There appeared to be several questions which I knew would be hard to answer:

■ Could "Whiplash" and his associates manage this company?

■ Were the principals essentially broke and looking for work? If the company can only raise a moderate amount of money, will the money be used for salaries?

■ Were the personal habits of the managers a danger to the financial well being of the company? In short, would the corporate treasury be spent in the bar?

■ Was the market for this "pump" limited to a few major manufacturers of machinery as it seemed to be? To be a supplier for major manufacturers is a dangerous proposition under any circumstances. A tiny company like Godot Inc. might have to wait forever for an order and the major manufacturer could even steal the concept.

■ Were major corporations eager to use the technology?

■ Even if a major venture capitalist, which Jack and I were not, provided money to start production, how much money would be

Waiting For Godot

"By the way, has the million dollar cheque from the multi-national arrived yet?" Charolais The Manager asked Tony The Accountant while I breathlessly waited for a reply.

RAMPAGING BULLS: Outfox Promoters At Their Game On Any Penny Stock Market

needed to market this product nationally and internationally? How many trade shows would the marketing team need to attend? How many exhausting meetings would the sales team need to attend with cynical buyers from major manufacturers who hate their jobs? Jack and I guessed that even if the company produced several "pumps" the sales effort would require two to three times more money than Charolais had estimated.

■ Suppose Godot Inc. needed substantially more than $300,000 to develop the product and distribution but couldn't raise more than $300,000? Would investors lose their initial $300,000 investment?

In short, Jack and I were nervous about this deal. We didn't even know how to get involved since there was no trading going on in the stock. If Jack and I were to invest in Godot Inc. would we be doing it out of sympathy? You should have heard Bungee going on about this "pump" as if it was the greatest thing ever invented.

"These guys will get financed. Trust me. You can buy the shares at two cents. The shares could be worth as much as $1 when they complete their financing," said Bungee. I didn't have the heart to criticize Bungee by asking him why his brokerage firm hadn't financed this deal.

Jack and I decided to go for drinks at The Last Tango Bar with the board of directors one more time a few days later. We wanted to make a big show out of placing an order to buy 50,000 shares at two cents in a cross from the board of directors. We phoned Bungee from the bar. Everyone heard the conversation. We were heroes for a day. At two cents per share our investment was $1,000 each. I didn't want to do it. Jack insisted.

"We can afford to help the needy. These people can use the money to buy food," Jack said.

"You mean beer," I said.

Jack felt sorry for the Godot Inc. team. Our buying spree created a blip in the trading chart. Then there was an eerie silence. The company reverted to being a "Flatliner".

I was afraid to ask if the company was named after Nobel Prize winning author Samuel Beckett's play *Waiting For Godot*. This strange play, about people waiting for Godot to arrive only to be disappointed when he doesn't show, is an excellent way to describe companies listed on penny stock markets which are waiting for a miracle. These companies have so many common factors with Godot Inc. that Jack and I have taken to describing them as "Waiting For Godot".

"Aren't you guys trying to develop a company that needs much more than $300,000 for production, marketing, advertising, and distribution in a world that demands kickbacks and bribes?" I asked Charolais.

"You must be kidding. If we were to ask for too much everybody would laugh at us," he said in a serious outburst. I didn't have an answer to that. Charolais was willing to allow an unsuspecting investor to sink $300,000 into his deal with the knowledge that the money was inadequate to get the job done. Was this honest? Stupid? Desperate? I phoned Bungee.

"I think Charolais is desperate and not as honest as you think," I said.

Godot Inc. needed big money to get the job done. Big money is also absolutely necessary to develop excitement among investors. With big money a Rampaging Bull could turn Godot Inc. into a hot stock. Unfortunately, there are many companies competing to raise money, attract Rampaging Bulls, and change the world while making everyone rich. Charolais would have to improve his style or find a bigger concept with a chance to appeal to a mass audience. That is why he and his team are still Waiting For Godot to save them.

Don't conclude from this sad story that all honest people on penny stock markets are losers. Far from it. There are many companies that are willing to do things right instead of taking short cuts like criminals and incompetents. These companies might evolve into real growth companies. The important thing is to determine if a stock promotion will offer a capital gain as the share price increases in the short term. If the company turns into a long term success, that's gravy. The Godot Inc. stock was not trading. Therefore, we should not have bought the stock. But Jack is a sensitive man. And I'm Jack's friend. We each lost money on Godot Inc. because the managers never convinced anyone else to invest. Live and learn.

That was also the day that Jack decided to open his own restaurant.

"I learned something today. If the Last Tango Bar, a real hole, can stay in business I'm sure I can open a bar that will do better," said Jack. I tried to tell him restaurants and bars are too risky for anybody who isn't willing to work 20 hours a day for no money during the first few years.

"I have a secret marketing strategy," he said. I didn't believe him.

"You are already a part owner of my new bar," he said. "I'm giving you a $1,000 interest in my new restaurant to compensate you for your loss in Godot Inc.," he said.

You and I now know that Jack's secret marketing strategy involved recruiting Holstein as a regular customer. It was risky, but brilliant. That's Jack for you—a *daredevil* beanstalk climber who invited me along for the climb twice.

In Search of Warriorpreneurs

19

. . . Almost Impossible To Find

I invited Bungee, Milan, Oswaldo, Jack, Dave, and Victor to lunch. I don't know why I hadn't called a board meeting of my friends earlier.

Our investing techniques were less than well thought out. We seemed to be investing aimlessly. Our investments at times made sense, at times made no sense, and at times seemed like sheer insanity. We had to develop a plan.

Jack thought I needed a good night's sleep when I picked him up.

"You're cranky. What are you expecting from this lunch, a vision?" he asked. I took a deep breath.

"You have to admit we should have never invested in Black Box Enterprises, Godot Inc., and Minor Achievement. We were unbelievably lucky to have made money on B.H. Beane International," I said.

"We were Naive Beginners. We are now well beyond that stage," Jack, The Diligent Trader, said.

Everybody was waiting for us at the Cheeky Monkey Restaurant, a restaurant that featured low calorie entrees. We always went to the Cheeky Monkey Restaurant when we wanted to hide from everyone or to get Jack out of his restaurant. Everybody knew I was in a black mood. They just didn't know how black my mood was.

"Thank you for coming. We can't keep investing like lazy supine losers forever, to quote Holstein. Penny stock markets are too dangerous for that. Eight out of 10 initial public offerings are bankrupt within two to five years. We have to get organized. We need a plan to find the winners," I said.

"Oh! Oh! I think we are going to get a presentation," said Bungee. Everybody laughed.

"It may have occurred to you that we are on thin ice. We can evaluate some investments. The rest of the time we seem to base our actions on hunches. The quality of our due diligence is very poor. We treat promoters as if they are handing us the Ten Commandments," I said.

"Bungee thought Godot Inc. was worth checking even though the managers are alcoholics! Oswaldo and Milan thought the Criminal Incompetents managing Black Box Enterprises were going to promote the stock to $20! Geez! I'd like to quote a phrase from Holstein. 'You are all lazy supine bastards.' We need to do better," I said.

Everybody, including the server standing by our table, was looking at me.

"You guys know Holstein?" she asked in awe. We all groaned.

I ordered the low-fat pizza that featured green peppers and tomatoes. Fresh vegetables always put me in a better mood. I have a knack for picking restaurants that offer good salads and unusual entrees. I even wrote a book about it once.

"Doesn't it occur to you that our stock picking skills are weak. Why can't we buy penny stocks that turn into winners, get listed on major stock exchanges, and turn investors into millionaires?" I said.

"For God's sake," said Bungee. "You are asking for winners every time we discover a potential investment on the penny stock market. That is impossible. The penny stock market is risky and difficult to predict. That is why they call it high risk speculation," said Oswaldo.

"No investor should have more than five to 10 percent of his or her capital in penny stocks at any given time because he or she has to learn the ropes," said Milan.

Diligent Trader Gets Irritated

"We are a bunch of lazy supine losers. We have no plan; no strategy. We have to do better," I said as a Diligent Trader to my brokers and friends .

RAMPAGING BULLS: Outfox Promoters At Their Game On Any Penny Stock Market

"We are in the penny stock market because we can't afford to invest on senior exchanges. The average price of a stock on these senior exchanges varies, on average, between $10 and $100 with a median price of $30. You can buy 150 shares at $30 per share for $5,000. None of us will get rich doing that. Let's say the share price goes up 10% in a year from $30 to $33. You will earn $450 and assume a lot of risk," said Bungee.

"You also have to be careful with mutual funds," Milan said.

"The higher the rate of return they promise, the more risk there is. Some funds are extremely volatile—and dangerous for security minded people. You still have to be a careful mutual fund shopper. Some funds will charge you as much as 9% to get in or as much as 9% to get out.

"Mutual funds over the past 20 years have been fairly secure. That is why all of us have some money in mutual funds as a diversification," said Milan.

"But mutual funds aren't any fun. We need the adrenalin rush of a big hit as young ambitious people. Penny stocks are for people who want to risk something in hope of making a killing. Mutual funds are primarily for people who need to conserve their capital with some growth," Bungee said.

"Everybody needs a good speculation to put colour in their cheeks and zest in their step. Sometimes you make money and sometimes you lose money," said Milan.

My brokers were warming up for serious debate.

I held up my hands.

"Whoa! Why can't we find some investment opportunities with the odds in our favour?" I said.

"We'll know when Holstein launches his next promotion. What more do you want?" all three brokers said in unison. Vic and Dave ate their soup and watched me make trouble.

"That's it?" I asked in disbelief. "Is Holstein our only hope? Holstein isn't the only Rampaging Bull. There are others. Go find them! What about uncovering some companies managed by Successful Entrepreneurs? Warriorpreneurs? There are all sorts of worthwhile initial public offerings and penny companies being promoted on senior or junior stock exchanges," I said.

Bungee laughed aloud.

"You want us to find every company that has Warriorpreneurs or Rampaging Bulls; that has money; that has a commercial product; that is or is almost distributing its product; and that offers investors a fair chance to earn large capital gains," said Bungee.

"Yes," I said.

The brokers looked at each other. They were shocked that I would be so demanding.

"You want the best of all possible worlds every time out," they said in unison.

"Excuse me," I said. "I want you guys to do more homework, more due diligence. There are 1,000 companies listed on our small junior stock exchange. At least 200 companies trade shares every day. Several companies move to senior stock markets every year. I don't remember ever discussing these winners with any of you! Let's focus on those. You can't be that lazy for God's sake," I said.

Oswaldo sighed.

"We can do that. The shares, however, trade between $2 to $10. These prices are too risky for small traders. The idea is to buy penny stocks at much lower prices. Most penny stock deals on the verge of becoming a success are seriously over priced. They are generally very risky and out of reach of smaller traders at the precise moment they become interesting to major investors.

"The small trader can lose a lot of money if the penny stock company doesn't achieve steady and growing revenues when its share prices have been bid up through promotion," said Oswaldo.

"Most heavy rollers like to promote a penny stock only after they and their friends pick up the inexpensive shares. That's why good penny stock investment opportunities, on their way to being emerging growth companies, are hard to find," said Milan.

"When the stock price is bid up, the pretentious promoters come out of the woodworks and peddle their stocks to pension funds, mutual funds, strangers, and believers like us," Milan said. I smiled.

"For God's sake," said Milan looking at me. "He wants us to hit the pavement and knock on doors," he added. I nodded my head.

"I want you to ask the hard questions. You haven't been doing that up to know," I said. They glared at me.

"Look at these questions. We can use them as our Due Diligence Test. I think they are good," I then handed them the list below.

■ A. THE DUE DILIGENCE TEST

■ Our Due Diligence Test is a set of 64 questions that we also call The Warriorpreneur Test and/or The Rampaging Bull Test—depending on what you're looking for. The test has two sections and five sub-sections.

■ Answer yes or no to every question.

■ If the answer is yes, assign a score from one to five. The higher the number you assign, the more truthful or plausible the positive quality is! A score of +5 means that you believe the positive quality to be 100% true.

■ If the answer is no, assign a value from -1 to -5. The lower the number, the more truthful or plausible the negative quality is! A score of -5 means you believe the negative quality is 100% true.

■ The first major section, Personality Background, has two sub-sections dealing with the promoter's and managers' ability to share and get the job done.

■ The second major section, The Big Picture, has three sub-sections dealing with the company's organizational structure, the market for the product and the stock, and the product's characteristics.

■ You will need practice to answer the questions properly. Beginners tend to be too liberal with their answers because they don't want to be rude. Remember: nobody but you need ever look at your scores. Be as tough as you need to be.

■ If you have substantial experience with the stock market there is a danger you will answer the questions too negatively because of your previous bad experience. Lighten up. Be fair.

■ You must do some investigation to answer these questions properly. The questions also require an intuitive understanding of people rather than hard cold statistics which managers tend to hide anyway. You can answer the questions after meeting with brokers, promoters, managers, and regulatory authorities.

■ If you don't have adequate data or if the question is irrelevant to the company skip the question. You won't nullify the test if you can't answer a few questions. The more questions you answer, of course, the more meaningful the result.

■ A lot of the questions are somewhat subjective or intuitive. It's hard to get hard information on penny stock companies. But most penny stock investments are subjective anyway. The questions will sharpen your ability to evaluate a good deal. You might want to work closely with your broker to get a handle on potential penny stock investments.

■ If a company is not promoting its share price either with a bona fide professional promoter or by cultivating deep and abiding friendships with brokers, analysts, the press, and government then the company will get low scores and not qualify as a capital gains investment opportunity.

■ It is almost impossible for incompetent people to get a high score and it is almost impossible for competent people to get a low score on the Personality Background portion of the Due Diligence Test.

■ If, for instance, you think that the board of directors is an independent body of people which cares about investors then you will answer yes to question number one. If you have met the board and watched them operate, you can give them the highest possible grade, +5. You believe the board has the highest degree of integrity. If, on the other hand, you feel the board is not independent of the promoter and the managers, you will assign a lower score and perhaps even a negative score. This allows you some flexibility in your scoring. You can hedge on your positive or negative attitude toward the board of directors.

■ In short, our Due Diligence Check List will help you reveal Warriorpreneurs, Successful Entrepreneurs, Criminal Incompetents, and Rampaging Bulls.

■ B. THE DUE DILIGENCE TEST

1. Personal Background = The "Y" Score
    i. The Ability To Share Sub-Total (benevolence)
    ii. Ability Sub-Total (competence and courage)
    iii. Personal Background Total Score= The "Y" Score

2. The Big Picture = The "X" Score
    i. The Market Sub-Total
    ii. The Product Sub-Total
    iii. Corporate Organization Sub-Total
    iv. The Big Picture Total Score

1. Personal Background = The "Y" Score

i. The Ability To Share (benevolence)

1. Is the board of directors an independent group of people who can protect shareholder interests and act as a sober check on the promoters and managers?

> *B.H. Beane International, No; Score: -4*
> *Black Box Enterprises, No; Score: -4*
> *Minor Achievement, Yes, with doubts; Score: +2*
> *Godot Inc., No; Score: -2*

2. Are the promoters benevolent? Are the promoters humane people who want to do the right thing for investors, employees, clients, and suppliers by paying their debts, honouring their promises, and paying dividends?

> *B.H. Beane International, No; Score: -5*
> *Black Box Enterprises, No; Score: -4*
> *Minor Achievement, No; Score: -3 (Birmingham is greedy)*
> *Godot Inc., Not Applicable (no promoter)*

3. Are the managers benevolent? Are the managers humane people who want to do the right thing for investors, employees,

clients, and suppliers by paying their debts, honouring their promises, and paying dividends when possible?

B.H. Beane International, No; Score: -1
Black Box Enterprises, No; Score: -2 (will do anything)
Minor Achievement, Yes, with doubts; Score: +2
Godot Inc., Yes; Score: +3 (they seem like decent people)

4. Are the company's promoters respected by brokers and most investors?

B.H. Beane International, Yes; Score: +5
Black Box Enterprises, Yes with doubts; Score: +2
Minor Achievement, No; Score: -2 (Birmingham, isn't powerful)
Godot Inc., Not Applicable

5. Are the company's manager, president, or consultants respected by brokers and investors?

B.H. Beane International, Yes; Score: +3 (Asian immigrants o.k.)
Black Box Enterprises, Yes; Score: +4 (engineers o.k.)
Minor Achievement, Yes; Score: +2
Godot Inc., No; Score: -5

6. Does the promoter have humble, simple tastes that encourage him or her to spend investor dollars wisely?

B.H. Beane International, No; Score: -5
Black Box Enterprises, No; Score: -2 (slobs who like money)
Minor Achievement, No; Score: -1 (broker likes good life)
Godot Inc., Not Applicable

7. Are the salary and stock options of the top penny stock company managers less than 15 times the salary and options of the receptionist/secretary and/or the blue collar workers and/or the lowest paid managers? You might keep in mind that some executives of major corporations are bleeding their companies and investors with salaries and stock options 150 to 300 times greater than their blue collar or office staff! These managers of many well known companies are probably malignant narcissistics!

B.H. Beane International, No; Score: -5
Black Box Enterprises, No; Score: -4
Minor Achievement, Yes; Score: +2
Godot Inc., Yes; Score: +5 (everybody is poor)

8. Do promoters or managers become involved in community work to win public acclaim? This is a clue as to whether they will skip town.

B.H. Beane International, Yes; Score: +5
Black Box Enterprises, No; Score: -4
Minor Achievement, Yes; Score: +1 (weak involvement)
Godot Inc., No; Score: -5 (too poor to care)

9. Do managers have a clean record with the securities commission, the stock exchange, or the police?

Note: Jack and I didn't think of checking the managers of these four companies. Therefore, we didn't assign values.

10. Do promoters have a clean record with the securities commission, the stock exchange, or the police?

Note: Jack and I didn't think of checking the managers of these four companies with these agencies. Therefore, we didn't assign values.

11. Do the managers and promoters involve the whole team in strategy and decision making, with appropriate rewards, rather than simply give orders from the top? never fly into a rage when they don't get their way? treat employees with respect?

B.H. Beane International, No; Score: -5 (rage and dominance)
Black Box Enterprises, No; Score: -4 (ditto)
Minor Achievement, No Score; (we don't know)
Godot Inc., Yes; Score: +5 (losers feel safe in group)

12. Do managers and promoters have an "active" open door policy for employees to hear ideas and complaints?

B.H. Beane International, No; Score: -3
Black Box Enterprises, No; Score: -5 (forget it)
Minor Achievement, Yes; Score: +2
Godot Inc., Yes; Score: +5 (losers feel safe in group)

13. Do managers and promoters return investor and customer phone calls or at least make themselves available for comment?

B.H. Beane International, Yes; Score: +2 (when convenient)
Black Box Enterprises, Yes; Score: +1 (when convenient)
Minor Achievement, Yes; Score: +4 (never many calls)
Godot Inc., Yes; Score: +5 (they never know who might invest)

14. Is there little or no personal, racial, sexual, or ethnic tension between the top managers and/or promoters that might destroy the company once it makes money? In short, do the top managers get along and respect each other?

We didn't consider this very important question. We will in future especially in a situation like Holstein versus Van Guilder.

15. Are managers and promoters willing to put things in writing that formally commits them to promises made?

B.H. Beane International, No; Score: -2 (only when forced)
Black Box Enterprises, No; Score: -4 (almost never)
Minor Achievement, Yes; Score: +2 (not sure)
Godot Inc., Yes; Score: +5 (they'll do anything to get money)

16. Do managers and promoters believe that you will hire and pay for a lawyer to enforce your rights if you have to? This is a very subjective question.

B.H. Beane International, No; Score: -2
Black Box Enterprises, No; Score: -2 (ditto)
Minor Achievement, Yes; Score: +1 (maybe)
Godot Inc., Yes; Score: +3 (maybe)

17. Are managers and promoters interested in developing a good reputation for whatever reasons?

B.H. Beane International, Yes; Score: +4 (longer term strategy)
Black Box Enterprises, No; Score: -4 (promoters no)
Minor Achievement, Yes; Score: +3 (they want to do it right)
Godot Inc., Yes; Score: +5 (they'll do anything to get money)

1. Personal Background "Y" Score

i. Ability To Share Sub-Total

If the score is positive the investor should expect decent treatment. If the score is negative the investor can expect rude and crude treatment and policy decisions which ignore investor interests. The investor should then behave like a professional trader. Buy and sell the stock with ruthless and lightning speed.

■ **B.H. Beane International,** Score: -13 (shares when convenient)

■ **Black Box Enterprises,** Score: -32 (very greedy)

The promoters and managers at Black Box Enterprises and B.H. Beane received negative scores for their ability to share. They prefer to scoop profits for themselves instead of sharing profits with investors. Holstein is smarter and prepared to put on a show of being generous in the short term to help B.H. Beane International attract investors.

■ **Minor Achievement,** Score: +15

The Minor Achievement managers seem to have the right spirit.

You might invest when managers arrange financing.
■ **Godot Inc.,** Score: +24
The managers at Godot Inc. don't have anything to share at this time even though they act as if they would if they could. They should be evaluated at each step of their progress to make sure their greed doesn't get the better of them if they get money.

1. Personal Background

ii. Ability To Get It Done (competence and courage)

18. Is an experienced promoter involved? Is he able to move the share price above the market average?

> *B.H. Beane International, Yes; Score: +4*
> *Black Box Enterprises, Yes; Score: +3*
> *Minor Achievement, No; Score: -3*
> *Godot Inc., No; Score: -5*

19. Do managers have experience as successful business people or some special knowledge to make the company a success?

> *B.H. Beane International, Yes; Score: +2 (Van Guilder o.k.)*
> *Black Box Enterprises, Yes; Score: +3 (engineers o.k.)*
> *Minor Achievement, Yes; Score: +2.5*
> *Godot Inc., No; Score: -5*

20. Do *managers* consider developing this company to be a dream for which they will commit time, be patient, and work hard? In short, are managers dedicated?

> *B.H. Beane International, No; Score: -2*
> *Black Box Enterprises, Yes; Score: +4*
> *Minor Achievement, Yes; Score: +4*
> *Godot Inc., Yes; Score: +3*

21. Do *promoters* consider developing this company to be worthy of their time, patience, and hard work? In short, is the promoter dedicated to this deal? Will promoters keep shares and options or dump them on the market?

> *B.H. Beane International, Yes; Score: +5 (promoter's money)*
> *Black Box Enterprises, Yes; Score: +1 (ditto)*
> *Minor Achievement, No; Score: -3 (broker not dedicated)*
> *Godot Inc., Not Applicable*

22. Can the promoter or management raise money? Have their previous deals been a success for the company and or investors?

B.H. Beane International, Yes; Score: +5
Black Box Enterprises, Yes; Score: +3.5
Minor Achievement, Yes; Score: +2 (lots of struggling)
Godot Inc., No; Score: -5

23. Do promoters have that special something defined as talent? raw cunning? intelligence?

B.H. Beane International, Yes; Score: +4
Black Box Enterprises, Yes; Score: +2 (moderate at best)
Minor Achievement, No; Score: -2
Godot Inc., No; Score: -5 (hopeless)

24. Do managers have that special something defined as business talent? Raw cunning? Intelligence?

B.H. Beane International, No; Score: -2 (managers flunkies)
Black Box Enterprises, Yes; Score: +2 (engineers not worldly)
Minor Achievement, Yes; Score: +3 (hotel is real)
Godot Inc., No; Score: -5 (hopeless)

25. Do managers pay attention to details required to implement the strategic vision?

B.H. Beane International, Yes; Score: +3 (could be better)
Black Box Enterprises, Yes; Score: +2 (technical knowledge)
Minor Achievement, Yes; Score: +4 (it's a real deal)
Godot Inc., Hard to establish

26. Do promoters pay attention to the small details that make a promotion look and feel sophisticated?

B.H. Beane International, Yes; Score: +3 (short term)
Black Box Enterprises, No; Score: -3 (too selfish)
Minor Achievement, No; Score: -3 (Birmingham worries about his clients first, not the company)
Godot Inc., Not Applicable

27. Are *promoters* mentally and emotionally stable; without debt, marital, financial, addictive, or dysfunctional personality problems (other than narcissism)?

B.H. Beane International, Yes; Score: +4 (malignant narcissism is not a disadvantage to developing a good short term promotion although it is a major disadvantage to developing a long term successful company)
Black Box Enterprises, No; Score: +1 (insecure but smart)
Minor Achievement, Yes; Score: +2
Godot Inc., Not Applicable

28. Are *managers* mentally and emotionally stable without marital, financial, addictive, or dysfunctional personality problems? (other than narcissism)

> *B.H. Beane International, Yes; Score: +2 (Van Guilder O.K.)*
> *Black Box Enterprises, Yes; Score: +3 (as far as we know)*
> *Minor Achievement, Yes; Score: +3 (we think)*
> *Godot Inc., No; Score: -5 (alcoholism)*

29. Do managers encourage staffers to set priority projects and encourage them to tackle one thing at a time?

> *B.H. Beane International, No; Score: -2 (unfocused)*
> *Black Box Enterprises, Yes; Score: +3 (as far as we know)*
> *Minor Achievement, Yes; Score: +1 (hoteliers are obsessive)*
> *Godot Inc., No; Score: -5 (alcoholism)*

30. Do managers and promoters avoid creating unnecessary panic, stress, and fear?

> *B.H. Beane International, No; Score: -4*
> *Black Box Enterprises, No; Score: -3 (ditto)*
> *Minor Achievement, No; Score: -3 (hoteliers spread fear)*
> *Godot Inc., No; Score: -1 (the whole team drinks)*

31. Are the insider trading reports filed on time?

> *Didn't think of asking.*

32. Are most insiders holding their stock because they believe in the company?

> *Never checked.*

1. Personal Background "Y" Score

ii. Ability To Get Things Done Sub-Total

B.H. Beane International, Score: +24

Black Box Enterprises, Score: +21.5

Minor Achievement, Score: +6.5

Godot Inc., Score: -33

1. Personal Background Total "Y" Score

iii. The Personal Background Total Score

(Ability To Share) + (Ability To Get Things Done)

■ **B.H. Beane International, Score:** (-13) + (24) = +11

B.H. Beane International and promoter Bob Holstein have the skills to get things done over the long term although they might not. B.H. Beane's and Holstein's excellent ability to get it done score is offset by the poor ability to share score. This contradiction shows that Bob Holstein and B.H. Beane International may qualify for Rampaging Bull status. The B.H. Beane and Holstein score shows that there is sufficient talent to achieve things, but insufficient interpersonal skills to sustain the achievement.

■ **Black Box Enterprises, Score:** (-32) + (21.5) = -10.5

The Black Box Enterprises reflects the promoter's ability to attract some investors and develop a short term promotion even though he has no intention of sharing the profits.

■ **Minor Achievement, Score:** (+15) + (6.5) = +21.5

Minor Achievement has a good Personal Background score because the scores for sharing and getting things done do not offset each other. This company is worth watching over the long term.

■ **Godot, Score:** (+24) + (-33) = -9

The score for Godot Inc. reflects the hope of moderately honest guys that they will get a chance to prove themselves with other people's money. They shouldn't hold their breath.

2. The Big Picture "X" Score

The Big Picture score "X" summarizes the state of the market, the product, and the company.

i. Market

33. Is the share price well below the average price per share on this stock market that might allow a trader to earn a capital gain? The question should be asked just before you buy.

B.H. Beane International, No; Score: -4 (Beane passed market average almost immediately)
Black Box Enterprises, No; Score: -4 (above average quickly)
Minor Achievement, Yes; Score: +2.5
Godot Inc., Yes; Score: +5 (share price as low as it can go)

34. Does the nature of the product allow for an extended promotion (longer than one year) which will allow investors time to buy and sell the stock in an orderly way?

B.H. Beane International, Yes; Score: +4
Black Box Enterprises, Yes; Score: +3

Minor Achievement, Yes; Score: +2 (hotel real)
Godot Inc., No; Score: -4 (too undeveloped)

35. Can investors and traders get excited by this penny stock's concept as original, innovative, and breathtaking?

B.H. Beane International, Yes; Score: +4
Black Box Enterprises, Yes; Score: +2 (depends on investor)
Minor Achievement, No; Score: -4
Godot Inc., Yes; Score: +1 (maybe)

36. Have any penny stock concepts similar to this one been successful stock market promotions?

Sorry. We didn't even think about asking this. We will in future.

37. Are economic conditions in the product's market segment healthy?

B.H. Beane International, Yes; Score: +3 (farms need help)
Black Box Enterprises, Yes; Score: +3 (people buy hi-tech)
Minor Achievement, Yes; Score: +3 (yes, tourism)
Godot Inc., Yes; Score: +4 (multi-nationals have money)

38. Does the company enjoy a monopoly in its market or potential market?

B.H. Beane International, Yes; Score: +4 (if it works)
Black Box Enterprises, No; Score: -4
Minor Achievement, No; Score: -4
Godot Inc., Yes; Score: +2 (multi-nationals can compete)

39. Is the potential market for this product large?

B.H. Beane International, Yes; Score: +4
Black Box Enterprises, Yes; Score: +5
Minor Achievement, No; Score: -2
Godot Inc., No; Score: -3

40. Is there a demand "today" for this company's product because nobody else has yet managed to satisfy the public? Would you buy this product?

B.H. Beane International, Yes; Score: +4
Black Box Enterprises, Yes; Score: +2 (must have quality)
Minor Achievement, No; Score: -1 (hotels are common)
Godot Inc., No; Score: -2 (not yet)

2. The Big Picture "X" Score

i. Market Subtotal

B.H. Beane International, Score: +19
Black Box Enterprises, Score: +7
Minor Achievement, Score: -3.5
Godot Inc., Score: +7

The scores indicate that B.H. Beane seems to have the best opportunities to market its products. Black Box Enterprises also has a huge market although there seem to be many hurdles facing the company in the marketplace especially well established competitors.

Godot Inc. is in for some tough times as it tries to develop and market its product while Minor Achievement is operating in a market with many competitors where it is hard to get and edge.

2. The Big Picture "X" Score

ii. Product

41. Is the product still a fantasy (score -5); in the conceptual stage (score -4); in the prototype stage (score -3); in the testing stage (score -2); in market test stage (score -1); in preliminary production (score +1); in full production (+2); in local distribution (score +3); in national and local distribution (score +4); attracting larger market share (+5)? If this is a resource company, are reserves proven and substantial?

B.H. Beane International, Score: -2
Black Box Enterprises, Score: -1 (looking good)
Minor Achievement, Score: +4 (the hotel is real)
Godot Inc., Score: -1 (testing with multi-nationals)

42. Can the product be priced to compete with similar products?

B.H. Beane International, Yes; Score: +4 (no competition)
Black Box Enterprises, Yes; Score: +4
Minor Achievement, Yes; Score: +3
Godot Inc., Yes; Score: +3

43. Is the patent adequate or extensive enough to prevent predatory practices by competitors?

B.H. Beane International, Don't Know
Black Box Enterprises, Not Applicable
Minor Achievement, Not Applicable
Godot Inc., Not Sure

44. Can the company sell this product successfully even if it doesn't have patents?

B.H. Beane International, Yes; Score: +3
Black Box Enterprises, Yes; Score: +3
Minor Achievement, Yes; Score: +4
Godot Inc., No; Score: -2 (big companies might produce it)

45. Is the government regulatory approval process (i.e. food, drug, and financial agencies) easy and quick? Is there little or no chance for major liability and damage suits?

We didn't consider this. We will in future.

2. The Big Picture "X" Score
ii. Product Sub-Total

B.H. Beane International, Score: +5 (could be a popular product; product exists)

Black Box Enterprises, Score: +6 (ditto)

Minor Achievement, Score: +11 (the hotel is very real)

Godot Inc., Score: 0 (needs development)

2. The Big Picture "X" Score
iii. Corporate Organization

46. Is this project easy for the company to develop?

B.H. Beane International, No; Score: -4
Black Box Enterprises, No; Score: -3
Minor Achievement, Yes; Score: +1 (but not too easy)
Godot Inc., No; Score: -4 (very difficult)

47. Can this company finance future growth from earnings?

B.H. Beane International, premature, no revenues.
Black Box Enterprises, premature, no revenues.
Minor Achievement, No; Score: -3
Godot Inc., premature, we don't know

48. Do promoters have a personal investment in the project or promotion?

B.H. Beane International, Yes; Score: +4
Black Box Enterprises, No; Score: -4
Minor Achievement, No; Score: -5
Godot Inc., Not Applicable

49. Do managers have a personal investment in the project or promotion?

B.H. Beane International, No; Score: -2 (all Holstein's money)
Black Box Enterprises, Yes; Score: +3
Minor Achievement, Yes; Score: +3
Godot Inc., Yes; Score: +2

50. Does the company have enough money in the bank to do what it wants? Is the company spending enough money to get the job done?

B.H. Beane International, Yes; Score: +5
Black Box Enterprises, Yes; Score: +4
Minor Achievement, No; Score: -3
Godot Inc., No; Score: -5

51. Is the working capital per share greater than the market value of the share?

We didn't check this at the time. We will in future.

52. Is the long term debt covered by working capital, cash, or one year's income?

B.H. Beane International, Yes; Score: +5
Black Box Enterprises, Yes; Score: +4
Minor Achievement, Yes; Score: +2 (mortgage is current)
Godot Inc., No; Score: -5 (debts are piling up, no cash)

53. Have earnings increased steadily over the past three years?

B.H. Beane International, Not Applicable
Black Box Enterprises, Not Applicable
Minor Achievement, Yes; Score: +3
Godot Inc., Not Applicable

54. Have sales increased steadily over the past three years? This sounds similar to the previous question about increased earnings, but it isn't. A company can have declining sales and increasing earnings or increasing sales and declining earnings.

We didn't discuss this question because only Minor Achievement had a sales history.

55. Are current assets (cash, accounts receivable, materials, and inventories) twice the size of current liabilities and financial claims payable during the year?

We didn't check this. We will in future. This is an excellent test of solvency.

56. Does the company have good labour relations and employees who have a vested interest in the success of the company?

B.H. Beane International, Not Applicable
Black Box Enterprises, Not Applicable
Minor Achievement, We don't know
Godot Inc., Not Applicable

57. Does the company have a team, other than promoter and manager, with talent, training, and abilities?

B.H. Beane International, No; Score: -2 (the whole thing may have been run by Holstein out of a briefcase in his fancy car)
Black Box Enterprises, Yes; Score: +3 (several experts)
Minor Achievement, Yes; Score: +3 (hotels always have a team)
Godot Inc., Yes; Score: +2 (even if they do drink a lot)

58. Can capital markets, local and foreign, finance this deal if they want to?

Sorry. We weren't thinking about this as much as we could have.

59. Are local stock and financial brokers willing to finance the company's program?

B.H. Beane International, Yes; Score: +2 (most money must come from foreign sources because too much money is needed)
Black Box Enterprises, Yes; Score: +1 (local financiers have no expertise in electronics)
Minor Achievement, Yes; Score: +2 (maybe in future)
Godot, No; Score: -3 (only if Godot gets purchase orders from manufacturing firms)

60. Are foreign and major brokers willing to finance the company's program?

B.H. Beane International, Yes; Score: +4 (right up their alley)
Black Box Enterprises, Yes; Score: +2 (foreign financiers could help if it is a good deal)
Minor Achievement, No; Score: -2 (would have to thrill them!)
Godot Inc., No; Score: -5 (they have their local Godot companies)

61. Is the company focused on one project?

B.H. Beane International, Yes; Score: +4 (good focus)
Black Box Enterprises, Yes; Score: +2 (three similar products)
Minor Achievement, Yes; Score: +4
Godot Inc., Yes; Score: +4

62. Is the audit firm independent and honest enough to tell the truth? This is the hardest question to answer. Our score is based on hindsight.

> *B.H. Beane International, No; Score: -4 (Holstein never works with honest people)*
> *Black Box Enterprises, No; Score: -4*
> *Minor Achievement, Yes, with doubts; Score: +1*
> *Godot Inc., Yes; Score: +5 (the poor can't bribe)*

63. Does the corporate accountant decline bribes or incentives. You may never find out until it's too late.

> *B.H. Beane International, We don't know*
> *Black Box Enterprises, We don't know*
> *Minor Achievement, We don't know*
> *Godot Inc., We don't know*

64. Does the company have an office, a listed telephone, and a receptionist?

> *B.H. Beane International, Yes; Score: +5 (tres cool)*
> *Black Box Enterprises, Yes; Score: +3*
> *Minor Achievement, Yes; Score: +5 (it's a real hotel)*
> *Godot Inc., Yes; Score: +1 (I guess it's an office)*

2. The Big Picture "X" Score

iii. Corporate Organization Sub-Total

B.H. Beane International, Score: +17 (Beane has money)

Black Box Enterprises, Score: +11 (Black Box needs organizing)

Minor Achievement, Score: +11 (Minor has something happening)

Godot Inc., Score: -8 (Godot needs help)

iv. The Total "X" Score

■ **B.H. Beane International Score:** (add market, +19; product, +5; and corporate organization, +17) equals +41.

This company could be a winner from the looks of it. The scores reflect the cash rich position of the company. This is important if the company expects to succeed. However, a careful review of the product and corporate organization scores shows that a truly competent and able team would have scored much higher. The share price could go through the roof in the short term until the truth comes out about the larcenous nature of the team. There is doubt about B.H. Beane's ability to develop a commercially accepted product.

■ **Black Box Enterprises Score:** (add market, +7; product, +6; and corporate organization, +11) equals +24

These people look like they have a chance with a highly commercial product until you review their scores carefully. Their share price will do something—but not for long because their market is very competitive.

■ **Minor Achievement Score:** (add market, -3.5; product, +11; and corporate organization, +11) equals 18.5

Minor Achievement's score reflects an active business that requires many disciplined people to keep it running. The company has some potential with a thriving property but needs money to become a growth company. The share price will go nowhere unless the managers raise money.

■ **Godot Inc. Score:** (add market, +7; product, 0; and corporate organization, -8) equals -1

The shares won't trade unless managers raise money or sign contract. Stay away, but keep a watchful eye if contract is signed.

■ C. INTERPRETING THE SCORES.

The over all scores from the Due Diligence Test are ranked in declining order below:

■ **Warriorpreneurs** and their deals will score highest on our Due Diligence Test. Don't delude yourself into thinking that the bright con man who you happen to meet at the side of the road is a Warriorpreneur. The Warriorpreneur is about as rare as you might imagine. The Warriorpreneurs will get a high positive score on the Personal Background test as people of integrity and ability to get things done. Their deals will get a high positive score on The Big Picture Test.

The high scores indicate a strong possibility that this person has the ability and the deal to make money for investors. The Warriorpreneur believes in excellence as a goal and not just a word to throw around in polite conversation. If every business leader were like this, working people would be in heaven.

■ **Successful Entrepreneurs** get moderate or low positive scores for their ability to share because these people can be as greedy and self-serving as economic prophet Adam Smith predicted 200 years ago. They will usually get a high positive score for their ability to get things done. Their deals, markets, and corporate organization will get a high positive score on The Big Picture test. The good scores show a strong possibility that these people have the ability and the deal to make money for investors.

The Successful Entrepreneur should get a higher overall score than The Rampaging Bull and a lower overall score than the Warriorpreneur. Successful Entrepreneurs, as managers of true growth companies, are also uncommon people with whom you might enjoy good times between "outbreaks of backstabbing". Excellence is an idea that a successful entrepreneur might take to heart—but you shouldn't hold your breath. When these people have an "outbreak of backstabbing" they justify the existence of the labour union movement.

■ **The Rampaging Bulls** will generally get a negative score for their ability to share because they can't part with anything they have. The Rampaging Bulls, however, will get a moderate or high positive score for their ability to get things done. Their deals will usually get high positive scores on The Big Picture test. This accurately reflects the reality of the malignant narcissistic whose dominant personality quirk is arrogance with a heavy dose of greed and anger. This self serving person, however, is still competent and committed enough to get a lot done— at least for a short period. This also means that The Rampaging Bull can develop a superior stock promotion even if the product is non-existent. The Rampaging Bulls are more common than truly Successful Entrepreneurs and Warriorpreneurs but much rarer than Criminal Incompetents, Minor Achievers, and Waiting For Godots.

The concept of excellence is something that The Rampaging Bull uses in conversation often though he or she has no idea what it means. The Rampaging Bulls, as greedy self indulgents, can and do cause serious labour strife because of their attitudes.

■ **Quick Note:** You must learn to differentiate between the Successful Entrepreneur, The Warriorpreneur, and The Rampaging Bull. They all appear similar to the untrained eye because their overall scores tend to be good although the breakdown of the scores shows very important distinctions. There is a difference between these people whether you accept this or not. Your investment results will improve dramatically if you learn the difference.

■ **The Criminal Incompetents** will score high negative scores for their ability to share because they are essentially "greedy bastards". The Criminal Incompetents will get moderate or low positive scores for their ability to get things done and moderate scores for their deals on The Big Picture test. This accurately reflects the greedy and self serving nature of the Criminal Incompetent who is able, at the very minimum, to promote an initial public offering or penny stock for a short period. Criminal Incompetents are very common and give stock markets a bad name.

The concept of excellence is a cloudy idea to the Criminal Incompetent who lacks respect for working people, unions, or himself.

■ **Minor Achievers** will get a high positive score for their ability to share because they are generally "ordinary people". Minor Achievers will get a moderate or low positive score for their ability to get things done and usually mid-range scores scores for their deals in The Big Picture Test. This reflects accurately the honesty and integrity of small businesspeople who don't or won't think big enough to get investors excited about the possibility of growth in their industry. The Minor Achiever company may, however, grow into a big deal over a long period, sometimes by the second generation in a family business thanks to evolution and hard work.

Minor Achievers are very common. Their main goal is to develop a business which offers a handsome living, weekends off, and an afternoon of golf once a week. They hate the danger

inherent with growth and risk taking. Excellence to them means having a peaceful life without a lot of stress. Minor Achievers may have the right attitude. These people rarely have anything to do with labour unions because they have such small operations.
■ **Waiting For Godots** will generally get high positive scores for their ability to share; negative scores for their ability to get things done; and negative or very low positive scores on The Big Picture Test. This reflects accurately the lack of personal skills and the poorly thought out deals they are involved in. These people are as common as grass, gripe about everything, and are generally honest but a major "pain in the ass". Waiting For Godots should get real jobs, get on with their life, and be excellent employees for some worthwhile company.

20 | The Vision Continues

. . . The Formulas

Everybody loved my questions.

But Bungee, Milan, Vic, Dave, and Jack were getting cranky.

"How do we use these questions in a practical way? Who is going to keep track of answers for 64 questions?" asked Bungee.

"If you don't do anything but answer the questions and evaluate the scores you will be miles ahead of any other investor. But I have also developed three formulas which apply The Due Diligence Test results. It's fun. It's helpful," I said.

They all groaned.

"God. This is math!" said Jack looking at my second handout. Everyone laughed except for me.

"Come on. Give me a break. I need just a few more minutes of your time for crying aloud," I said. They all groaned.

"When a share price reaches a *peak* there is usually very little time to sell off large holdings as the share price starts to decline, rapidly or slowly. The goal of every professional trader is to know when he or she can begin an orderly and leisurely sale of one's share position in a company. This orderly and leisurely sale of a stock position is one of the great joys in life.

"Therefore, the share price predicted by our formula offers the typical investor a margin of safety. This is the share price at which the investor can feel safe for awhile. Once the share price goes higher than the price predicted by the formula, the investor should start selling and/or short selling. If the share price is below the price suggested by the formula, you can still buy," I said.

The share price from the formulas is a median price—neither the highest or lowest price but one that will appear a few times. A typical stock promotion might offer share prices that are higher or lower than the share price our formula pumps out.

Our first formula is for a penny stock company *with no* earnings or revenues and our second formula is for a budding growth company *with* earnings or revenues. The formulas, as you might imagine, are not exact because nothing in the stock market is. These easy to remember formulas do, however, offer excellent clues about the nature of a company, promoters, and managers.

The formulas assume that the most important factor in the share price of a growth and/or penny company is the quality of the promoter and/or promotional campaign instead of the company's or economy's vital statistics or story. This should make sense if you have grasped our theme throughout this book.

We'll restate our case just in case you missed our message. We believe that the nature of the stock market has changed dramatically in the past 30 years as more people promote and buy stock for an expected future value as opposed to the stock's present value. This strange and crazy fad of investing in potential future earnings has made the stock market a money machine for an ever growing army of promoters and con men. They prey on greedy and naive investors eager to put money into pipe dreams. This phenomenon, by the way, extends to all five dozen sovereign states that now have stock markets.

You should no longer think of the stock market, and especially the penny stock market, as a place for investors to bid against each other at random. To succeed, you must behave as if stock prices are heavily influenced by the actions of the Rampaging Bulls or other promoters who work hard to manipulate the stock market, public opinion, and regulatory agencies.

This is not an easy concept to stomach. All regulators, governments, and brokerage firms still cling tightly, for instance, to the fiction that stock markets offer a level playing field for everyone.

This, on the evidence, is not true for penny stock markets and may not even be true for senior markets.

Rampaging Bulls and other promoters have to manipulate the stock market because, if they didn't, very few stocks would trade on any markets.

We don't, however, think that all promotions are larcenous conspiracies like Holstein's effort for B.H. Beane International. Far from it. That is why we have gone to so much effort to discuss the various types of companies and promoters on penny and senior stock markets. We believe in promotion. Most people need leadership and direction. That is why a successful company needs a great promoter to harness many directionless people to support its product or stock—sometimes for everyone's benefit.

Don't get intimidated by the formulas. They are easy to use and easy to understand. Let's do this step by step.

■ A. DETERMINING THE "X" FACTOR

The Big Picture score is used to figure out the company's underlying strength and weakness. This "X" score acts as a hindrance or support to the promoter's abilities and efforts. Therefore, the Big Picture score needs to be transformed into an "X" factor for our formula. Here is how we do it.

We assume that a score of 24 from the Big Picture Test is equal to an "X" factor of one. A score of 12, for instance, is equal to an "X" factor of .5. A score of 36 is equal to an "X" factor of 1.5.

If the Big Picture Test score is negative, the company still has value. Assign an "X" factor between .01 and .04 depending on how negative the score is. We have a longer explanation for this which we will omit for now.

Any company with an "X" factor greater than one has a chance to grow with its own earnings and revenues.

The "X" factor can never be bigger than 6.5. If we give a company perfect "five" scores for each of the 32 questions in the Big Picture Test, the total "X" score is 160 divided by 24 which equals an "X" factor of approximately 6.5. Most "X" factors will be under "two".

For B.H. Beane International we assign a factor of 1.7 for "X" because the X score was 41; for Black Box Enterprises we assign a factor of "1" for "X" because the X score was 24; for Minor Achievement we assign a factor of .77 for "X" because the X score was 18.5; and for Godot Inc. we assign a factor of .04 for "X" because the "X" score on the Big Picture test was "-1".

◾ B. THE NO INCOME PENNY STOCK

1. The Formula

Our formula for the median share price of a penny stock that has no revenue or earnings is: **Big P= (small p) [(X) (Y)] (T).**

2. What The Formula Means

◾ The "Big P" is for the median share price that might be reached at some point either during the first, second year, or third year of the promotion. This share price is neither the highest, nor the lowest.

◾ When the (X)(Y) scores from our Due Diligence Test are high, look for the Big P price to increase. When the (X)(Y) scores are negative we drop them from the equation entirely. We are looking for deals and promoters which have positive scores and can help us earn capital gains.

◾ The (small p) is for the share price before the stock promotion. The pre-promotion share price, (small p), for a company with no earnings, by the way, is already a moderately promoted price. We have developed a game to help us always remember this. If a penny stock company has no earnings, we simply assume that the company has one cent per share in earnings. Therefore a penny stock with no earnings but trading at 20 cents, in our game, has a price earnings ratio of 20 which is high; at 50 cents per share has a price earnings ratio of 50 which is very high; and at $2 per share has a price earnings ratio of 200 which is outrageous, and so on.

This is a game we play to help us stay conscious and realistic when the promoters tell us a penny stock trading at $2 is really worth $10 or $20 although there are *no* earnings.

All investors hope promoters and management can create a company that will achieve earnings to justify the promoted share price and perhaps justify an even greater share price in the future. The idea, as far as we know, is to make rich all those buying early.

■ The "X" stands for a factor derived from The Big Picture Test score in our Due Diligence Test. The "X" factor enhances or discounts the promoter's Personality Background score "Y".

■ The "Y" stands for the Personality Background score taken directly from our Due Diligence Test that reflects the promoter's ability to get things done and his ability to share.

■ The "T" is the length of the promotion in years and can only have six values: 1, 1.5, 2, 2.5, 3, or 3.5. These numbers reflect and approximate what happens over time. The longer a promotion lasts, the more people get attracted to a stock. Any promotion that lasts two years usually attracts substantial buying and can have a share price twice as high as the first year's share price. It takes time to develop momentum and critical mass for a truly powerful promotion.

If the stock promotion is still going on in year four, which is very rare, we drop the "T" from our formula to read as follows: Big P=(small p)[(Y)(Z)]. The result for "Big P" will be much lower in year four to reflect the expected share price drop if the company fails to produce promised revenues and earnings.

Do not confuse how long a company has been in business or listed on an exchange with how long the stock promotion has lasted. These are two different things.

3. The Results

Let's try using the formula for these three companies with no earnings, Big P= (small p) [(X) (Y)] (T)

■ Year One—B.H. Beane International: (.30) [(1.7)(11)] (1)=$5.61

■ Year Two—B.H. Beane International: (.30) [(1.7)(11)] (2)= $11.22

■ Year Three—B.H. Beane International: (.30) [(1.7)(11)] (3)=$16.83

■ Black Box Enterprises: (.60) [(-)(-)] (1)= .60

■ Godot: (.02) [(-)(-)] (1)= .02

These results will change over time. Dramatic things can happen. That's why we have developed a computer program so you can update your scores faster. Fill out our two-page order form at the back of the book.

The B.H. Beane International promotion lasted at least three years when it reached a share price of about $25. We were involved during the first two years. Only big rollers should have bought B.H. Beane International in the third year of the promotion. Short sellers were in full operation every step of the way during year two and three that featured severe share price swings.

No unsophisticated investor should buy a penny stock after the second year of a promotion. Most investors get restless and cranky if they wait longer than three and half years for revenues to start flowing to a highly promoted company. The promoters and managers can keep investor expectations bottled for a while. By the third year investors get restless as they demand results, sales, earnings, and great expectations realized.

A share price of $5.61 in year one offered a certain margin of safety even if the price was risky as it moved higher in fits and starts, peaks and valleys. This year one price is absolutely the highest price a Careful or Professional Trader should consider on a penny stock market which probably has lower average prices.

The penny stock trader might have bought B.H. Beane International at well under $11.22 in year two only if he or she was a Diligent Trader, as we were, and had become convinced that the promoter had staying power and energy. You will remember that the share price fluctuated dramatically on its way to $20 in year two. Anybody buying at more than $16.83 in year three could have lost a fortune when the promoter induced several selling panics, when the investing public got bored and sold to collect profits, or when short sellers launched an attack.

Anybody selling from $5.61 all the way up to $20, as a Diligent Trader or Professional Trader, would have made a fortune at a leisurely pace—the goal of all speculators.

We recommend that you reduce all formula figures by 20% to 30% in a highly promoted stock to reduce the danger and risk.

You will remember that we drop the "XY" numbers if the promoter/manager's "Y" score is negative like we did for Black Box and Godot Inc. You should always figure out the "X" score anyway. A company with good fundamentals can get a great promoter.

The Black Box Enterprise promotion, which lasted less than one year, offered investors a margin of safety when the share price was 60 cents. The stock peaked much higher and then dropped very quickly. Any investor who got in at 60 cents or less could have made money rather than lost money as most people did who bought in at much higher prices.

The Waiting For Godot share price of two cents essentially reflects the price of the share throughout the period in question. The stock didn't trade except when Jack and I bought.

■ C. Companies With Earnings

1. The Formulas

Our formula to predict the median share price of a budding growth company *with earnings* offers equally fascinating results. We use Minor Achievement's financial results to illustrate the formula.

■ **Formula One** for companies with earnings:

$$P = (e) [8.5 + 2(X)(Y)]$$

■ **Formula Two** for companies with earnings:

$$P = (e) \left[\frac{37.5 + 8.8(X)(Y)}{i} \right]$$

2. An Explanation of the Formulas

■ i= current and prevailing interest rate for Triple A bonds. When you plug in values for "i" don't use decimal points, just whole numbers. For instance, 8% is not .08 in the formula but 8.

■ e=current earnings per share are $0.03 for Minor Achievement.

■ The "X" represents a factor derived from The Big Picture Test in our Due Diligence Test. This score enhances or discounts the promoter's Personality Background "Y" score. Our "X" factor for Minor Achievement is .77.

■ The "Y" stands for the Personality Background score which reflects the promoter's ability to get things done and his ability to share. Our "Y" score is 21.5.

■ (X)(Y) = growth as a percentage. This corporate growth as a percentage is our *best guess* about what other people believe, what you think will happen, and what might actually happen. We estimate that this company will grow by 16.5% a year in the short term (.77 x 21.5) because a good marketing program can fill all the rooms eventually during peak season.

■ The P is for a median share price that supposedly reflects the value of the stock if the company grows at the (X)(Y) rate.

You'll notice that the shares of a company *with earnings but no growth* will trade at a multiple of 8.5 times earnings in the first formula. At a current interest rate of 8%, the shares of a company *with earnings but no growth* will trade at a multiple of 4.688 times earnings in the second formula.

3. Results

Let's plug in the numbers for Minor Achievement Inc. which is the only company of the four we discussed with earnings. An "X" factor of less than one shows the company is not a growth company. We do, however, assume Minor Achievement might grow during the next few years. The Personal Background "Y" score suggests managers behind Minor Achievement might attract investors to buy other hotels.

Formula One: P = (.03)[8.5 + 2(.77)(21.5)] = $1.24
Formula Two: P = (.03)[37.5+8.8(.77)(21.5) /8] = $0.69

As you can see, Minor Achievement is apparently a reasonable buy below 69 cents and a risky buy between 69 cents and $1.24, and a sell at $1.25. Minor Achievement could trade between 69 cents and $1.24 because many investors will assume the hotel will get higher occupancy levels next year and that managers might raise money to expand soon. You will remember that the current price is around 45 cents to 55 cents. The share price will increase but slowly.

The evaluation for Minor Achievement should be repeated at least twice a year or after every financial statement. Our software package can help you update scores quickly.

The price/earnings ratio (P/E ratio) for Minor Achievement is $1.24 divided by $0.03 equals 41 for formula one and $0.69 divided by $0.03 equals 23 for formula two.

Experts tell us that acceptable price earnings ratio vary over time. Consider the following P/E ratios:

■ a decaying industry: 2.5 to 5
■ stagnant industry: 4 to 10
■ older growth industry: 7.5 to 25
■ vigorous growth industry: 25 to 75
■ growth and glamour industries: 50 to 1,000 (which is nuts!)

Tourism in the Canadian Rockies is still a growth industry which means Minor Achievement is reasonably priced at a P/E ratio near the high end of an older growth industry and the lower end for a vigorous growth industry. The best bet is to consider buying Minor Achievement shares well below 69 cents and ideally between 10 to 20 cents less per share—the current price.

4. Roots

We have adapted our two formulas for penny stock companies *with earnings* from the formulas originally developed by Benjamin Graham, David L. Dodd, and Sidney Cottle.

The formulas are discussed in their 1934 book *Security Analysis* which went through several editions. This book evolved into the easier to understand *Intelligent Investor*, first published in 1950 and last revised in 1973 shortly before Benjamin Graham's death.

These three authors, as fathers of modern security analysis, have influenced an entire generation of value investors including some well known pension and mutual fund managers.

The original Graham-Dodd-Cottle formula for determining what you should pay for a growth company's shares was simple but elegant: P= e [8.5 + 2(g)].

The three analysts, however, reminded all their readers that determining "g" or the growth rate for a company over several years was full of dangers. The "g" depended on many factors including the interest rate, the quality of management, the economic environment, the market, dividend payments, patents, and so on. The original formula was eventually updated to account for the impact of interest rates.

The second formula is still elegant, simple, and exciting:

$$P = (e)\left[\frac{37.5 + 8.8(g)}{i}\right]$$

The challenge, as you might imagine, after a careful review of these formulas is to calculate the value for "g" or the annual percentage growth rate of earnings over the next seven years. We believe we have discovered the answer to this problem.

■ D. THE SOFTWARE PROGRAM

The great mutual and pension fund managers used, or use, their intuitive skills to figure out which companies will grow dramatically to make big money for investors. What about the rest of us now that promotion, hype, and double talk are the norm?

Do you accept the company's promotional literature which claims that the company will grow at 20% per year. Do you accept analyst reports that the company will grow at 10% per year. Do you discount every analyst prediction by half to determine the growth rate? Do you ignore emerging growth companies that have not been reviewed by analysts even though shares trade at lower prices before analysts issue reports?

Will you fill out our Due Diligence Test faithfully with pencil and paper? Will you feel like making changes once you have painstakingly completed it once? Who knows? That is why we have developed a unique software package which you can use on your IBM compatible or Macintosh personal computer. The 3.5 or

5.25 inch disks are designed to help you store information efficiently on each company and to make changes easily and quickly. We think our software program, incorporating the methodology of Chapter 19, *In Search of Warriorpreneurs*, and Chapter 20, *The Vision Continues*, will help you become a good speculator able to pick winners. Just duplicate the two-page order form at the back, complete it, and mail it to us. We will include a free update in the price.

■ E. SOME QUICK TESTS

As you develop your expertise in the market you will discover that the experts have many ways of evaluating companies and stocks. Most of these tests are for more senior companies with earnings and dividends but can apply to many junior companies. We've included a few of them here for fun. You can even use our (X)(Y) scores in one of the tests.

1. Quick Test One:

One of the best ways to figure out if the share price is a candidate for buying or short selling is to ask yourself the following question:

Would my associates and I buy the entire company, if we had the money, at a price equal to the current market value of all outstanding shares (price per share times the number of shares)?

The answer is usually a big fat no. The market capitalization is usually much higher than the book value or even the future earnings potential of the company within the next few years.

2. Quick Test Two:

Determine the share price/cash flow per share ratio? If this ratio is greater than nine think about selling your position. If this ratio is less than nine, consider buying shares. This is one of those mystical-historical rules in the stock market. We offer you this rule as a way to get you to think about more elements than just earnings. Cash flow is harder to fake; earnings can be manipulated.

This ratio is fully explained in the books we suggest for further reading and is often irrelevant for penny stocks that usually have no cash flow.

3. Quick Test Three:

Is the share price/gross sales per share ratio less than 4? If this ratio is less than 4, buy shares. If this ratio is greater than 4, sell your shares. We offer you this rule as another way to get you to think about more elements than just earnings. Sales can't be faked; earnings can be faked.

This ratio is fully explained in the books we suggest for further reading and is also often irrelevant for penny stocks.

4. Quick Test Four

For companies which pay dividends, you might try a formula which mutual fund manager John Neff, we are told, developed and used to get superior results. Add the dividend yield (d) plus the expected growth rate (g) and divide by the price-earnings ratio (p/e). If the result is two or larger than two, buy the stock; if the result is less than two, wait. This formula essentially divides what you might get by what you pay.

A company whose dividend yield is 5%, whose expected growth is 10%, and whose price/earnings ratio is 10 has a result of 1.5 with this formula. This company might not be a good buy.

We won't explore this formula since many growth companies and most penny companies don't have dividends. We do suggest that you might try substituting our $(X)(Y) = g$ factor into this formula. You should be aware also that this strategy requires extreme patience during a period when every stock is too expensive because of speculative frenzy.

◼ F. BACK TO THE STORY

Everybody was silent. I knew I had stunned them.

They were amazed that I could explain the share prices so well with the formulas and numbers from the Due Diligence Test.

I did tell them that I had the benefit of 20-20 hindsight. The trick, of course, is to evaluate accurately a company before the share price moves up or down.

"I knew there was a point to this lunch," Bungee said.

"I want this group of explorers to search out public companies on penny markets and investigate them thoroughly. We will then evaluate them with The Due Diligence Test. If each of us evaluated the same company, the results might all be different. We will, however, agree on the general strengths and weakness of a company which in the end is all we need," I said.

"I am looking for companies whose managers and promoters can make things happen and share the profits with me. What do you say?" I asked.

"Count me in," said Milan. "Your methods might have some merit. I have to get the hang of it. There have to be holes in the theory somewhere," he said.

I agreed.

"There are. The theory has a few rough spots largely because we are trying to do what many think is impossible—to evaluate formally a penny stock company. You can help me work out the bugs. We can work as a team," I said.

"The seeming impossibility of it all shouldn't stop us from trying. We have to approach the Due Diligence Test with a clear head. Beginners are too generous in their evaluations because they don't want to think badly of others. Experienced investors are too cynical or bitter because of their past failures," I said.

"Keep a clear head. Recognize that many questions require intuitive skill. Learn to trust your instinct. Try discounting your final score for $(X)(Y)$ by 20% to 30% until you get the hang of it, just to be safe," I said.

"God knows, we all need an edge in the stock game," said Oswaldo.

"I think The Due Diligence Test and formulas are also valid for emerging growth companies on senior stock exchanges. If analysts have already reviewed a company you like, incorporate their thoughts in The Due Diligence Test," I said.

"There is one problem. Many analysts avoid commenting in writing about a manager's integrity, benevolence, skill, and ability to get things done because of libel laws. The analyst's brokerage firm also needs to keep good relations with major companies and industries. Many analysts use vague and confusing code words to describe company management or ignore the whole topic of management. The analyst might focus heavily on the Big Picture—the economy, market demand for the product, financing, marketing, etc.

"Your goal is to find the good analysts in your brokerage firm and learn how to work with them. Ask analysts how they did on their most recent three or four predictions. The great analysts like to share their information with brokers and clients. Encourage analysts to answer the Due Diligence Test—informally and off the record of course. This will give you a more complete and realistic evaluation of the company. Many good analysts want to co-operate because they need the respect of brokers in their own firm," I said.

"A full analysis of a company has to incorporate subtle details about management's greed, ability to get things done, benevolence, and integrity. An investor owes it to himself or herself to get the real dirt on company management. Short and long term growth for penny and emerging growth companies hinges on the determination, integrity, and skills of the managers much more than on the Big Picture outlook," I said.

My brokers groaned.

"You have no idea about the corporate politics involved in developing an analyst's report. The analysts are under severe pressure from all sides. Their brokerage firm's managers don't want to rock the boat; brokers want the dirt; clients want performance; and public companies need support," they all whined.

"Promise analysts that you won't advertise their personal views on the managers of companies being evaluated. Then make sure you don't. Present your analyst's opinion as your opinion to clients. The analysts can't possibly get in trouble then," I said.

"You are advocating the establishment of two sets of analyst reports—one formal and written, the other informal and verbal. Very few analysts will do that for every broker in the firm because some brokers are major whiners and could ruin an analyst's career," said Bungee.

"Not at all. I'm trying to figure out the *claim to fame/claim to shame* ratio by asking all the hard questions in our Due Diligence Test. The idea is to account for all the good things and divide them by all the bad things. If the number is greater than one then you have a candidate worth watching," I said.

"How many more of these ratios are you going to dream up," Oswaldo asked.

"I hope you don't promote this claim to fame divided by claim to shame ratio to any anal-retentive financial professionals. They don't understand intuitive tests. They are more comfortable with hard numbers," said Oswaldo.

"Work with analysts who have courage and who trust you. The more diligent, honest, and able the managers and promoters, the more investors are attracted," I said.

Vic and Dave just shook their head.

"Oh God! You and Jack don't have families. We can't afford to lose money. I'll play along this year with $1,000. That is all I can afford to speculate," said Dave.

I told him that's all anybody needs if they know what they are doing. Vic waved at the server.

"You amaze me sometimes," Vic said.

"You know my methods, use them. My throat is dry," I said. Vic ordered me a beer.

"I think you are working too hard. Relax a bit. You are starting to sound like Sherlock Holmes," Vic said.

I laughed. Sherlock Holmes could have been a superb penny stock speculator because he understood the diabolical and narcissistic mind.

21 | An Indefinite Conclusion

. . . You've Got To Be Strong

This is a good time to summarize.

Unfortunately, I don't feel like it. Jack and I made so many stock trades, good and bad, that it's hard to prepare a score sheet. So there isn't any point in pretending there is a conclusion to this story—that would be a case of "premature articulation" if you know what I mean. Our story is unfolding. We are ahead of the game and we expect to do better as we learn "The Business". If you stay in touch we'll keep you posted.

Bungee, Milan, Oswaldo, Vic, Dave, Jack, and I are still trying to discover "hot stocks". It's more fun, and the odds are better, than betting on horses, greyhounds, lotteries, bingo, consumer contests, or charity casinos.

Everybody's life is exactly the same as before except for Jack's. His bar has become a big success because he knows how to make people feel at ease. The rest of us are still doing what we have always done even though I never did tell you what Vic, Dave, and I do for a living. Oh well, we'll get into that next time. We always meet in Jack's Bean Stock Bar where the staff has been instructed to charge us "Happy Hour Prices".

But there is one vignette I want to share with you before I sign off. I saw Holstein on the street during lunch a few months after he came back from his holidays with his wife. I was standing on a street corner waiting for the light to turn when he walked up while talking on his cellular phone and holding his cigar in his other hand. I said hello. He looked at me. Then he recognized me.

"Jack's friend," he said.

"Mr. Holstein," I said.

"I'm not that much older than you. My friends call me Bob," he said.

"Bob", I mumbled. We stood there quietly thinking about something witty to say.

"So how's it going?" he asked.

"Good. And it's mainly because of you," I said instinctively, knowing I should have kept my mouth shut.

Holstein looked surprised.

"I just want to thank you for giving us an opportunity to learn so much during your stock promotion," I said.

"You made money?" he asked slowly. I nodded. He was pleased.

"Good, very good. A lot of people whine because they don't make as much money as they think they should or they think they deserve. Their greed makes them crazy," he said. I nodded sympathetically and avoided mentioning all the people who lost money on his promotions.

"Everybody thinks the world, society, government, or God owes them something. I have news for them. Nobody gave me anything until I went out to get it. That's the way it is. Sometimes you have to take," he said warming to his topic with just a slight edge in his voice.

I laughed. I couldn't help myself. I recognized, in that moment, that Holstein was a product of many hard to understand motivations. The only thing I could do was enjoy his company and keep my distance. If I got any closer to him I knew he could trample me by accident or by design.

He was waiting for me to explain why I laughed.

"You are right, of course. Some of us just don't know how to get what we want, how to close a deal, or how to take what's ours. So you shouldn't mind if some people need to keep a close eye on you for a chance to piggyback their way to a fortune," I said. He laughed.

"Are you still driving your eight cylinder domestic car?" he asked. I nodded, surprised that he remembered our conversation from the first time we met.

"I got rid of all my fancy imported cars. I've leased three domestic cars. I'm not sure I'll enjoy them as much. But I tell everybody your story about domestic eight cylinders being superior to imported four cylinders. Everybody thinks I'm a patriot," he laughed.

"No way," I said.

"Yes way," he said.

"You and the rest of the piggies can go for a ride on my back whenever you want. In fact, I'll give you lots of advance warning the next time I start a stock promotion. Just keep it confidential," he said while looking me in the eye. He half smiled. He knew that *I knew* that he knew that I would discuss his new deal with everyone.

Then he said something about chicken droppings, poultry manure, incineration, steam, and electrical energy. I didn't understand a word of it. I did know that I would get the full story about his new stock promotion soon enough. There was no rush in *scooping* this information, if you know what I mean. He invited me to visit him any time I needed advice. I believed him. Then Holstein said goodbye. People like me helped him get ahead. I felt good—not because I had a new friend, which I didn't, but because I knew I was on the right track. I understood what so few people understand. If you want to get rich you have to make your own deals. The Rampaging Bulls can be involved, but at a distance so they can't trample you by accident or design.

I knew his "hot tips" in the future might be nothing more than lies and that he would behave the same way he has always behaved in the past—like the Rampaging Bull that he is. But I could approach him anytime to bounce around business ideas and get his criticisms, if not his money.

I was happy because he knew that I knew all this. I was no longer a Naive Beginner. The Rampaging Bull would now look me in the eye and be wary. I am a step closer to understanding the heart of darkness and the secret of success. My adventure is just beginning.

And then I did something stupid. Just before we parted I asked him something I had meant to ask the first time I met him.

"Bob, what does the B.H. in the company name stand for?" I asked. Holstein laughed loudly.

"You mean Jack never told you! Bob Holstein's 'magical' Beane stock," he said while laughing his way across the street. I couldn't believe it. Jack and Oswaldo both knew this and had neglected to tell me. I heard Holstein laughing a half-block away. I was pissed off.

What else can I tell you?

There is one thing. Two months later I saw Holstein drive by in his car. I waved. He waved and laughed—like a small boy caught in a lie. I laughed also. He was driving a fancy-schmanzy four cylinder imported car. Some people can never change their behaviour. You and I have to *recognize* this reality and *beat* the Rampaging Bulls at their own game.

22 | The Epilogue

. . . The Rampaging Bull Is Everywhere

You might have guessed by now that we think the Rampaging Bulls are causing most of the world's problems. This is a very personal opinion which we didn't emphasize earlier. We have dedicated this book to making you a better speculator in the penny stock market, not changing the world.

Yet the stock market is a microcosm of the whole world. If it's true in the stock market, it's true in other segments of society. If the Rampaging Bull is a danger in the stock market, then the Rampaging Bull is a danger everywhere.

Unfortunately, you can't beat the Rampaging Bulls elsewhere as easily as you can in the stock market. But this doesn't mean that you and I shouldn't try. We want to maintain peace, order, and good government.

We do, however, recognize that we have to be realistic. Maybe my favourite rock star Bruce Springsteen is right when he sings his hit tune, *Human Touch*:

> "Tell me in a world without pity,
> Do you think what I'm askin's too much,
> I just want something to hold on to,
> And a little of that human touch,
> Just a little of that human touch."

◼ A. THE EARLIEST RAMPAGING BULLS

The Rampaging Bulls have been around for a long time. Consider the Old Testament *Book of Ecclesiastes* which scholars think to be the pen name of Solomon (King of Israel 973 B.C. - 933 B.C., ancestor of Jesus).

Ecclesiastes, which means member of the legislative assembly in Greek, says he is depressed because the world is full of malignant narcissistic "jerks" who take advantage of defenceless people. Consider his thoughts:

■ "The oppressed are crying and no one helps them. The oppressors have power on their side. I envy those who are dead and gone. They are better off than those who are alive."

■ "It is better to have only a little, with peace of mind, than to be busy all the time with both hands trying to catch the wind."

■ "Don't be surprised when you see government oppress the poor and deny them justice. Every official is protected by the one over him and both are protected by still higher officials."

■ "People save up their money for when they need it, lose it all in some deal, and finish with nothing for their children."

■ "I have seen wicked people buried and in their graves, but on the way back from the cemetery people praise them."

■ "Stupid people are given positions of authority."

■ "Only someone too stupid to find his way home would wear himself out with work."

■ "Dead flies can make a whole bottle of perfume stink."

■ "As long as people live, their minds are full of evil and madness. Then they die."

Ecclesiastes, though he wasn't a happy camper as an Old Testament king, was humble and more hip than any modern commentator. Was he or was he not warning us about The Rampaging Bulls?

Ecclesiastes, who was also a terrific speculator, advised his clients to invest in foreign trade and to diversify investments in case of war. We think he would have made a fortune in the modern stock market.

The father of modern economics, Adam Smith (1723-1790), said that businesspersons often conspire to limit free trade and a free market. Here's the exact quotation: "People of the same trade seldom meet together, even for merriment and diversion, but the conversation ends in a conspiracy against the public or in some contrivance to raise prices." *Wealth Of Nations,* Vol. I, Book I, Ch. 10, Part 2.

Wasn't Smith, the father of capitalist economic theory, warning us about malignant narcissistics? about the Rampaging Bulls? about giving anyone absolute power? Isn't his warning playing itself out every day? Smith wanted us to free markets which would make it impossible for the malignant narcissistics to take over!

Karl Marx (1818-1883), a mentally disordered man who ignored his own family's well being, constantly raged against evil malignant narcissistics! He even designed a plan to outlaw businesspersons as a class of people because he thought they were supremely evil. His plan backfired as the malignant narcissistics and psychopaths changed their way of doing business by joining his movement. Former businessmen and other hangers on, as malignant narcissistics, subverted, converted, and took over his movement to enslave half the world. These political busybodies killed 50 to 100 million people in many countries as part of their evangelization.

The history of religious organizations has countless perverse examples of how malignant narcissistics made people suffer for pleasure—certainly not for the glory of God.

The New Testament *Book of Revelation* warns us about the soon to arrive " hot" promoter with a big mark on his head. This "hot" promoter is supposed to seduce us into a stupid promotion on our way to "hell". There are so many stupid promotions, including the "New World Order" movement, that they may all be connected by computer modem to the *Prince Of Darkness.* Isn't the New Testament warning us about malignant narcissistics?

If you review the books and movies we recommend in our abridged reference list you will see that virtually every great thinker and writer has been preoccupied with this topic.

You would think that we, as a species which wants to survive, might have learned how to handle supremely arrogant and malignant people in the past 3,000 years. So why haven't we?

■ B. HANDLING THEM IS HARD!

The narcissists, malignant or not, are almost impossible to handle. You can't appeal to the Rampaging Bull's humanity. These people are heartless. You have to resist and/or defeat the heartless—not reform them!

Biologists, zoologists, anthropologists, and historians tell us that one in 20 or five percent of people exhibit "dominant traits". The literature on this is enormous. These "dominant" people usually *need* to be boss, sit in huge chairs, make big decisions, bang their desks, and be liked by people they abuse.

We shouldn't conclude that all "dominant" people are personality disordered. This would be far fetched for anybody to conclude. But have you *ever* met a "dominant" person who behaves in a benevolent, kindly, humane or "normal" manner? People who have a *deep need* to be boss do *not* qualify as "normal" people regardless of what this word means to you. Dominant people, personality disordered or not, tend to abuse "friends", associates, employees, spouses, children, cats, dogs, old people, and the environment. Perhaps what passes for the modern personality disorder may be nothing more than psychology's way of defining the "highly twisted" version of the dominant person.

So how do you cure or handle this person? You can't.

Most people shrug their shoulders and say "that's the way it is". Other people join political movements managed by "good" narcissistics to get rid of "bad" narcissistics. This usually makes more problems than it solves.

If you are involved in business as an ethical person, there is only one thing you can do in an uncharitable environment: pick the battlefield. Arrange to compete with malignant narcissistics in an open market, like the stock market.

You are, usually, on your own.

You can also help yourself and your family by *being* self-reliant which can include some very energetic initiatives; *teaching* others how to be self-reliant; *helping* the weak; and *not* being seduced by countless pop culture promotions which want to scoop your hard earned dollars.

There are other defences. We offer them as secondary options and/or for your personal enjoyment:

■ **The Scrooge Gambit**—Summon the ghosts of Christmas Past to terrify the malignant narcissistic into reforming like Ebeneezer Scrooge in Charles Dickens' story, *A Christmas Carol*. This is hard to do in a clinical setting at 4:30 p.m. on a sunny afternoon.

■ **Watch Less Television**—The malignants have taken over the tube and pushed out almost every wholesome program. There are so many perverse programs about abuse, betrayal, murder, and mayhem that we don't understand how anybody can claim children aren't being affected?

■ **Union Option**—Support the union movement and help union members fight against two sets of malignant narcissistics who have set themselves up as employers and as "supposed" union leaders. If it isn't one damn thing, it's another.

■ **The Good Man/Good Woman Initiative**—Every non-union company has at least "one good man" willing to stand firm against the rage of the malignant narcissistics. Support and promote this one good man or woman who will defeat the Rampaging Bulls as a fair, benevolent, courageous, and able leader.

■ **The Wild West Solution**—Run the malignant narcissistics out of town if they don't own the town. If the malignant narcissistics own the town, then you leave. Don't run. Leave slowly on horseback, down the centre of mainstreet, your gun hand hanging loosely by your thigh, and your guns in full view. This is a much more popular solution throughout the world than you might think. This solution explains why there will be problems in the world for the next 1,000 years.

■ **Start Your Own Company**—You can develop a hiring policy which screens out the Rampaging Bulls? Why not? They don't want to work for you anyway. They want to take your company and kick you out. Nobody will ever accuse you of discrimination. Remember to keep your organization lean and mean, under 20 people.

■ **Be Realistic**— You have to contol your expectations of people as you develop a few "supportive and loving" friends. You will never have more than a "handful of friends" because *you* won't devote time for this unless you are a very rare person.

■ C. PROBLEMS CAUSED BY BULLS

The Rampaging Bulls cause problems everywhere. Consider these examples:

First: *Newsweek* reports that as many as 100 million people live in bondage despite shrieking denials from the many guilty countries. Four *Newsweek* correspondents, apparently, spent 1991 interviewing people living in bondage throughout Africa and Asia. If you pull out your calculator you'll discover that 100 million slaves represents two percent of the world's population. What about all the other people who are living in near bondage? in feudalism? in debt? in poverty?

Are not slave owners personality disordered malignant narcissistics? Are governments which protect slave owners malignant narcissistic? Should these countries be expelled from the community of nations? Will there be a community of nations if all the abusive slave owning states are booted out? If your country does business with a country that allows slave ownership, feudalism, and rampant abuse is your country an accessory to a major crime against humanity?

Second: The U.S. Congressional Budget Office, The Federal Reserve Board, *The New York Times*, and economists at The Massachusetts Institute of Technology tell us the richest one percent of households are scooping more than their fair share of the economic pie however you define the phrase "fair share". Consider this:

- The *top one percent* of households in the U.S. increased their ownership of all private net worth from 31 percent to 37 percent from 1983 to 1989.
- The *top one percent* of households increased their family incomes by 77 percent from $315,000 to $560,000 from 1977 to 1989.
- The *average* household income in the U.S. grew 4 percent to $36,000 during this time period.
- The income of the *bottom* 40 percent of households in the U.S. actually dropped in this period.
- The *bottom* 90 percent of households, now about 84 million, own $4.8 trillion in net worth (after you deduct liabilities).
- The *top one percent* of households, now about 834,000, own $5.7 trillion in net worth (after you deduct liabilities). Good grief!

Doesn't this explain why voters are cranky and become involved in riots, demonstrations, and other surly behaviour. Doesn't this explain the burning of Detroit in 1967 or Los Angeles in 1965 and 1992 by poor people. This surly behaviour, by the way, is happening in every country which has wealth and income statistics similar to that of the U.S.—one of the many rich countries that have perfected public piety and private greed into a refined art.

These skewed income results *do not* prove that one percent of U.S. citizens, or citizens of other countries with similar statistics, deserve all the money because they are so talented. These results prove these unfair income and ownership statistics can happen only because of three reasons:

- A lot of narcissistic people, malignant or not, are actively lobbying law makers in an aggressive, vicious, and self-indulgent way to stack the rules in their favour.
- A lot of narcissistic people, malignant or not, are concocting some very successful promotions to scoop all the money.
- A lot of narcissistic people, malignant or not, are trying both strategies: concocting successful promotions *and* lobbying law makers to stack the odds in their favour.

Isn't anyone, by definition, who actively tries to scoop all the money anti-social and narcissistic? You tell me!

Third: The richest twenty percent of the world's population has increased its share of wealth and/or gross domestic product and/or money by 12 percent from 70.2 percent in 1970 to 82.7 percent in 1992 according to *the* United Nations Human Development Report.

The poorest 60 percent of the world's population has lost ground and now has about six percent of the world's wealth and/or gross domestic product and/or money. This is tragic.

Are most of the world's people stupid, undeserving, incompetent? The answer, clearly, is no. The richest countries got that way because they have better weather, more resources, fewer disease carrying pests, fewer tropical storms, fewer deserts, fewer droughts, fewer locusts, fewer jungles, and other factors in their favour.

The world's ordinary people are starving, sick, and abused. About 20 percent of the world's 5.4 billion people in 1992 (8.3 billion by 2020 AD) are physically sick or malnourished in any two week period according to the World Health Organization. About 50 million people, or one percent of the population, die from disease every year according to the World Health Organization.

The top 10 diseases from the most common to least common are hepatitis B, tuberculosis, anemia, hookworm, roundworm, diarrheal diseases, whipworm, malaria, iodine deficiency, and schistosomiasis.

Parasitic diseases, for instance, are so widespread that entire regions of the world are being laid waste. In fact parasites may be the biggest danger to the security and existence of homo sapiens in Africa, Asia, South America and many parts of southern Europe. Tourist guide books, which are full of lies, never discuss this nightmare of disease that plagues most of the world.

The richest countries are also rich because they have conspired and lobbied to keep the poorest countries poor by not sharing wealth. The World Bank says trade restrictions reduce poor countries' income by $75-billion each year. This is more than poor countries receive in foreign aid. The poor countries will continue to be poor!

Aren't leaders of rich countries self indulgent malignant narcissistics? Aren't you and I, who live in the rich countries, an accessory to this greedy behaviour by our leaders who are casting a dark shadow on our future? What are our leaders afraid of? Sharing? Losing votes?

Won't narcissistic behaviour by the richest countries create more unrest, civil war, terrorism, insurrection, riots, desperation, and screaming headlines as the poor lash back? What happened to charity? benevolence? the spirit of Christmas? Leaders of rich countries will be inspiring riots wherever they visit.

I can't believe leaders in the European Economic Community, the U.S., and Japan are discussing a "New World Order". The world's biggest countries are talking about power, money, networking, and a new cartel. This is completely nuts! This is also what Adam Smith, father of capitalist thought, predicted would keep happening over and over again. Only malignant narcissistics who don't care about the *dark record* of the past 78 years can dream about this! The "New World Order" promoters, in short, want to scoop as much as they can for themselves and their tribes as they create "New Narcissism", "New Imperialism", and "New Abuse." They don't care about the wars they will cause again and again. The world is going to be in more trouble during the next 100 years than it has been during the previous 100 years. The rich will continue to build barriers against the eight billion poor people expected on the planet in less than 40 years. Nothing is changing! "Ordinary" people, however you define them, will continue to be crushed the way they always have. Ecclesiastes' words, or the wisdom of Solomon, may ring true forever.

■ **Fourth:** *Newsweek* also says seven percent of male psychiatrists and three percent of female psychiatrists in the U.S. *admitted* to abusing, usually sexually, their patients.

"Even more disturbing, 65 percent of therapists said they had treated patients who had been sexually involved with previous therapists—nobody knows how widespread abuse of patients is because studies rely on *anonymous* surveys," *Newsweek* also reported.

How many mental health professionals are self-indulgent, vain, critical, perfectionist, greedy, easily angered, abusive, unfeeling, and controlling people? We think one to ten percent! Isn't a therapist who abuses patients, by definition, himself or herself a mentally disordered anti-social?

■ **Fifth:** Adults who abuse children are by definition, we think, personality disordered, psychopathic, or suffering from some other serious mental disorder, curable or incurable. Child abusers as a rule, we think, don't understand what they are doing and/or have little emotion or feeling for others. They are totally preoccupied with themselves which means they are narcissistic, malignant or not.

"Child abusers have trouble relating to other people. They treat others like objects to be used," say representatives of the Sexual Behaviour Clinic in Kingston, Canada. The clinic also says that the number of abusers has not been reliably estimated.

The Toronto *Globe and Mail* newspaper reports: "The multiple child abuser is *far removed* from the stereotype of a trench coated pervert nosing around school yards. The child abuser is likely to be a community leader who is well established and respected as a volunteer organizer of camping trips, sports events, or music and drama lessons."

Child abuse, by the way, *includes* the controlling and mean-spirited parental and institutional behaviour made famous by writers Charles Dickens and Mark Twain, in novels such as *Great Expectations, Tom Sawyer, Oliver Twist,* and *Huckleberry Finn.* Their ideas on child abuse have been mirrored in countless books and movies including those starring Shirley Temple who always made me cry. Poor Shirley Temple! She always had a malignant narcissistic guardian to defeat! Yet these themes are still relevant.

The International Labour Organizaton tells us that 10% to 30% of the world's children are forced to work long hours in abusive conditions. Are the employers and governments which allow this malignant narcissistic? psychopathic?

The U.S. National Committee for Prevention of Child Abuse tells us that about 2.7 million cases of child abuse were *reported* in the United States during 1991. Let's assume the U.S. population is about 250 million; there are 2.5 people per home; one case of reported child abuse occurs per home; and five cases of child abuse are not reported for every one that is. This might mean five to 10 percent or more homes are "managed" by dominant and/or personality disordered people who abuse children.

Some Canadian mental health groups estimate that all forms of child abuse are much higher and almost an epidemic as one in four girls and one in six boys under 18 are abused mentally and/or physically. The British Columbia Health Ministry, for instance, studied 30 Canadian multiple child abusers who molested 2,099 children. The abused continue the cycle of violence and abuse others. Can this cycle of abuse reach a point in the next 100 years when every other child on the planet is abused physically or mentally? What a thought.

■ **Sixth:** What about spouse abuse? Are people who abuse their spouses anti-social personality disordered? How many of these people are there? How do they behave with others in their professional career? Can a wife beating public prosecutor perform his duties adequately?

■ **Seventh:** More than a dozen nations and tribes have suffered one hundred million people killed in genocidal frenzy this century at the hands of religious, political, and ethnic malignant narcissistic and psychopathic leaders. Yet there is a world wide conspiracy by twisted intellectuals to deny *any* genocide ever took place on planet earth. Homo sapiens are obviously having problems accepting the idea that there is a small, but powerful and unfeeling, percentage of their kind determined to rape and pillage forever.

■ D. FINAL COMMENT

You may have to "gird your loins" like an Old Testament warrior for your own personal struggle to improve yourself and for the apolitical rage of the poor during the next 50 years as the world's population doubles to 10 billion.

I'm confident that you can evolve, change, help the poor, and justify the ancient belief that "this is a still a beautiful world despite all the sham and drudgery". Unfortunately, a self-improvement program requires constant effort—something which few people want to do and no malignant narcissistic is even considering. No wonder some futurists are already telling us that homo sapiens will become extinct faster than dinosaurs—flatulence or no flatulence.

Hunter S. Thompson (author, atypical American, a dedicated non-member, recluse, and rebel with a cause) may have been right all along. The "hypocrites, degenerates, and atavistic bastards" may have already taken over. Thompson echoes playwright William Shakespeare who said "the mass of men lead lives of quiet desperation". This is identical to Ecclesiastes.

While we wait for planet Earth to self-immolate you might consider the following:

■ Make money on the stock market and help somebody!

■ Work with entrepreneurs running small companies to escape the "horrors" of the big companies.

■ Stand up to Rampaging Bulls like the warrior that you are. It will hurt at first. You will eventually learn how to do it with a sure step and perhaps even enjoy it.

You will know when you have arrived because you won't have a membership in any organization; you'll team up with a few like-minded friends who believe excellence is a worthy goal and can be achieved only in small groups; and you'll be ready to "short sell" the Rampaging Bull's position.

I am starting a physical fitness program. I have to be in shape to write my next book and to beat the Rampaging Bulls and Criminal Incompetents wherever I find them.

23 | # An Eclectic Reference

. . . With Appropriate Comments

FICTION

▪ Charles Dickens (1812-1870), **The Christmas Carol** (1843); also several classic movies—a Rampaging Bull repents, after seeing terrifying ghosts, and becomes benevolent; only known cure for narcissism.

▪ Fyodor Mikhailovich Dostoyevsky (1821-1881), **The Brothers Karamazov** (1879-1880); **Crime and Punishment** (1886)—an indictment of narcissism and unfeeling intellectual snobbery.

▪ Samual Langhorne Clemens a.k.a. Mark Twain (1835-1910), **Huckleberry Finn** (1884); **The Man That Corrupted Hadleyburg** (1900)—about malignant narcissism, moral decay, con men, and lynch mobs.

▪ Sir Arthur Conan Doyle (1859-1930), **Sherlock Holmes** (1887-1927)—a consulting detective and biographer tackle malignant narcissistics.

▪ Rudyard Kipling (1865-1936), **The Man Who Would Be King** (1889); Nobel Prize 1907; also a movie—two engaging narcissistic confidence men dupe a small nation into making them Godkings but forget to get out in time.

▪ Fingal O'Flahertie Wills a.k.a Oscar Wilde (1854-1900), **The Portrait Of Dorian Gray** (1891)—a malignant narcissistic deals with the devil and gets rich.

▪ Abraham Stoker (1847-1912), **Dracula** (1897)—a malignant narcissistic/psychopathic, but charming, con man sucks blood and controls others.

■ **Robin Hood,** circa 1377 in Peirs Plowman and ballads of the day; also major 1922, 1938, and 1991 movies—a local hero and friends free their country from a malignant narcissistic prince and sheriff.

■ Margaret Mitchell, **Gone With The Wind** (1936); 1937 Pulitzer Prize; a narcissistic, "partially" psychopathic southern beauty needs to dominate.

■ **Citizen Kane,** 1940; directed by and starring Orson Wellcs (1915-1985); nominated for nine Academy Awards—a malignant narcissistic makes money and abuses everyone.

■ Samuel Beckett, **Waiting For Godot** (1952, 1956); 1969 Nobel Prize— "theatre of the absurd" play about people who learn about themselves while waiting for something to happen.

■ **The Invasion Of The Body Snatchers**; 1956 and 1978 movies directed by Don Siegel and Philip Kaufman—a paranoid conspiracy to replicate and replace humans by unfeeling aliens.

■ Mordecai Richler, **The Apprenticeship of Duddy Kravitz** (1959); also a 1974 movie—a narcissistic youth wants to own land and win respect.

■ Anthony Burgess, **A Clockwork Orange** (1962); also a 1971 movie directed by Stanley Kubrick; a New York Film Critics Best Film Award—a malignant narcissistic and/or psychopathic rapist punk tries to reform.

■ Aleksandr Isayevich Solzenitsyn, **A Day in The Life Of Ivan Denisovich** (1962); **Cancer Ward** (1968); **Gulag Archipelago** (1973-1976); 1970 Nobel Prize—chronicles spread of malignant narcissistic and psychopathic behaviour.

■ Mario Puzo, **The Godfather** (1969); also Academy Award winning movies—cranky malignant narcissistics like to own everything and have their hands kissed.

■ Robertson Davies, **Fifth Business** (1970)—two friends drift apart as one pursues his narcissistic quest for fame and fortune while the other pursues a spiritual life.

■ **The Sting** (1973); directed by George Roy Hill; seven Academy Awards—two loveable con men turn the tables on narcissistic personality disordered mobsters.

■ **The Tin Men** (1987); directed by Barry Levinson—two malignant narcissistic but strangely endearing aluminum siding salesmen prey on naive homeowners.

■ **Wall Street** (1987); directed by Oliver Stone; one Academy Award—a malignant narcissistic corrupts everyone he meets.

■ **Dirty Rotten Scoundrels** 1988); directed by Frank Oz; starring Steve Martin and Michael Caine—narcissistic weasels have fun.

■ Tom Wolfe, **Bonfire of the Vanities** (1990); also 1991 movie—malignant narcissistic gets punished.

■ **Other People's Money** 1991 movie; based on play by Jerry Sterner—a short malignant narcissistic abuses everyone while eating donuts in stretch limousines.

NON-FICTION

■ **Kong Fu Zi a.k.a Confucius** (551-479 B.C.), **The Analects**—how to achieve success and peace.

■ **Lao Tze** (6th century B.C.), **Tao Te Ching (The Way Of Life)**—how to achieve success and peace.

■ **Old Testament** (with special reference to **Ecclesiastes**)—how to defeat malignant narcissistics.

■ Apostles Matthew, Mark, Luke, John, and Paul, **The New Testament**—how to achieve success and peace.

■ Christian monks, **The Philokalia** (circa 200 A.D.)—how to achieve success and peace.

■ Niccolo Machiavelli (1469-1527), **The Prince** (1513)—realistic suggestions about achieving success in a world plagued by narcissists.

■ Adam Smith (1723-1790), **An Inquiry Into The Nature And Cause Of The Wealth Of Nations** (1776)—how to defeat malignant narcissistics disguised as businessmen.

- Charles Mackay (1814-1889), **Extraordinary Popular Delusions And The Madness Of Crowds** (1841)—malignant narcissists seduce people into war.
- Karl Marx (1818-1883) and Friedrich Engels (1820-1895), **The Communist Manifesto** (1847) and **Das Capital** (1867); Friedrich Wilhelm Nietzsche (1844-1900), **Also Sprach Zarathustra** (1883-85); Adolf Hitler (1889-1945), **Mein Kampf** (Vol. 1, 1925 and Vol. 2, 1926)—four busybody psychos and/or malignant narcissistics plan to enslave mankind.
- Montague Summers, **The Vampire in Europe** (1929)—in his words "a review of the monstrous things just beneath the surface of our cracking civilization"; in our words, how people explained narcissists and psychopaths before they understood them.
- Benjamin Graham (1894-1976), **The Intelligent Investor** (Harper & Row, 1949, revised frequently until 1973)— by Benjamin Graham, David L. Dodd, Sidney Cottle, and Charles Tatham— how to find value before everyone else.
- John Maynard Keynes (1883-1946), **General Theory of Employment, Interest, and Money** (Harcourt, 1936)—how to promote your way out of economic depression by getting people to spend their money before anybody notices the debt.
- Melanie Klein, **Contributions to Psychoanalysis** (McGraw Hill,1964)— insights into borderline personalities.
- George J.W. Goodman a.k.a. "Adam Smith", **The Money Game** (Random House, 1967); **Supermoney** (Random House, 1972)—how to be a winner by understanding the big picture.
- Robert Ringer, **Winning Through Intimidation** (Los Angeles Book Publishing Co., 1973)—how to defeat malignant narcissistics and become a warrior.
- Otto Kernberg, **Borderline Conditions and Pathological Narcissism** (Jason Aronson Press, 1975)—a learned work.
- Christopher Lasch, **The Culture Of Narcissism** (W.W. Norton Company, 1978)—a deep book about malignant narcissistics.
- Tom Peters, Robert Waterman, **In Search of Excellence** (Warner, 1982)—A noble effort but impossible for most big companies.

■ Burton Malkiel, **Random Walk Down Wall Street** (W.W. Norton Co., 1973); **Winning Investment Strategies** (W.W. Norton, 1982)—excellent review of the efficient market theory.

■ Jeffrey Little and Lucien Rhodes, **Understanding Wall Street** (Liberty Hall Press, 1978, 1980, 1987, 1991)—an authentic handbook.

■ M. Scott Peck, **The People Of The Lie: The Hope For Healing Human Evil** (Simon and Schuster, 1983)—best description of evil.

■ Colin Wilson, **A Criminal History Of Mankind** (Grafton Books, 1984)—how malignant narcissists destroyed and will destroy everything.

■ Jerrold.Maxmen, M.D., **The New Psychiatry** (New American Library, 1985)—an update on the conventional wisdom.

■ Kenneth Fisher, **The Wall Street Waltz** (Contemporary Books, 1987)—90 stock market charts, covering two hundred years.

■ Hunter S. Thompson, **Songs Of The Doomed** (1990); **Generation Of Swine** (1988); **The Great Shark Hunt** (1979); **Fear And Loathing In Las Vegas** (1971)—manic stories about malignant narcissistics.

■ Diane Francis, **Contrapreneurs** (Bantam-Seal Books, 1988)—a review of Canadian Criminal Incompetents.

■ Peter Lynch with John Rothchild, **One Up On Wall Street,** (Simon & Schuster, 1989)—superb investing tips for senior stocks and markets before analysts get involved.

■ Richard Saul Wurman, Alan Siegel, and Ken Morris, **The Wall Street Journal Guide to Understanding Money & Markets** (Prentice Hall Press, 1990)—an intriguing graphic explanation.

■ Richard Goldfarb, **Bluff Your Way In Psychology** (Centennial Press, 1990)—an entertaining review for Naive Beginners.

■ M. Hirsh Goldberg, **The Book Of Lies: History's Greatest Fakes, Frauds, Schemes, and Scams** (Quill Book, 1990)—title covers it.

24

Financial Sources

. . . Randomly Selected List

NORTH AMERICA

CANADA

- **Toronto Stock Exchange**, 2 First Canadian Place, Toronto, Ontario, M5X 1J2; Fax: 416-947-4662.
- **Montreal Stock Exchange**, Box 61, 800 Victoria Square, Montreal, Quebec, H4Z 1A9; Fax: 514-871-3533.
- **Vancouver Stock Exchange**, Box 10333, 609 Granville St., Vancouver, British Columbia, V7Y 1H1; Fax: 604-688-6051.
- **Winnipeg Stock Exchange**, 2901—One Lombard Place, Winnipeg, Manitoba, R3B 0Y2; Fax: 204-947-9536.
- **Alberta Stock Exchange**, 21 Floor, 300 Fifth Ave. S.W., Calgary, Alberta, T2P 3C4; Fax: 403-237-0450.

USA

- **Boston Stock Exchange**, One Boston Place, 38 Floor, Boston, MA 02108, USA; Fax: 617-523-6603.
- **Cincinnati Stock Exchange**, 49 East 4th Street, Suite 205, Cincinnati, OH; Fax: 513-621-4963.
- **Document Retrieval** from SEC and at least a dozen companies including Bechtel, 1570 Shady Grove Rd., Gaithersburg, Maryland, 20877, Phone: 301-258-4300; or Disclosure Inc., 5161 River Rd., Building 60, Bethesda, Maryland, 20817, 301-951-1300.
- **Midwest Stock Exchange**, 440 LaSalle St., Chicago, IL 60605, USA; Fax: 312-663-2162

■ **National Association of Securities Dealers (NASDAQ)**, 1735 K St. NW, Washington, DC 20006-1506, USA; Fax: 202-293-6260.

■ **Pacific Stock Exchange**, 310 Pine St., San Francisco, California, 94104 and 233 South Beaudry Ave. Los Angeles, California; Fax: 415-393-4202.

■ **Philadelphia Stock Exchange**, 1900 Market St., Philadelphia, PA 19103, USA; Fax: 215-496-5653.

■ **Pink Sheets**, an over the counter trading network for 20,000 companies managed by privately owned National Quotation Bureau, Jersey City, NJ.

■ **The Securities and Exchange Commission (SEC)**, Public Reference Branch, 450 Fifth St. N.W., Washington, D.C., 20549, USA; several services and publications available.

■ **United States Department of State**, Country Officers, 2201-C St. N.W., Washington, D.C., 20250; Phone: 202-632-9552; experts offer background information on foreign countries.

■ **COSTA RICA - National Stock Exchange**, Box 1736-1000, San Jose; Fax: 506-55-0131.

■ **MEXICO - Mexican Stock Exchange**, Reforma 255, Colonia Cuauhtemoc, CP 06500, Mexico DF; Fax: 52-5-5-91-05-34.

PACIFIC OCEAN

■ **AUSTRALIA - Australian Stock Exchange**, 9 Floor, 87-95 Pitt St., Sydney, NSW 2000; Fax: 61-2-235-0056.

■ **NEW ZEALAND - New Zealand Stock Exchange**, 8 Floor, Caltex Tower, 286-292 Lambton Quay,Wellington; Fax: 64-4-731-470.

■ **PHILIPPINES - Manila Stock Exchange**, Prensa Corner Muelle de la Industria, Binondo, Manila; Fax: 63-2-47-11-25.

EUROPE

■ **FRANCE - Paris Stock Exchange**, Societe des Bourses Francaises, 4, Place de la Bourse, F-75080 Paris Cedex 02; Fax: 33-1-40-26-31-40.

■ **GERMANY** - **Frankfurt Stock Exchange**, Borsenplatz, Postfach 10-08-11, D-6000, Frankfurt-am-Main 1; Fax: 49-69-2197-455.

■ **GREECE** - **Athens Stock Exchange**, 10 Sophocleous St., 105 59 Athens,; Fax: 30-1-3213983.

■ **DENMARK** - **Copenhagen Stock Exchange**, Nikolaj Plads Six, Box 1040, 1007 Copenhagen K; Fax: 45 33 12 86 13.

■ **ITALY** - **Milan Stock Exchange**, Via Camperio, 4, 20123 Milano; fax: 39-2-8534-4640.

■ **NETHERLANDS** - **The Amsterdam Stock Exchange**, Beursplein 5, 1012 JW Amsterdam; Fax: 31-20-24-80-62.

■ **SPAIN** - **Barcelona Stock Exchange**, Paseo Isabel II no.1, 08003 Barcelona; Fax: 34-3-401-37-57.

■ **UK AND IRELAND** - **International Stock Exchange Of The United Kingdom and The Republic Of Ireland (ISE)**, The Stock Exchange, Old Broad St., London, EC2N 1HP, United Kingdom; Fax: 44-71-374-0504.

CARIBBEAN

■ **BARBADOS** - **Securities Exchange of Barbados**, 6 Floor, Central Bank Building, Church Village, St. Michael; Fax: 809-429-8942.

■ **JAMAICA** - **Jamaica Stock Exchange**, Box 621 Bank of Jamaica Towers, Kingston; Fax: 809-92-25770

AFRICA

■ **KENYA** - **Nairobi Stock Exchange**, Box 43633, Nairobi; Fax: 254-2-729349.

■ **NIGERIA** - **Nigerian Stock Exchange**, 2/4 Customs Street., Box 2457, Lagos; Telex: 23567 STEX NG

■ **SOUTH AFRICA** - **The Johannesburg Stock Exchange**, 17 Diagonal St., Box 1174, Johannesburg, 2000; Fax: 27-11-838-1463.

MIDDLE EAST

■ **ISRAEL** - **Tel-Aviv Stock Exchange**, 54 Ahad Ha'am St., Tel-Aviv 65202, Israel; Fax: 972-3-662704.

■ **JORDAN** - **Amman Financial Market**, Box 8802, Amman, Jordan; Fax: 962-6-686830.

■ **KUWAIT** - **The Kuwait Stock Exchange**, Box 22235, Sufat, 13083; Fax: 965-2420779

ASIA

■ **HONG KONG** - **Hong Kong Stock Exchange**, 1 Floor, One and Two Exchange Square, Central, Hong Kong; Fax: 852-810-4475.

■ **INDIA** - **The Bombay Stock Exchange**, Phiroze Jeejebhoy Towers, Dalal St., Bombay, 400-001; Fax: 91-22-2028121.

■ **JAPAN** - **Nagoya Stock Exchange**, 3-17, Sakae 3-Chome, Naka-ku, Nagoya 460; Fax: 81-52-241-1527.

■ **KOREA** - **Korea Stock Exchange**, 33, Yoido-dong, Young-deungpo-ku, Seoul 150-010; Fax: 82-2-780-6421.

■ **MALAYASIA** - **Kuala Lumpur Stock Exchange**, 3 & 4 Floor, Block A, Exchange Square, Off Jalan Semantan, Damansara Heights, 50490 Kuala Lumpur; Fax: 60-3-255-74-63.

■ **PAKISTAN** - **The Karachi Stock Exchange**, Stock Exchange Building, Stock Exchange Rd., Karachi; Telex: 2746 kasex pk.

■ **SINGAPORE** - **Stock Exchange of Singapore**, 1 Raffles Place, 24-00 OUB Centre, Singapore 0104; Fax: 65-535-0985.

■ **TAIWAN** - **Taiwan Stock Exchange**, 2-10 Floor, City Building, 85 Yen Ping South Rd., Taipei; Fax: 886-2-391-5591.

■ **INDONESIA** - **Jakarta Stock Exchange**, Jalan Medan Merdeka Selatan #14, Jakarta, Pusat 10110; Fax: 61 21 35 04 42.

SOUTH AMERICA

■ **ARGENTINA** - **Buenos Aires Stock Exchange**, Sarmiento 299, 1353, Buenos Aires; Fax: 54-1-312-9332.

■ **BRAZIL** - **Rio de Janeiro Stock Exchange**, Praca XV de Novembro No.20, 20010, Rio de Janeiro, RJ; Fax: 55-21-221-2151.

■ **COLOMBIA** - **Bogota Stock Exchange**, Apartado Aereo 3584, Bogota; Fax: 57-1-281-3170.

■ Thanks

Many very talented and skilled people have contributed to the production of this book and have offered background information in good faith. A few, for many complex reasons, prefer to remain anonymous. We thank everyone who has made this book possible. Any conclusions based on the background information gathered from various sources are solely the responsibility of the author and the publisher.

Production

- ■ Cartoons - Bob Devan
- ■ Cover Design - The Image Brokers, Dean McKenzie, Barry Anderson, Louis Krynski, Dave Whamond.
- ■ Pre-press Production - Colour Four Graphic Services, Fred Potter, Mike Cramer, Sharon Woodward.
- ■ Typesetting and Composition - Network Composition Systems
- ■ Photography - Jude Dillon
- ■ Marketing/Distribution - Ingrid Epp, R. Hlady, H. Cybulski, J. Starkman, P. Rasmussen, M. & R. Mills, S. Thistlethwaite.

Background Information

- ■ Mark Wayne, founder of a $110 million Canadian mutual fund, Chartered Financial Analyst, lawyer.
- ■ Jim Lucyk, president of Clarendon Investments Inc., engineer, businessman.
- ■ Brad Denis, a professional stockbroker with Burns Fry Ltd.
- ■ Don Ritchie, floor trader for 25 years on three stock exchanges - Montreal, Vancouver, and currently Alberta.
- ■ Tony Fulgenzi, a professional stockbroker with McDermid, St. Lawrence, Chisholm Ltd.
- ■ Kathleen Jost, national director and manager of a discount brokerage firm owned by a major bank.
- ■ Steve Cochrane, a professonal stockbroker with Levesque Securities Inc.
- ■ Sam Chu, a professional stockbroker with Charlton Securities Ltd.
- ■ Dan Markovich, vice-president investment policy and research for a large pension fund.
- ■ Barb Fraser, an investigator with the Alberta Stock Exchange.
- ■ Eden Oliver, a lawyer with the firm of Osler, Hoskin, Harcourt.
- ■ John Koop, a Certified Management Accountant.
- ■ Mark and Mila Tadich, wise managers and entrepreneurs.
- ■ Greg Justice, country bar owner, former broker and banker.

■ Order Form

Part One
(Duplicate and Mail)

Check		Amount
☐	Please send me ___ copies of The Due Diligence Software Package at $17.95 Canadian each: There are no shipping, packaging, and sales tax charges to Canadian residents for a limited time. One-free update included in price. This introductory offer is subject to change or cancellation without prior notice. Circle Macintosh or IBM and 3½ or 5¼ disk format.	$
☐	Residents of all other countries please enclose $3.00 Canadian for each software package to cover shipping, handling, and packaging costs:	$
☐	I want the bulk order offer. They are great gifts. Please send me 10 x ___ = ___ books at $7.95 Canadian each: For every ten books I order as a Canadian resident the publisher will pay shipping, handling, and sales tax if applicable; and include a free eleventh book and "glossy cover" suitable for framing. This 30% introductory discount is subject to change or cancellation without prior notice. Place single orders with your local book seller.	$
☐	Residents of all other countries add $1.50 Canadian for each book ordered as part of the bulk order offer to cover shipping and handling. An eleventh book and "glossy cover" will be included free for every ten books ordered:	$
☐	We want the author to speak to our business, social, men's, women's, and youth club. Send details.	
☐	I want to order the cartoons in the book enlarged and colourized. The cartoons make excellent gifts and are suitable for framing. Send details.	
☐	Send me information on your special reports which update the work in **RAMPAGING BULLS**.	
	Total Canadian Enclosed:	$

■ Order Form

Part Two
(Duplicate and Mail)

"The Due Diligence Software Package really works. I like it," The Rampaging Bull said to Jack.

(Print Clearly) Ship This Order To:

_____

Name

_____

Address

_____

City   Prov/State   Postal Code/Zip

_____

Daytime phone number (with area code)

Enclose Part One and Part Two of this order form with your Canadian funds cheque or money order in an envelope and mail:

Special Orders, Elan Publishing Inc.,
Box 21009, Dominion Post S.W.,
Calgary, Alberta, Canada, T2P 4H5

◼ About The Author

Alexander Tadich has earned three university degrees; has worked for three daily newspaper chains; has been on the board of three public companies; and is currently writing his third book on a theme which develops some ideas mentioned in **RAMPAGING BULLS:** *Outfox Promoters At Their Own Game On Any Penny Stock Market.*

The author is a penny stock *trader*, is a communications and business consultant to a handful of "highly literate" managers; is an entertaining public and seminar speaker; and can be found in out of the way coffee shops discussing the possibility that "aliens" are more benevolent than "homo sapiens" and are forced, therefore, to remain reclusive and unidentified.

Tadich understands the nature of "bulls", "bears", and "buffaloes" better than any modern commentator. He actually rode, in a moment of well documented passion, a sweaty 1,800 pound stampeding buffalo; wrestled an 800 pound bear which later ripped someone else's finger off; and fought a "rampaging" bull with extremely long and sharp horns.

"Stay in touch.
There's more,"
the author promises
his readers.